# SPEECH

## Content and Communication

# Speech

## *CONTENT and*

## *COMMUNICATION*

CHARLES S. MUDD
MALCOLM O. SILLARS
*San Fernando Valley State College*

Chandler Publishing Company
*124 Spear Street, San Francisco, California 94105*

# PREFACE

For the majority of college students, a one-semester or a one-quarter course in speech is their only formal training in oral communication. The greatest number of such courses take either a public speaking or a "fundamentals of speech" approach. This book is designed for use in the former: it is a text for a beginning course in public speaking.

The materials covered in this book and the principles discussed are recognizably traditional. We have given greater emphasis, however, to certain aspects of public address which are, it seems to us, often slighted in texts intended for use in a beginning course. The chapter on audience analysis (especially the section on how to use audience analysis) and the chapter on finding issues contain, we think, important principles not usually given sufficient emphasis in the beginning course. The chapters on argument stress the rhetorical aspects of persuasion and build on the concept of probability. Our approach to public speaking, then, can be seen to be audience oriented.

We have based the book on the assumption that the significant difference between beginning and advanced courses should lie not in the principles and skills developed but in the degree to which they are developed. Consequently, this text may be used not only in a one-semester or a one-quarter course, but in the traditional full-year course as well.

Users may and will cover the material in any order they see fit. In our courses, we find, the following chapter sequence in reading assignments fits nicely into a usable pattern. Such an order suggests a certain sequence in speaking assignments as well.

Chapters I, III, and II, which we approach in that order, are introductory. They help to get the class under way.

Chapters VI, VII, VIII, IX, and XVII may be grouped for a unit in informative speaking.

Chapter XIX and assignments in speaking to explore fit in well after informative speaking and re-emphasize material covered in that unit.

Chapters XII, XIII, XIV, and XV discuss principles important throughout but may be covered in a unit with Chapter XVI and assignments for speeches to entertain.

Chapters IV, V, X, XI, and XVIII form a block of materials most relevant to persuasive speaking. We think speaking to persuade should be the culmination of the course.

The writers are grateful for the comments and criticisms of colleagues who read portions of the manuscript. We are especially indebted to Professors Willard Bellman, James Egbert, Donald Henze, Charles Kaplan, Fred McMahon, Robert Rainey, and Jerome Richfield. They have contributed significantly to whatever merit the book has; they have no share in any shortcomings or errors. Mr. Robert Canny of the Library Staff of San Fernando Valley State College gave generously of his time.

Permission to reprint certain copyrighted material was kindly given. Acknowledgment is made at appropriate places in the text.

C.S.M.<br>M.O.S.

# CONTENTS

# ILLUSTRATIONS

# MATERIALS

# SPEECH

## Content and Communication

# Chapter I

# INTRODUCTION

In 1900, the editor of an anthology of famous American speeches expressed the opinion that there had been no great public speaking during the thirty-six years since the Civil War. He reasoned that because America had solved her significant problems with the formation and preservation of the Union, there had been and would be no crises to inspire great speaking. And yet, he had lived through the period of America's greatest industrial expansion, labor strife, agricultural discontent, scientific advancement, and religious upheaval; he had watched the political battle of imperialism, and he had heard such men as William Jennings Bryan, Robert G. Ingersoll, and Henry Ward Beecher speak out on topics of massive importance.

Not only did this critic grossly err in judging the past but his view of the future was also naive. The first six decades of this century have seen issues raised on a scale never before imagined. War has destroyed many millions of people. Great economic problems have cast shadows over large areas of the world. Minority groups have successfully pressed for more rights than they ever before enjoyed. The powerful irrationality of fascism and the persuasive conspiracy of international communism threaten the world.

All who live in the middle years of the twentieth century are aware that this is an age of danger. But what is surprising in that fact? To be alive is to be in danger—of death, if of nothing else. Every period in the history of civilization has been faced with problems. The significant point, then, is not whether there will be problems, nor what forms they will take. The important

question is, how are they solved? Inherent in the creed of western
democracy is the notion that people can best solve their problems
through the medium of popular rule, the rule of an enlightened
and sensible majority. As historian Carl Becker has put it,
"Democratic government rests upon the principle that it is better
to count heads than it is to crack them."

For this reason, western democracy has always put a high value
on freedom of speech. It has assumed that all ideas must be dis-
played and examined so that the people can make a decision.
The nation, therefore, needs wise men and great speakers in
every age to educate against ignorance, to analyze problems, to
provide workable solutions, and to mobilize majority opinion.
These difficult tasks are not the province of statesmen, scholars,
and the clergy alone. If democracy is to function well, the responsibility for it falls upon all citizens and particularly upon
those who would claim the right to lead.

In a 1952 presidential campaign address, Adlai E. Stevenson
said to a television audience,

Struggle is the primary law of life. You struggle and you survive.
You fail to struggle and you perish. . . . Your salvation is in
your own hands, in the stubbornness of your mind, in the te-
nacity of your hearts, and such blessings as God, thoroughly tried
by His children, shall give us. . . . The task is yours. Yours is
a democracy. Its Government cannot be stronger or more tough-
minded than its people. It cannot be more inflexibly committed
to the task than they. It cannot be wiser than the people. As citizens of this democracy you are the rulers and the ruled, the law
givers and the law abiding, the beginning and the end. Democracy is a high privilege, but it is also a heavy responsibility whose
shadow stalks, although you may never walk in the sun.

As well as any piece of spoken rhetoric we know, this expresses
a realistic basis for understanding why men must speak to the
public.

Public life (and not only public life) is lived in an atmosphere
of solving problems: social, economic, political, moral, and many
others. Solving them calls for using the human ability to reason,
an ability that is a priceless property of man. In reasoning to
solve their public problems, people must communicate with one

another, must speak to the public. Speech supports reasoning citizenship.

Many people feel powerless to take part in the operations of a free society. Perhaps this is as serious a fault as the failure to see the problems of society. You have heard these men talk. The ones who say: "What can you do about it? All the decisions are made by a few men at the top." "All that most people want in America today is to conform to the mass." "You can't do anything to change conditions." "We're all controlled by professional manipulators who take our pulse, read our minds, chart our subconscious and then condition our responses to their will." In a very real sense, these are all variations on the old theme, "You can't fight City Hall." Certainly no man should ignore the fact that there are people who want to control him. There are great pressures on every American to act as the television advertiser, the so-called social leader, and the superpatriot think he should act.

Many are easily discouraged and confused. The many have always been easy to discourage and confuse; this weakness is what dictators and demagogues count on. But for those who take the opportunity to say something worthwhile in even a small voice to a little group to lift spirits and to clarify thought, an age of danger is an age of excitement. Surely a democracy is dependent upon having a substantial segment of the society who see its problems and offer means for resolving them. Wherever an educated person is found, in business, in education, in government, in the professions or in the home, he must have the ability to perceive and to speak. This ability is one unit in the major objective of education: to add to the community another person with insight into its problems and with ability to help solve them.

Liberal education, we are told, is primarily an education in citizenship in the finest and deepest sense of that word. Regardless of what profession you may train for, your first obligation is to the fullest development of your own ability to recognize the human and social problems of the times and to offer constructive solutions for them. Society takes its measure of a man from the way he communicates his convictions. Can you say from your own experience that you respect a man or distrust him without thinking of what he says or how he says it? Of course not. Most of the evaluations you make of people are actually criticisms of what they say.

The truly educated man is one who communicates. He is not content to harbor his understanding; he demands the right to share his thoughts and feelings with others. But knowledge alone does not make an able speaker. The enormous amount of ineffective speaking one hears makes clear the fact that effective speaking requires more than having something to say. Successful speaking is an art; it is learned through study, practice, criticism, and experience.

It may seem reasonable to think that a person should learn to speak well just from speaking often. After all, he normally begins to talk between the ages of one and two and spends the rest of his life practicing. Unfortunately, however, long practice in conversational speaking somehow fails to prepare one for more public communication. It fails to do so in spite of the fact that there is no essential difference between a private speech situation and one that is public. Both speech situations require the use of skills common to both. But informal speaking often lacks merit and, even when it does not, the easy mode of address that should characterize private speech does not carry over into a public situation. All speaking demands skill, and skill usually requires training of one kind or another. For all save a tiny few, training is needed to develop the skills needed for effective and successful public speaking.

Perhaps the need to communicate does not seem so immediate. Your relationship to great issues and to audiences may seem remote, rather like a World Series game: viewed at first hand by some, read about by more, seen by millions on television, but played by relatively few. Not so—public and world affairs do affect you, and in a democracy you act in the drama, in part at least, in relation to how much you want to act.

Your conversations, your speeches, your criticisms of the speaking of others all have a part in determining the intellectual and political climate of the nation and, eventually, the actions of its leaders. Even the speeches you give in class have an effect. The presence of any audience, large or small, formal or informal, provides an opportunity and a responsibility for a speaker. Your class should be viewed as more than a training situation; it is also an opportunity for you to fulfill your obligations as a communicator.

Learning from classroom speaking experiences will be improved if you realize that each such speaking assignment is also a real-life one. It does not occur to many beginning speakers that the class they address is an audience, subject to the same kind of ideas and feelings as any other audience. In a speech class you speak to a group of real human beings. Don't ever forget that. Think of your class as you would any other audience you are called upon to address. You may feel that your classroom listeners are different because they will criticize you. But *all* audiences criticize speakers. Therefore, search out criticism. Make this situation work to your advantage. Keep a careful record of the criticisms you get from your instructor and your classmates. Then use this information to improve your later assignments. You will never get such useful help from any other audience.

## QUESTIONS

1. What function does a speaker on public issues have in a democracy?

2. What is "a priceless property of man?" For what purpose is it used?

3. What part does speech play in one of the major objectives of education?

4. Comment on the idea that good speakers are born, not made.

5. Is your speech class more than a training situation? Why?

# THE BEGINNING SPEECHES

I. Selecting a subject and a purpose for the speech
II. Organizing the speech
   A. Organizing the body of the speech
      1. Chronological order
      2. Geographical or spatial order
      3. Topical order
   B. Organizing the conclusion
   C. Organizing the introduction
III. Supporting the ideas in the speech
IV. Delivering the speech
   A. Modes of delivery
      1. Speaking from manuscript
      2. Speaking from memory
      3. Speaking impromptu
      4. Speaking extemporaneously
   B. Characteristics of good delivery
      1. Directness
      2. Spontaneity
      3. Vitality
      4. Intelligibility
   C. Practice
V. Summary, questions, and exercises

*Chapter* **II**

## THE BEGINNING SPEECHES

Proficiency in the art of speech grows out of the combination of understanding and experience, of theory and practice. Which should be taught and studied first? If a student waits until he has a good background of theory before he begins to make speeches, his speaking suffers from lack of practice; if he makes speeches from the beginning, he lacks the guidance of theoretical knowledge.

To begin speaking at the outset seems the better choice. The theoretical basis of your speaking will admittedly need development, but the value of practice is great, and your knowledge of theory will grow as you examine the principles of speaking in greater detail.

It will be helpful and necessary to learn enough of the theory to do a satisfactory job early in the course. This chapter is intended to meet that need by examining briefly four elements that are present in any effective speech: subject, organization, supporting material, and delivery.

### Selecting a Subject and a Purpose for the Speech

On any speaking occasion, two restrictions will limit your choice of a subject. You will be limited by the need for finding a subject that will be of interest to both you and your audience, and you will be limited in the amount of time you will have to speak.

Because of the restriction in time, the general subject you choose must be narrowed in scope so that it can be adequately discussed in the length of time allowed. The narrowed subject is then further narrowed by phrasing it as a *statement of specific purpose* which indicates what you intend to convey to your listeners about the subject.

*General Subject:* Transistors
*Specific Subject:* How a transistor works
*Specific Purpose:* To inform the listeners about the way in which the phenomenon of electron borrowing makes transistor radios possible

*General Subject:* Skin diving
*Specific Subject:* Skin-diving equipment
*Specific Purpose:* To inform the audience about the minimum equipment necessary for the beginning skin diver

*General Subject:* Capital punishment
*Specific Subject:* The effect of capital punishment on crime
*Specific Purpose:* To persuade the audience that capital punishment is not a deterrent to crime

Notice how concrete these statements of specific purpose are. Each points to one clear-cut effort and excludes any others. Compare them with the following statements of purpose which are alleged to be specific but are multiple, diffuse, and therefore badly drawn:

*Specific Purpose:* To inform the audience of the popularity of the transistor radio and how it works, especially how it uses electron borrowing

*Specific Purpose:* To inform the audience of the equipment necessary for skin diving and how skin diving is not only safe but fun

*Specific Purpose:* To persuade the audience that capital punishment does not deter crime and, as a matter of fact, that no severe punishment is effective, even with children in the home

All three of these statements of purpose are poor. They show that the speaker does not have a clear, single purpose in mind. Instead, he has some vague notions about what his subject will be. The statement of purpose must be carefully drawn because it will be used as a guide to test the organization and material of the speech.

## Organizing the Speech

Your speech will be organized into three parts: an *introduction,* the *body,* and a *conclusion.* The body is organized first, because it bears the primary responsibility for accomplishing the purpose of the speech. The introduction and the conclusion are developed after the body of the speech has been prepared.

### ORGANIZING THE BODY OF THE SPEECH

If human beings were able to use some method of direct psychic communication such as that commonly called "mental telepathy," it would perhaps be possible for your listeners to receive a whole complex of ideas in a single perceptive flash. Since audiences do not have this ability, however, you must build understanding in your listeners piece by piece. To accomplish what is specified in your statement of purpose, you will need to partition the body of your speech into an organizational pattern of main points that will bring order to the materials and clarity to the ideas. Together with their supporting material, these main points constitute the body of your speech. We mention three organizational patterns here. These, and others, will be discussed further in Chapter XVII, Speaking to Inform.

*Chronological order.* The sequence of main points in the body of the speech may be arranged in the order of their occurence in time.

> *Specific Purpose:* To inform the audience about Germany's submarine-warfare policy in World War I
>
> I. February 1915, declared the British Isles a war zone

    II. May 1916, pledged not to sink ships without
       warning
    III. January 1917, commenced unrestricted subma-
       rine warfare

***Geographical or spatial order.***    The sequence of main points
in the body of the speech may follow the order of their arrangement in space. The points occur in the speech in the same order
in which the listener might visualize himself moving physically
from one to another.

    *Specific Purpose:* To inform the audience about the
      organization of the library

      I. The reserve room and the library are on the first
        floor.
      II. The card catalog, reference books and periodicals
        are on the second floor.
      III. The general book collection is on the third and
        fourth floors.

***Topical order.***    The main points in the body of the speech
may be a list of the important parts of the idea discussed by the
speaker. Added together, these parts or "topics" make up the
whole idea.

    *Specific Purpose:* To inform the audience about the
      nature of the three major regional dialects of
      American English

      I. The Eastern dialect
      II. The Southern dialect
      III. The General American dialect

  In speeches to persuade, the body is organized in what may
be thought of as a form of topical arrangement. The body of the
persuasive speech contains arguments to demonstrate the truth
of what the speaker is trying to prove.

    *Specific Purpose:* To persuade the audience that prices
      at the college book store are too high

      I. The book store has increased its prices every year
        for the past three years.

II. The book store made an excessive profit last year.

III. The same books cost less at neighboring colleges.

## ORGANIZING THE CONCLUSION

After you have organized the body of the speech, you will want to plan a *conclusion* to pull together the main ideas in the speech. One customary and effective way to end a speech is with a brief summary which recalls for the audience the specific purpose of the speech and the main points that develop it. A summary conclusion is particularly valuable in speaking because a listener cannot go back and rehear as a reader can go back and reread.

## ORGANIZING THE INTRODUCTION

The last section to be developed is the introduction, even though it is to be spoken first. In preparing a speech, the introduction is left until last because once the body of the speech and the conclusion are prepared, you know what you want to say to the audience. You will then be able to prepare an introduction that is more directly related to the ideas contained in the speech.

The introduction has two essential parts. First, there is some interest factor: a story, incident, description, startling statement, or quotation which will catch the attention of the audience. This interest factor should be immediately pertinent to the subject of the speech because its primary function is to arouse interest in what you are going to say and to direct that interest toward the purpose of the speech.

The second major part of the introduction is the subject sentence. This is a statement which expresses the specific purpose of the speech in an informal oral style.

> *Specific Purpose:* To inform the audience about the way in which the phenomenon of electron borrowing makes transistor radios possible

> *Subject Sentence:* Behind the transistor radio is a phenomenon of electron borrowing which makes it possible for the engineer to give us this little miracle.

## Supporting the Ideas in the Speech

The statement of specific purpose and its subpoints constitute the definite idea you want your audience to have. But ideas become meaningful to an audience only when they are *interesting* and *clear*. Examples, statistics, quotations, and arguments all help to make your ideas more clear, interesting, and believable. Always use *at least* one item of such specific material in support of each important point in the body of the speech. (Usually, two or more pieces of supporting material are necessary and desirable.) This specific material will help you to make the ideas you have developed more precise and vivid and thus serve to clarify the subject, add interest, and establish belief.

When you have determined the content and organization of the speech, you may want to prepare some notes to help you in delivery. Whatever notes you use should be in outline form. Here is an example of standard outline form and an indication of how it is used.

INTRODUCTION
I. Interest factor
II. Subject sentence

BODY
I. First main point of the speech
A. Supporting material
B. Supporting material
II. Second main point of the speech
A. Supporting material
B. Supporting material
[And so on]

CONCLUSION
I. Summary statement noting the purpose
A. First main point
B. Second main point
[And so on]

## Delivering the Speech

The ideas, organization, and supporting details in any given instance of communication can be the same whether the communication is written or spoken. Except for some few differences in style (the way language is used), what most distinguishes writing from speaking is that a speech must be delivered. Indeed it doesn't become a speech until the moment of delivery. Consequently, delivery is an important part of effectiveness in speaking. It is the vital, physical means by which ideas are transmitted to a listener. The first decision that must be made about delivery is what kind of delivery to use.

## MODES OF DELIVERY

Four different methods of delivering a speech are commonly recognized. These four methods (or modes) of delivery differ from each other according to the kind of preparation the speaker makes for the delivery. If the language of the speech is thoroughly prepared in advance, the speech can be delivered either from a *manuscript* or from *memory*. On the other hand, when the specific language which will be used in the speech is not chosen before the moment of delivery, the speech will be either *impromptu* or *extemporaneous*.

**Speaking from manuscript.** There are three kinds of speaking occasions that may legitimately call for a speech to be read from manuscript.

The first of these is the making, by a person in a position of responsibility, of a statement so important that mistakes must not be permitted to occur. When the President of the United States speaks for this country to the world, even a simple slip of the tongue or a momentary lapse of control over his own emotions might have far-reaching and serious consequences. Similarly, an ambassador to the United Nations will very frequently deliver a prepared statement from manuscript.

An occasion of great formality may demand a polish in the speech that cannot be expected except through complete preparation of language beforehand.

The third kind of occasion that may make use of a manuscript desirable occurs whenever there are strict time limits put upon a speaker. The length of time a speech will last is much more easily determined when the speech is in manuscript, and the time can much more easily be adhered to when the speech is delivered from manuscript. The most common instances of this sort can be observed in broadcasts over radio and television. The very strict time schedules of these broadcast media require a speaker to meet a specific time limit.

Apart from these kinds of occasion, however, a manuscript ought not to be used. It is totally unlikely that such demands for precision in wording will arise in a public-speaking class or, for that matter, in any of the speaking that all but a few will be called upon to do in the future.

Besides being on most occasions unnecessary, manuscript speaking has certain quite definite disadvantages. William Jennings Bryan, commented on these in connection with his Madison Square Garden speech in 1896, accepting the nomination as Democratic presidential candidate:

I was compelled to choose between an extemporaneous speech, which would be less concise and comprehensive, and a speech which, because read from manuscript, would disappoint the audience. I knew, too, that in order to secure an accurate report of the speech in the daily papers it would be necessary to furnish a copy in advance of delivery, and I knew that if delivered from memory it would be taken down in shorthand and compared with the copy furnished to the press. After weighing the relative advantages of, and objections to, the two modes of delivery, I concluded that it was the part of wisdom to disappoint the few thousands who would be in the hall in order to reach the hundreds of thousands who would read it in print. Having decided to use my manuscript it was necessary to make the speech as brief as possible because the crime of reading a speech increases in heinousness in proportion to its length.

The most effective kind of speaking takes place when someone with a *thought,* a meaningful idea, expresses that thought in simple, direct, straightforward language to an audience with which he is making close visual and psychological contact. This contact is extremely difficult to achieve in speaking from manuscript. Moreover, a manuscript is totally lacking in flexibility.

The speaker who uses it ties himself to a set pattern of words and denies himself any opportunity for adapting to his audience during the course of a speech. For these reasons, unless it is absolutely necessary to do so, a speech should not be delivered from a manuscript.

*Speaking from memory.* In preparing a speech to be delivered from memory, a speaker will ordinarily write out a manuscript, practice from it until he knows it by heart, and then will deliver the speech from memory. This kind of speaking has few of the advantages but carries with it all of the disadvantages of the manuscript mode of delivery. Unless he is a reasonably accomplished actor, the speaker delivering a talk from memory will find it difficult to maintain close contact with the audience. Even if he is a good actor, or recites well, he will be burdened with the same lack of flexibility from which a manuscript speaker suffers. There is, moreover, another disadvantage to speaking from memory. If the speaker forgets, he is lost. We say, categorically, *never* memorize a speech. If the occasion demands that kind of preparation, prepare a manuscript and use it instead.

*Speaking impromptu.* An impromptu speech may be defined as one for which a speaker has made no immediate preparation. He is called upon to speak unexpectedly and the things he says are said on the spur of the moment. It is probable that nearly everyone has at one time or another imagined himself in a speaking situation wherein he is required to "think on his feet," and (since everyone sees himself as the hero of his own daydreams) has come through admirably, swaying masses of people, crushing opposition, the epitome of impromptu eloquence. The picture is unrealistic.

We are not saying that such skill is undesirable or impossible to attain. It is, however, hard to come by. Henry Ward Beecher, after delivering a splendid talk which seemed to be completely impromptu, was asked how long he had prepared for it. The answer: he had been preparing for the talk for forty years.

Except when the speaker is given no warning, no speech

should be delivered impromptu. A speaker should take every opportunity to prepare as thoroughly as time will allow. If he is called upon to speak with no preparation, he should remember that the same principles of organization and support apply to all speaking. If at all possible, he should take a few moments to think through what he will say and perhaps to jot down a few notes. Even if he must react at once, he should remember that the major function of a speech is to introduce an idea, develop it, and finish discussing it—conclude. In this way, even the most hastily prepared talk can be given the quality of order.

*Speaking extemporaneously.*          Under ideal circumstances, all public address would be extemporaneous. In this mode of delivery, the ideas, organization and supporting material of a speech are thoroughly prepared in advance. Moreover, the delivery of the speech is practiced as well. The only part of such a speech that is *ex tempore* (that is, grows "out of the time" or comes at the actual moment of delivery) is the *language.* This is chosen in much the same manner as the language of an impromptu speech. The difference between impromptu speaking and extemporaneous delivery, other than the thorough preparation of the content of the latter, is in the fact that the extemporaneous speech has been "talked through" several times. The speaker does not write the speech in full, nor does he make any effort to learn or memorize the language he will use in delivery. Indeed, each time he practices the speech, he will use different language and work toward a more precise and clear statement of his ideas. When finally he delivers the speech, the speaker is so thoroughly familiar with what he intends to say that he can in a very real sense "ad lib" the language that will be most effective for his audience, his subject, and the occasion of his speech.

It is apparent that extemporaneous delivery has the greatest number of advantages and the fewest disadvantages of all the four modes of delivery. It lends itself to direct visual and psychological contact with the audience. It can have all the spontaneity and immediacy of casual conversation without the disorganization that often characterizes conversation. It affords the speaker great flexibility in meeting the specific and yet shifting demands of his audience. Extemporaneous speaking is the principal concern of this book and all of what is said in it is most directly applicable to this mode of delivery.

## CHARACTERISTICS OF GOOD DELIVERY

A highly communicative pattern of language and delivery appears in the everyday conversational speech of a large number of persons who do not carry over this quality into public-speaking experiences. This fact is unfortunate, for good delivery, even in formal situations, needs all the best qualities of good conversational speech.

*Directness.* Good conversational delivery is *direct*. A speaker talks to his audience. He chooses words which listeners will understand. He looks directly at them. He does not look over their heads, nor out the window, nor through them as if they were not there. He recognizes that they *are* there and he talks to them with much the same delivery and language he would use if they were guests in his home.

*Spontaneity.* Good conversational delivery appears to be *spontaneous*. That is, it sounds as if the speaker is talking about the ideas for the first time. It reveals the enthusiasm which he has for his own ideas and the sincerity of his desire to communicate.

*Vitality.* Good conversational delivery has *vitality*. It usually involves variety in voice and bodily action which provide cues to the audience about the relative importance of the materials in a speech. Vitality in delivery demands the kind of gesture and movement which the speaker would naturally use to emphasize a point in ordinary conversation. Some people, it is true, do not gesture very much. But nearly everyone gestures more than he realizes. As an experiment, pay some attention to what you and others do in everyday speaking situations. You may be surprised to see how much gesturing is done. In general, gestures serve two functions: they help the audience to measure a speaker's emotional involvement in his subject; they help the speaker to clarify and emphasize his ideas.

*Intelligibility.*    Good conversational delivery is readily *intelligible*. Nothing a speaker says will make much sense if it is difficult for his audience to hear. But to make the members of an audience "hear" the speaker must make them *listen*. Doing so requires that his voice must be more than merely audible. A speaker's voice should not only be loud enough to be heard, but more, it should be loud enough to command attention in spite of the many normal distractions he may expect. To hold the attention of his audience, he must be able to contend with such competitors as a noisy air conditioner in the rear of the room or with a group of small boys playing ball outside an open window.

Besides *audibility,* there are other qualities of good speech that contribute to the intelligibility of delivery: *Articulation* (the formulation of individual sounds) should be clear and precise without being stilted. *Pronunciation* should be acceptable; it should follow the standard usage of the educated members of the speaker's community.

## PRACTICE

An audience will judge your speech as it is delivered, so you need to prepare it in terms of that delivery. In practice, listen to the speech as it might be heard by the audience.

When you have what you think is the final draft of your outline, practice speaking from it several times to set the ideas in your mind. Don't write the speech out or try to memorize it. Use the words that come to you at the time of each practice delivery. The oftener you practice during the preparation period, the better you will be able to find the words to get the reaction you want from the audience.

## SUMMARY

Develop your beginning speeches through attention to these four basic steps: subject, organization, supporting material, and delivery. Formulate a specific purpose. Study the possible ways to divide the speech into its main points. Search for the right supporting materials to make the ideas clear, interesting, and acceptable to your audience. Practice while you are preparing the final outline and after it has been established.

There is no mystery to successful communication. Consistent attention to the basic steps of speechmaking can free you from the frustration of unsuccessful efforts to communicate.

## QUESTIONS

**1.** From the general subject "Education" select a specific subject suitable for a short informative speech. Prepare a statement of specific purpose and a subject sentence.

**2.** Give an example of each of the three types of order for the body of a speech.

**3.** What is the purpose of an introduction?

**4.** Why should a speech have a conclusion?

**5.** What are the two factors mentioned in the text which make ideas most precise and vivid for an audience?

**6.** What mode of delivery is preferable and why?

**7.** What are the characteristics of good delivery?

## EXERCISES

**1.** From an issue of *Vital Speeches* magazine or a volume of A. Craig Baird's *Representative American Speeches,* select a speech and briefly outline it showing the division of the speech into introduction, body and conclusion and the main points in the body. Then write a few paragraphs analyzing the speech, noting the following:

(a) Would the beginning of the speech arouse interest?
(b) Is the subject sentence clearly stated?
(c) Does the speaker have enough or too many main points in the body?
(d) How does he conclude his speech?

2. Organize and deliver a three-minute informative speech explaining to your classmates some historic or scenic location within one hundred miles of the college.

3. From one of the general subjects mentioned below or from others assigned by your instructor, select three specific subjects and phrase them into statements of specific purpose.

(a) Automobiles
(b) Dating practices of college students
(c) Juvenile delinquency
(d) United States foreign policy
(e) Psychology
(f) Athletics

4. Listen carefully to the delivery of an instructor's lectures in another class. Compile a list of the things about his delivery which aided your understanding and a list of the things which detracted from it. How many of the detracting factors do you suppose you would have noticed if you hadn't especially looked for them? How important do you think delivery is to a speaker?

# SELECTING A SUBJECT

I. How speech subjects come about
II. The general ends of speeches
    A. Speaking to entertain—to give enjoyment
    B. Speaking to inform—to bring about understanding
    C. Speaking to persuade—to influence belief or action
        1. Propositions of policy
        2. Propositions of fact
        3. Propositions of value
    D. Speaking to explore—to study a problem in search of a solution
        1. Problems of policy
        2. Problems of fact
        3. Problems of value
III. Selecting a good subject
    A. Qualities of a good speech subject
        1. Significance
        2. Appropriateness
    B. Speaker, audience, occasion, and subject
        1. Speaker
        2. Audience
        3. Occasion
IV. Summary, questions, and exercises
V. A list of possible subject areas

# Chapter **III**

## SELECTING A SUBJECT

The subject of a speech is the topic a speaker discusses. It encompasses the materials, ideas, and attitudes he wants to convey. The choice of a subject is an important influence on the speaker's effectiveness. This chapter will examine several factors which help to influence his choice.

### How Speech Subjects Come About

Sometimes a speaker's subject forces itself upon him. When Cicero prosecuted Catiline, and when Clarence Darrow defended Loeb and Leopold, neither lawyer was given the opportunity to choose the subject of his speech. Neither Abraham Lincoln nor Stephen A. Douglas had to ask for suggested subjects in their series of famed debates. Today, when members of Congress frame legislation, there is no problem of "What shall we talk about?" The issues are there to be analyzed and debated. In all of the above instances and in many others, the subjects of both written and oral discourse present themselves ready made and with a demand to be considered.

On other occasions, a subject is assigned to the speaker. Thousands of luncheon and dinner clubs, service clubs, patriotic organizations, political clubs, chambers of commerce, and professional and church groups are interested in hearing a speaker discuss subjects of local and current interest. In such cases, the speaker has less control over the choice of his subject. Ordinarily, the assigned topic will come within the realm of the speaker's professional competence.

In still other instances, however, a subject is of the speaker's own choosing. A candidate for political office recognizes a large number of issues, all worthy of attention; from these, he selects one for a speech. A minister has a wide range from which to select the topic for a particular sermon. The writer, scientist, educator, businessman, or artist who is asked to speak will ordinarily have freedom to select his subject.

In your speaking, then, some subjects will be important enough to demand your attention; others may be arbitrarily chosen for you; still others you may choose for yourself. Regardless of the part you play in the choice of your subject, you must be able to understand its nature.

A speech subject reflects not only what a speaker wants to give to his audience, but also what he wants his audience to give to him. To his audience he gives ideas, organized and supported. From his audience he wants a response. The subject of a speech and the response desired from an audience are closely related and determine the purpose of the speech. Selecting a subject requires an awareness of the different purposes a speaker may have. These different purposes are commonly called *the general ends of speeches.*

## The General Ends of Speeches

The number of recognized general ends has differed from time to time. The early writers on speech, men who taught and practiced the classical rhetoric of Greece and Rome, made it clear that they were concerned with only one kind of response from the audience—agreement with the attitude or action proposed by the speaker. This response was gained through argument, by offering the audience reasons for believing what the speaker said was true. The goal was *persuasion.* In later years, however, the list of general ends has grown as other writers have recognized other ends that speakers may have in view and other responses they may try to win. A speech may be said to

have as its purpose one or another of four general ends: to entertain, to inform, to persuade, or to explore. Each of these four
kinds of speaking seeks a specific response:

General
ends (the
speaker's
purpose)

$\left\{\begin{array}{l}\text{To entertain — } \textit{Enjoyment}\\ \text{To inform — } \textit{Enlightenment}\\ \text{To persuade — } \textit{Agreement}\\ \text{To explore — } \textit{Agreement and/or}\\ \qquad\qquad\quad \textit{enlightenment}\end{array}\right\}$

*The re-
sponse the
speaker
seeks*

## Speaking to Entertain—to Give Enjoyment

On many occasions, both formal and informal, a speaker will
have the sole purpose of entertaining his audience. Ordinarily,
he will use humor as the means. When the president of the
freshman class, for example, gives an after-dinner speech at the
annual class banquet, he may decide to entertain his audience
by building an amusing speech around the freshman's first experience with the college registration procedure. Mort Sahl,
whose rapid-fire stream-of-consciousness monologues have made
him a popular satirist, entertains his audiences. Though he
draws much of his humor from the foibles and incongruities he
sees in society, with a consequent strong undertone of social
criticism, the goal he seeks is the amusement of his audiences.

The speaking of Mort Sahl and many other comedians permits
us to make what will later become an important distinction between the use of ideas to create humor and the use of humor to
support ideas. A speech to entertain should not be confused with
an informative or persuasive speech which uses humor as a device
for arousing interest. The use of humor as a means of arousing
and retaining interest in a speech will be discussed at some
length in Chapter XVI, Speaking to Entertain.

## Speaking to Inform—to Bring About Understanding

When a speaker's purpose is to make something known to an
audience, to clarify ideas for them, to give them facts or infor-

mation, his general end is to inform. The response he wants from his audience is understanding: of an object, an operation, or a condition. To fulfill a requirement in a course on international relations, you might give a report on the organization and function of the Presidium of the Supreme Soviet of the USSR. In a report of this kind, you have no immediate concern for the attitude the audience might take toward the Presidium or toward the Soviet Union; nor do you care what your listeners might do with the information they get from you. Your sole concern is that they understand and remember what you say. *Understanding* and *retention* are the criteria of an effective speech to inform.

## SPEAKING TO PERSUADE—TO INFLUENCE BELIEF OR ACTION

A speech to persuade is the attempt to cause an audience to feel, believe, or act in a manner specified by the speaker. The subjects he speaks on, however, are not matters of assured agreement. The speaker, therefore, gives his audience reasons for adopting his own point of view.

To make persuasion necessary, the difference between the attitudes of speaker and audience need not be one of open hostility or even one of active disagreement. Look at the following instance: Irritated by the fact that you cannot find a clean table in the cafeteria because students frequently fail to bus their dishes, you decide to embark upon a clean-up campaign on the campus. You would need to persuade your friends to give active support to your campaign. The need is apparent, for otherwise the conditions you disapprove in the cafeteria would not exist.

The need for giving reasons (using arguments) to support a point of view indicates a significant difference between informative and persuasive discourse. An example will point up the difference between the two: suppose one were to propose an informative speech on the operation of the Security Council of the United Nations, but were to close that speech with an appeal for support of the United Nations. Such an appeal would be out of place in an informative speech. The goal of informative speaking is understanding; no effort is made to give proof. The subject of a persuasive speech, however, is a matter in debate and demands proof if the speech is to change belief. Certainly, persuasion is not likely to take place in an uninformed audience, but in almost every case, more than information is needed to persuade. When a speaker has not accurately defined his purpose for himself, he can hardly expect it to be clear to his audience.

Before his opinion on a subject is presented to an audience, a speaker should already have formulated it for himself. That opinion is worded as a statement which expresses the belief he asks his listeners to accept or the action he wants them to perform. These statements are called propositions. Depending on a speaker's purpose, they appear as propositions of *policy,* propositions of *fact,* or propositions of *value.* Let us look briefly at these three forms.

***Propositions of policy.***     One of the purposes of persuasion is to win approval for procedures, methods of operation, or modes of conduct which are more prudent or more expedient than those to be supplanted. When a speaker advocates a course of action, he is attempting to prove a proposition of policy. A proposition of policy is the statement which specifies a course of action (policy) and calls for its adoption. Here are two examples:

> The student council should establish a system of fines for students who neglect to bus their dishes in the cafeteria.
> Private citizens should build bomb shelters of the kind recommended by civil defense authorities.

***Propositions of fact.***     On many occasions, persuasion is needed to establish belief in a proposition that does not call for a change of policy. In such cases, a speaker's purpose may be to prove a proposition of fact. A proposition of fact is a statement which asserts that specified conditions or circumstances exist. Because a proposition of fact, like a proposition of policy, is debatable, it needs proof. It is a statement of what a speaker intends to prove. Examples:

The defendant is guilty as charged.

The Soviet Union will not permit open inspection of
facilities for testing nuclear weapons.

***Propositions of value.***     A proposition of value is a special
form of the proposition of fact. The difference between the two
is that the proposition of value expresses a judgment concerning
the goodness, rightness, quality, merit, *value* of an object or act,
whereas the proposition of fact does not. The value judgments of
a speaker are debatable and therefore they need proof. The
proposition of value makes a statement of the value judgment a
speaker intends to prove.

An increase in taxes will be detrimental to the American economy.

The American educational system is superior to the
systems of Europe.

The major distinction between propositions of fact and value
on the one hand, and propositions of policy on the other, lies in
the difference between what *is* and what *ought to be*. Propositions of fact and value assert that certain specified conditions or
qualities *exist;* propositions of policy allege that certain specified
modes of conduct *ought* to exist.

It has probably occurred to you to ask where these propositions come from, to want to know how they are found. To answer that question, we turn to the fourth general end of speaking.

## Speaking to Explore—to Study a Problem in Search of a Solution

When a problem exists with no immediate indication of an
acceptable solution, it must be explored. If, for example, you
and a group of friends wanted to run a candidate for the office
of student-body president, several problems would arise: Who
should your candidate be? How should you conduct his campaign? And so on. You and your friends would gather to explore
the subject for a better understanding of the problems involved
and to make decisions about them. As a result of the exploration,
you achieve understandings and beliefs you did not have before

your inquiry began. In talking about the campus election, for example, you might come to conclusions like the following: "The candidate who can get the Interfraternity Council behind him will swing the election." "Fred Byron is the best man to unite the Council behind him." "Fred Byron ought to be selected as our candidate for the office of Student Body President." "Fred's campaign ought to be built around the idea of getting for the students a more decisive voice in appropriating money from the student-activities fee." You will recognize that each of these conclusions is a proposition: the first, a proposition of fact; the second a proposition of value, and the last two, propositions of policy.

This example makes evident a relationship between speaking to explore a subject and speaking to inform or persuade: The new understandings and beliefs that are the outcome of exploration *become the propositions that you may, in speaking to others, choose to explain or to prove.*

Any proposition, then, is presumably the solution to some kind of problem. This fact implies that problems, like propositions, are of three kinds: problems of policy, problems of fact, problems of value.

*Problems of policy.*      A problem of policy is a question which asks for a formulation of policy. It asks what procedure, what method of operation, or what mode of conduct ought to be adopted. It says, in effect, "What should be done in order to improve such and such a problem situation?"

The question that phrases a problem of policy should be stated in such a way that it calls for a choice among several possible alternative courses of action. It does not ask for acceptance or rejection of any one proposal. This point can be clarified by an example. Suppose we were to ask, "Should the United States recognize Communist China?" The question is obviously concerned with a matter of policy. Is it not, then, a satisfactory question of policy? It is not, and for this reason: A policy that the United States might adopt toward Communist China is suggested in the very phrasing of the question. Instead of asking which one of *all* possible courses of action ought to be adopted, the question as stated demands a Yes or No answer with regard to *one* alternative proposal. As such, it is an invitation not to *explore,* but to *persuade.* A properly phrased problem of policy would read, "What should be the policy of the United States toward Communist China?"

**Problems of fact.**      A problem of fact is a question which asks what the conditions in a given situation are. We may ask, "What procedures does the Federal Reserve Bank employ in controlling credit spending?" Other examples range from such questions as "What were the causes of the Korean War?" and "What principles govern the operation of the neutron bomb?" to such simple matters as "What time is it?" and "What's for supper?"

**Problems of value.**      A problem of value is a question which asks about the merit or lack of merit in a person, an item, or an idea. A value judgment must be made before an answer can be given to such questions as, "What is the greatest play in the English language?" or "When did the most significant advances in science take place?"

A problem of value is to all intents and purposes a special kind of problem of fact. That is to say, a problem of value and a problem of fact both ask that a judgment be made. There is, however, a difference between the kinds of judgments that these two problems require. As the name implies, the problem of value asks for a value judgment; the problem of fact does not. An example will make the distinction clear:

> *Problem of fact:* In how many schools is art a required part of the curriculum?
> *Problem of value:* How important is art in the college curriculum?

To insure that problems of fact and value will be explored rather than debated, avoid phrasing them as questions that can be answered Yes or No. Instead of asking "Is the defendant guilty?" ask "Who committed the crime?" Instead of asking "Is Babe Ruth the greatest baseball player in the history of the game?" ask "Who is the greatest baseball player in the history of the game?"

## Selecting a Good Subject

An audience will probably not listen to a speaker if he fails to arouse an interest in what he says. An important step in creating the necessary interest is the choosing of a good subject.

### QUALITIES OF A GOOD SPEECH SUBJECT

A speaker will usually choose a subject he cares something about, but listeners have less choice in the matter. Even so, they are not forced to listen and often simply refuse to. It is apparent, then, that if a speech is to be successful it must be on a subject that is interesting both to the speaker and to his audience. This basic condition will be met by a subject that for him and for the audience is *significant* and *appropriate*.

*Significance.* For a home-economics major, the fact that the spool of thread for which she used to pay a nickel now costs fifteen cents is of considerably greater interest than it is to an art major whose creativity takes forms other than sewing. An anthropology major would go out of his way to hear a lecture on the Hopi Indian. A student of political science might gladly spend time tabulating returns of a campus election in which the anthropology major had perhaps not taken time to vote. All four students would respond sharply to news that tuition at their college was to be increased twenty-five per cent. In each of these instances, each student would be giving attention to some event which has significance for him.

The same condition applies to a speech subject. It will be of interest to an audience if it involves matters that are of significance to the audience. The greater the significance, the greater the interest. The listeners may not be aware of the extent to which the topic does concern them. Indeed, they may not have any feeling in the matter. This indifference does not mean the subject is necessarily a poor one. Instead, it means that the speaker must stimulate interest in his subject. He stimulates it by helping his listeners perceive the significance his topic has for them. Unless he makes clear why his listeners should be inter-

ested, unless he shows how and why the subject is of significance
for them, they will pay him little heed. Then it will not matter
that the subject offers information the audience has not had before or new insights into familiar ideas, or that the material of
the speech is organized with great clarity, eminently well supported, and delivered with superior skill.

*Appropriateness.*     A speech subject must not only be significant; it must also be appropriate for both the speaker and his
audience.

The subject a speaker chooses will be appropriate for him if it
is one on which he is competent to speak. His competence does
not have to exist before he chooses the subject. In fact, when a
subject is chosen, the speaker may know very little about it, may
be incompetent in the sense of not having detailed knowledge.
However, if he adds to his knowledge through study, then his
initial knowledge and his research can combine to make him
competent.

For the audience, a speech subject is appropriate on grounds
other than competence. Presumably, the very fact that the audience is as informed on a subject as the speaker constitutes good
reason for not choosing it as the subject for a speech.

The subject of a speech is appropriate only if the speaker can
hope to gain the response he seeks: enjoyment, enlightenment,
action, or belief. There is not much point in trying to get an
audience to do something it cannot do: normally high-school
students cannot vote for a sheriff. Nor is there much use in asking the audience to accept an attitude the speaker knows it is
highly probable they will reject: liquor dealers will scarcely en-
dorse prohibition. In other words, the subject of a speech will be
appropriate for the audience only if the speaker seeks a response
that he can expect to get.

## SPEAKER, AUDIENCE, OCCASION, AND SUBJECT

Every speaking situation is made up of four elements. These
are the *speaker,* the *subject* of his speech, the *audience* to whom
he speaks, and the *occasion* upon which he speaks. All four of

these elements closely influence each other in the development of the talk. In fact, taken together they *are* the speaking situation. Selecting a good subject is the first step in speech preparation, so let's see what influence the speaker, the audience, and the occasion have on the subject of a speech.

*Speaker.* It is clear that the first approach to the question, "What shall I speak on?" should be to ask, "What am I interested in?" The assumption that a good speaker can talk well on any subject is an erroneous one. Winston Churchill, one of the great speakers of the modern world, finds subjects in the political, economic, and social questions to which he has devoted his public life. He would not try to tell engineers how to build a bridge, or a group of biochemists how to build a laboratory for manufacturing antibiotics. These would not fit his interests or background. Of course, a good speaker is an avid reader and investigator. He pursues all kinds of knowledge, but he cannot be an expert on everything. He must, therefore, speak on the subjects which have interest and significance for him. His topics will be chosen from areas of his own greatest competence.

Begin, then, by searching your own experience, study, and thought. What are the subjects you know best, that you deal with most often, that you think about most? These are the areas in which you will be most competent. These will be your best sources of speech topics.

*Audience.* The second factor that influences the choice of a subject is the audience. A topic that provides new information or a new approach to familiar material is inherently acceptable. But listeners are not much interested in being told something they already know. In one speech class, a student delivered a well-prepared speech on Wendell Johnson's book, *People in Quandaries,* telling how its "new" idea of semantics had proved so significant to him and discussing basic principles of language usage which the semanticist teaches. The members of the class agreed that it was a "good" speech, but that it covered material they had all learned the semester before in Freshman English. Strictly speaking, then, it was not a good speech, because, although it was well chosen in terms of the speaker's interests and the nature of the subject, it was not well chosen for the audience. With a fresh view of the audience, the speaker was able to rework his speech, using materials which were not so well known to his listeners. On his second try he received a much better response.

Thus, when you have a subject that you can relate to your listeners, one that you can make interesting to them, and one to which you can bring a new approach and fresh materials, you will have a subject that meets the demands of your audience.

*Occasion.*      Usually it is a specific occasion which draws men and women together to form an audience. In choosing a subject a speaker must, therefore, consider the occasion. A thoughtful speaker would not deliver a partisan political talk at a church meeting any more than he would tell jokes at a funeral. An address delivered on Lincoln's birthday should indicate at least an awareness of the great president's philosophy and deeds, and on the Fourth of July some phase of patriotism is traditionally in order.

Some speakers, on the other hand, use the limitations of the occasion as an excuse for not taking a responsible part in the affairs of the community. Franklin D. Roosevelt's speech on the threat of aggression prior to World War II was delivered at the dedication of a Chicago bridge. It might seem better to have delivered this "Quarantine of Aggressors" speech at a foreign-policy meeting, and to have made his appearance in Chicago the occasion for a speech on public works. The demands of the times, however, *made* this a right occasion. Certainly the people of Chicago are interested in the question of war and peace. It might have been easy for the President to delay until Hitler marched into Poland two years later, excusing himself by saying that the right occasion for stating his views had never come along.

Similarly, you will be given many opportunities to voice your opinion on questions that concern you. Do not hesitate to let others know what you think because "the occasion is not right." This is an excuse rather than a reason. If you are to take your place as a responsible citizen, you must be willing to state your views on the pressing problems of the times. The world is full of people who are eager to shirk this responsibility.

## SUMMARY

The possible subjects for speeches are as many as there are ideas and people in the world. Regardless of whether his subject is assigned to him or whether he chooses it for himself, a speaker must understand the considerations that influence the selection if he is to get from his audiences the responses he desires.

The first step in his understanding is an awareness of the four general ends of speech: to entertain, to inform, to persuade, and to explore. Each of these ends, or purposes, is related to some response the speaker desires: amusement, enlightenment, action or belief.

With his general end in mind, the speaker can select his subject. He will look for one which is significant and appropriate. The speaker himself, his audience, and the occasion must all be considered when the choice of the subject is made.

## QUESTIONS

1. What are the general ends of a speech? Which one was the only one recognized in ancient Greece and Rome?

2. What are the differences among problems of fact, value, and policy?

3. Explain the two qualities of a good speech subject.

4. How does the audience help determine the subject of a speech?

## EXERCISES

1. Select some campus problem and, using the examples in this chapter as models, state it as a problem of policy. Rephrase it into a proposition of policy indicating what you believe should be done.

2. Phrase a proposition of fact and a proposition of value from the same general subject. Explain, by using these examples, the difference between fact and value.

3. Select one of the audiences below or one assigned by your instructor and make a list of five speech subjects which you believe would interest them. Write a brief note after each one indicating why you think this audience would be interested.

   (a) A church club you belong to.
   (b) An assembly of the high school from which you graduated.
   (c) The freshman class at your college.
   (d) An organization to which your parents belong.

4. Make a list of five general subjects you believe you are qualified to speak on and explain why you feel each would or would not be interesting to your classmates.

5. Examine the following list of statements and determine whether each is (1) a problem or a proposition; (2) concerned with policy, fact, or value; (3) properly phrased—and if not properly phrased, why not.

   (a) Girls aren't very reasonable.
   (b) Should we go to the movie?
   (c) What day does school open?
   (d) Who is the most valuable member of the football team?
   (e) What nation produced the most steel last year?
   (f) The United States should give economic assistance to Poland.
   (g) War is caused by greed.
   (h) What should our city do about the increase in crime?
   (i) Hasn't Senator Morgan lost the confidence of the people?
   (j) Which automobile is best for students?
   (k) What should be the college policy toward smoking on campus, or should there be one?
   (l) Wouldn't Doris make a beautiful Homecoming Queen?

## A LIST OF POSSIBLE SUBJECT AREAS

The following list is intended to assist you in thinking of a speech subject. These subjects will need to be narrowed. Each of these could be a subject for entertaining, informing, persuading, or exploring. Taking the first subject on education, for instance, you might choose one of these specific purposes:

*Entertain:* To indicate what a large university looks like to a very small freshman.

*Inform:* To inform the audience about the academic organization of Columbia University.

*Persuade:* To persuade the audience that students get a better education at a large university.

*Explore:* To inquire into what is the probable future role of the large university in America.

### Education

Large universities
Private vs. public education
Teaching a child to read
Federal aid to education
The place of athletics in education
The teaching of reading
Foreign and American colleges
Grading systems
Vocational aptitude
Junior colleges
Campus political parties

Small colleges
Progressive education
College students today
Revisions in the high schools
Foreign languages
Student government
Changes in education
Honors programs
Junior high schools
Counseling
Drop-outs

### World Politics

Disarmament
United Nations
Israel and the Arabs
Japan's economy
Dictators
Alaska and Russia
The Middle East
International spies
Underdeveloped countries
Russia's leaders
American tourists
Yugoslavia

Berlin
Africa
China
Cuba
Canada and the United States
India
Russia's army
Past wars
Propaganda
Ambassadors
Franco's Spain
Satellite nations

### National Politics

Military men in public office
Revisions of the Supreme Court
Constitutional amendments
Antitrust Laws
The Electoral College
Straight party voting
Lobbying
Social welfare
Wiretapping
Pump-priming

Should Congress be televised?
Presidential elections
How different are the parties?
Labor disputes
Ex-Presidents
Filibuster
State offices
Public power
Withholding tax
Closed shop

## Science

Great scientists
Ants
Microscopes
Photosynthesis
Growth
Man in space
Psychiatry and psychology
Radiation
Atoms

Should nonscientists study science?
Solid-state physics
Butterflies
Cell division
Perception
Dentistry
Fission
Disease
Computers

## Humanities

The value of the study of history
Great writers
How to understand poetry
"Time spent in reading is time lost from living"
Civil war
Transcendentalism
Semantics
Representational vs. abstract art
Huck Finn revisited
Should a novel have a happy ending?
The Trent affair

Liberal vs. technical education
Recent novels
Modern art
Sculpture
Does history repeat?
Rationalism
Bertrand Russell
Modern music
Popular fiction
Morality in art
Sigmund Freud
Movies made from novels

## Society

The Hopi Indians
The ideas of an ethnic group
"All men are created equal"
The police force
Subliminal advertising
Personal liberty
Distinctive features of American society
Television give-away programs
"A woman's place is in the home"
Human beings are unalike
Social Security
Marriage laws

New roles for women
A double standard?
Are Americans disliked?
High salaries for entertainers
Polish wedding
Racial barriers
Science in advertising
Traffic accidents
Capital punishment
Juvenile criminals
Divorce
Retail price control

## Religion

The sermon in Protestantism
What is a saint?
Varieties in Judaism

"The Great Awakening"
Mohammedanism
Hinduism

Psychology and religion
The education of the clergy
The symbolism of the Mass
The election of the Pope
Puritanism in New England

Religious wars
Zoroastrianism
Confucianism
Science and religion
Buddhism

## *Definitions*

Rumor
Gossip
Capitalism
The Great Plains
Liberal education
Morality

Ethics
Communism
Socialism
New Yorker
Loyalty
American

# FINDING THE ISSUES

I. Issues defined
II. Analysis—the method for finding issues
    A. Analyzing propositions of policy
        1. Finding the issues in propositions of policy
        2. Phrasing the issues
        3. Reducing the number of issues
        4. Classifying the issues (general issues)
    B. Analyzing propositions of value and fact
III. The five *loci* of potential issues
    A. Issues located in the first general question
    B. Issues located in the criteria
    C. Issues located in the relative importance of the criteria
    D. Issues located in the application of the criteria to evidence
    E. Issues located in the evidence
IV. How issues are used
    A. To indicate the lines of argument
    B. To group the arguments
V. Summary, questions, and exercises

# Chapter IV

## FINDING THE ISSUES

Ministers and salesmen, governors and fraternity presidents, lawyers and housewives all have ideas they want others to accept. You are barraged with efforts to persuade you: appeals and arguments of enormous variety. You try to persuade others, both individuals and groups: to accept the truth of something you believe; to value something you like; to do something you want done.

Suppose you and your friend Bob would like to take the same elective course so you can study together. You favor Anthropology. You might say:

> "A half dozen of the fellows in the fraternity are going to take Larssill's course in Anthropology next semester. Hal says Larssill's an easy grader; he doesn't even check on whether you do the reading. Last semester, he didn't call the roll half the time."

But Bob is a good student. He is not looking for a snap course; he wants one which will be worthwhile and interesting. He isn't worried about whether the professor is an easy grader. He likes to do the reading for the courses he takes. Although he recognizes that there are valuable insights to be gained from a study of anthropology, he has heard reports that the instructor is dull and fears that the course may be a bore. Therefore, while the arguments you have used seem plausible to you, they probably won't be convincing to Bob; they fail to deal with the specific questions that bother him.

41

## Issues Defined

Before you can expect to persuade Bob, you will need to find arguments that deal with the grounds upon which he disagrees with your proposal. This means that in persuasion you must find the points at which your position comes into conflict with his. These points of disagreement are called "issues."

In the question of whether Bob should take the course in Anthropology, his position is somewhat like the following:

> "I hear that Larssill is a very dull lecturer. He just stands up in front of the room and reads from those yellow pages he hasn't revised in twenty years; he doesn't even look at the class. I don't think it would be an interesting course."

The position you should take if you are to argue effectively must be somewhat along these lines:

> "Anthropology is an interesting subject. The course has field trips to Indian burial grounds and to museums. You're already interested in sociology, and Larssill's course covers the cultural background of this very area."

The *issue* Bob raises lies in the question: "Is Anthropology an interesting course?" If you argue on any grounds other than this issue that concerns Bob, your efforts are more than likely to fail.

Notice that both you and Bob express your attitudes about the Anthropology course in the form of *argument*. Both of you give *reasons* for the attitude. Moreover, when you take the position you should, the arguments directly oppose one another. In this relation you find the issue, that is, *the question over which the opposing arguments clash.*

## Analysis—the Method for Finding Issues

The process of finding issues is called analysis. Through analysis, a speaker discovers the points of controversy which he must resolve if a speech is to be effectively persuasive.

## ANALYZING PROPOSITIONS OF POLICY

When he sets out to prove that Communist China should be admitted to the United Nations, a speaker may find it necessary to prove that Nationalist China is not a symbol of democracy in Asia. By what process does he discover that he must prove the latter proposition? It seems remote from the speaker's basic purpose, but it can be an essential point in his proof. The speaker knows that his audience opposes the admission of Communist China to the United Nations on the following grounds:

> The nations of southeast Asia consider Nationalist China to be a symbol of democracy. Admitting Communist China to the United Nations would humiliate Nationalist China, discredit the symbol of democracy, and thereby weaken the confidence of southeast Asians in democracy.

To change the attitude of his listeners, the speaker must discover and remove the basic area of disagreement between his position and theirs. In the present instance, there are three points at which an issue may arise:

1. Is Nationalist China a symbol of democracy for southeast Asians?
2. Will the admission of Communist China to the United Nations discredit that symbol?
3. Will discrediting the symbol weaken democracy in Asia?

Examining these areas of potential difference, the speaker sees that he must agree with the audience that admission of Communist China to the United Nations will cause great discredit through loss of face for Nationalist China (a grave matter among eastern nations). He recognizes further that he must agree with the audience on the importance of symbols. Consequently, neither of these two questions is the issue. On the remaining point, however, speaker and audience do not agree. The *issue* lies in the question of whether Nationalist China *is* or *is not* a symbol of democracy among the nations of southeast Asia.

*Finding the issues in propositions of policy.*     An example will most easily explain the method of analyzing a proposition of policy. College fraternities have been a source of controversy on American college campuses for a very long time. From time to time, the proposal to abolish fraternities has been seriously advanced. When such a proposal is made, its discussion comprises both vigorous attack and ardent defense. If you become involved in the controversy, you will need to defend your point of view. No matter which of the opposing positions you take, here is how you can make an analysis of the proposition, "College fraternities should be abolished."

First draw a line down the middle of a sheet of paper. On the left side of the sheet list all the arguments you can find which support the proposal. On the right side, list the arguments that oppose the proposition. Match the opposing arguments by pairing them against each other:

| *College Fraternities Should Be Abolished* | *College Fraternities Should Not Be Abolished* |
| --- | --- |
| Standards for selecting members are poor. They are based on money, surface personality, and narrow identity of interests. | Standards for selecting members are high. Members are selected for their qualities of social adaptability, their character, scholarship, and leadership potential. |

An identical statement sometimes supports opposing views:

| *College Fraternities Should Be Abolished* | *College Fraternities Should Not Be Abolished* |
| --- | --- |
| Men who associate together as fraternity brothers are expected to give and receive mutual support. | Men who associate together as fraternity brothers are expected to give and receive mutual support. |

If nothing more is to be said on this point, there is no issue, and the matter should be waived—that is, left out of the discussion. There is no use taking a speaker's or an audience's time to labor a point that is not at issue. But don't forget statements of this kind; even waived matter can be useful in a speech. Save the note. (Moreover, as you may be eager to point out, the statements do clash when pertinent sentences are added, according to viewpoint: "This expectation leads to beautiful friendships" or "This expectation builds cliques and factions.")

An argument in one column or the other may appear to admit of no opposition:

| College Fraternities Should Be Abolished | College Fraternities Should Not Be Abolished |
| --- | --- |
| No apparent argument. | Members get jobs and make friends in strange towns through fraternity associations. |

It is unwise to assume that such unopposed arguments constitute waived matter. The offering of the argument suggests that an issue exists. To make the analysis complete, find an argument to answer the one that seems unopposed. In your reading or thinking about the controversy, you will usually find a suitable argument to clarify the issue. For example:

| College Fraternities Should Be Abolished | College Fraternities Should Not Be Abolished |
| --- | --- |
| This claim is a statement that fraternity members cannot verify. *Or* Fraternity membership is a false basis for selecting employees and friends. | Members get jobs and make friends in strange towns through fraternity associations. |

When you have eliminated waived matter and found opposing points of view on all the arguments, your analysis sheets will look somewhat like this:

| College Fraternities Should Be Abolished | College Fraternities Should Not Be Abolished |
|---|---|
| Fraternities discriminate against minority groups. Even where regulations no longer exist in constitutions, discrimination is practiced by "gentlemen's agreements." | Very few fraternities still have religious and racial restrictions in their constitutions. |
| Discrimination has no place on a college campus. | A man has a right to choose his friends. |
| ~~Men who associate together as fraternity brothers are expected to give and receive mutual support.~~ | ~~Men who associate together as fraternity brothers are expected to give and receive mutual support.~~ |
| The standards of selection are poor. They are based on money, surface personality, and sameness. | Fraternity members are selected for their personality, character, scholarship, and leadership. |
| Fraternity activities interfere with the study programs of the members. | Fraternities provide tutoring, require study hours, and in general watch the grades of their members. |
| Fraternities try to control the college activities for their own purposes. The member's first loyalty is to the fraternity, not the college. | Fraternity members are the strongest supporters of college activities. If they control, it is because they are more active than other students. |
| This is minor compared to all the damages they do the college by the actions noted above. | Fraternities do service projects for the college and the community. |

| College Fraternities Should Be Abolished | College Fraternities Should Not Be Abolished |
|---|---|
| This claim is a statement that fraternity members can not verify. *Or* Fraternity membership is a false basis for selecting employees and friends. | Members get jobs and make friends in strange towns through fraternity associations. |

***Phrasing the issues.*** After the analysis sheet is prepared, the points at which the two opposing sides clash are more easily seen. The next step is to phrase as a question the clash implied in each of the sets of opposing arguments. This is done in the same manner that the clash was phrased in the example of the anthropology class on page 42. The questions that result are the issues. For example:

| Fraternity activities interfere with the study programs of the members. | Fraternities provide tutoring, require study hours, and in general watch the grades of their members. |
|---|---|

The issue that separates the opposing positions is the question: "Are fraternity activities detrimental to scholastic achievement?"

Examine each of the issues to see that all are *clearly stated.* The following issue is badly drawn:

*Issue:* "How serious is the discrimination against minority groups?"

As it is phrased, the question presents no issue between clearly opposed points of view. Moreover, it assumes that there is discrimination when the very existence of discrimination is itself an issue that must be resolved.

***Reducing the number of issues.***     Not all of the issues that are discovered by your analysis of the proposition will need to be argued. The issues in any proposition should be reduced to the smallest number which will accurately identify the important elements of the clash.

Wherever possible, combine issues that seem to overlap. The following issues involve only one point of conflict:

> *Issue:* Do fraternities develop a social life restricted to their
>      own members?
> *Issue:* Do fraternities isolate their members from the normal
>      life of the campus?

Eliminate issues which seem trivial. The following clash is not central to the disagreement:

| Fraternities promote senti-mentality. | No, they don't, but why waste time arguing about that? |
| --- | --- |

Eliminate issues which seem to be irrelevant:

| Local chapters couldn't exist without help from the national fraternity. | Many local chapters and all unaffiliated fraternities operate without financial help from a national office. |
| --- | --- |

The issue exists: "Are college fraternities financially independent?" But it has no relevance to the proposition at hand.

When the job of analyzing the proposition is done, you will have a list of issues like the following:

> *Issue 1.* Do fraternities discriminate against people
>      because of race, color or creed? If it is admitted
>      that discrimination is practiced, substitute the
>      *issue:* is discrimination desirable on a college
>      campus?

*Issue 2.* (Apart from questions of race, color, or creed) do fraternities select members for the right reasons?

*Issue 3.* Are fraternity activities detrimental to scholastic achievement?

*Issue 4.* Is a fraternity member's first loyalty to this organization or to the college?

*Issue 5.* Are fraternity service projects significant compared with other strengths and weaknesses?

*Issue 6.* Does membership in a fraternity help a student after he leaves college? If it is admitted that membership is helpful, substitute the *issue:* Is fraternity membership a satisfactory basis for selecting employees and friends?

**Classifying the issues (general issues).** To persuade an audience to accept a proposition of policy, the speaker's proposal must meet the test of three general questions. The audience must be able to answer yes to these three questions before the proposition is proved.

1. Is the problem that underlies the proposition severe enough to warrant considering a change from our present course of action?
2. Is the proposed policy a more desirable means of meeting the problem than the policy now in operation?
3. Is the proposed policy workable?

These three questions are called the general issues of propositions of policy. They are general in that they are found in any policy clash. They embrace the specific issues, such as those listed above for the proposition that college fraternities should be abolished—the issues in the form that you hear argued in the dormitory, in the drugstore, on television programs.

The general issues are useful in two ways:

1. They help you to identify and interpret the specific issues you have discovered in your analysis.
2. They offer a means of grouping the specific issues by putting each one into a recognizable, workable class.

In an argument over the abolition of capital punishment, for example, some would contend that to abolish capital punishment would be desirable because innocent men are sometimes put to death (that is, the problem is severe). Others would say that the responsibility of determining another man's life or death is too heavy a burden for anyone to bear (again, the problem is severe). On the other side, you hear it argued that to abolish capital punishment would lead to an increase in crime (that is, the proposed policy is less desirable than the present one).

All these arguments relate to the first and second general issues. That is, each of the three arguments cited is concerned either with the severity of the problem or with the desirable or undesirable character of the proposal. Should you, then, when you take a position in the matter, press the issues of whether the proposed solution is workable? Not unless there are different views on workability: you are concerned with resolving the *issues that divide opinion.*

When you and an audience are agreed that it would be easy to abolish capital punishment simply by changing the law (the third general question), disagreement is limited to determining whether American justice is improperly maintained today (the first general question), and whether capital punishment is the most desirable means to maintain justice (the second general question). Is capital punishment visited on the innocent? Is the responsibility for taking life too serious for anyone to assume? Is the abolition of capital punishment the only way to maintain justice? Can't we change other laws? Can't we reform the judicial procedure? These and a number of other questions come into your listeners' minds. They become the basis of the specific issues, the ones which must be resolved to prove your case.

## ANALYZING PROPOSITIONS OF VALUE AND FACT

If you look back at the issues we have used as examples, you will recognize in them a common characteristic: in every instance, the question that states the issue must be answered with a proposition of value or fact. Then in order to resolve the issue, a speaker must be able to prove the proposition which states his position on the issue. Issues, in other words, are resolved and policy decisions are made on the basis of judgments of value and fact.

Proving a proposition of fact or value requires giving arguments to support it, arguments that will eliminate grounds the audience may have for rejecting it. Any issues that stand between speaker and audience must be resolved. The fact that there are issues in propositions of fact and value implies that they must also be analyzed before they can be proved. The same method of analysis is applied to both of these kinds of propositions.

There are two items in the statement of every proposition of value or fact. The first is the subject term, the idea, thing, or event to which reference is made. The second is the predicate term, the word or phrase or clause which says something about the subject term.

SUBJECT TERM    PREDICATE TERM

*Fact:*    The Soviet Union *is* a composite state.
*Value:*    The Soviet Union *is* warlike.

The first step in finding the issues in propositions of fact and value is to formulate a successful definition of the predicate term. This definition will serve as a set of criteria for evaluating the subject term. Analyze, for example, the proposition: "The Soviet Union is warlike." Here, "the Soviet Union" is the subject term. The predicate term is the word "warlike." A warlike nation might be defined as one which:

(1) takes direct aggressive actions against others,
(2) incites others to take aggressive actions against third parties, and
(3) operates presently in preparation for the time when it will commit one or both of the first two acts.

If these criteria satisfy a speaker as a definition of a warlike power, and if he is convinced that they will be acceptable to his

listeners, the next step is to apply them to the actions of the
Soviet Union.

The final step in the analysis is to make a judgment. If the
speaker can convince his audience that the majority of Soviet
actions fit the definition, he will prove that the proposition is
true.


## The Five Loci of Potential Issues

When there is disagreement on any proposition, each issue will
arise at one or another of five points. These are the *loci* of the
issues, the points where they are located. In analyzing a proposition he intends to prove, a speaker may expect to find in these
five regions of potential issues the conflicting attitudes that identify a division of opinion. The first region applies only to propositions of policy. The last four are the sources of issues that arise
from propositions of value and fact.

### ISSUES LOCATED IN THE FIRST GENERAL QUESTION

The first point at which conflict may be found is in the first
general issue:

> Is the problem that underlies the proposition severe
> enough to warrant considering a change from our
> present course of action?

This may be the locus of an issue in a policy proposition. No
proposal to adopt a *new* policy is likely to succeed unless there
is agreement on the need for a change from *present* policy. De-
baters generalize this issue in the question, "Does the need justify
the plan?" It may be agreed, for instance, that adequate health
facilities are lacking for many people in the United States; but in
analyzing the proposal to establish a Federal Health Insurance
program, we must ask whether the condition is serious enough
to justify a change.

## ISSUES LOCATED IN THE CRITERIA

There may be disagreement over the validity of the criteria. That is, an issue may arise over whether the predicate term of the proposition (of fact or value) has been defined. There are many speakers whose use of logic and evidence is good, but whose conclusions are based on standards that appear to be false. There is grave danger that issues will arise over definition unless such abstract terms as "good," "truth," "peace," and "prosperity" are defined with great care. In the 1956 political campaign, Republicans defined "peace" as the absence of Americans from active combat. The Democrats tried to apply the term to the broader base of general world conditions. No one disagreed that Americans were not fighting; they disagreed on whether this fact was a basis for saying that there was peace.

Apart from the matter of acceptable definition of terms, an issue can arise over criteria when there is a disagreement over whether a given criterion is acceptable no matter how well it may be defined. Expenditures for national defense are frequently attacked on the grounds that they consume far too great a proportion of the federal government's income. Often enough, these attacks are answered by saying, "It isn't a matter of cost." In other words, the whole idea of expense is rejected as a criterion for measuring the worth of a project.

## ISSUES LOCATED IN THE RELATIVE IMPORTANCE OF THE CRITERIA

Even when there is general agreement on the criteria that should be used in making a judgment, and even when the criteria are acceptably defined, an issue may arise over the relative importance (a proposition of value) the criteria should have in influencing a judgment. Suppose you were to evaluate a baseball player's ability using as criteria (a) hitting, (b) fielding, (c) running bases, (d) team spirit. You might, when comparing two men, find that one was a better hitter and base runnner but the other was a better fielder and had more spirit. The problem of deciding which is the better ball player can be solved only by deciding the issue of which of these characteristics (criteria) is most important.

## Issues Located in the Application of the Criteria to Evidence

A fourth area of potential issue is in the application of the criteria to evidence. Assuming that there was complete agreement at all three of the preceding points, there might very well be an issue at the point where the actual judgment of fact or value is made. The United Nations is much concerned of late with aggression. Any delegate to the United Nations will acknowledge that the elimination of aggression is a universally accepted criterion which guides that body in many of its deliberations. No issue there. You might even get markedly similar definitions of the term "aggression" from members of widely disparate political points of view. But ask several of these same members whether the Russians committed aggression in Budapest in October of 1956. There's an issue! Were the Russian soldiers aggressors, or were they neighbors come to rescue?

## Issues Located in the Evidence

At the base of all controversy is the possibility of disagreement over evidence (a proposition of fact). Such issues arise with great frequency between the Soviet bloc and the Western powers in the conflict known as the cold war. Were American planes flying over Soviet territory, or were they not? Were these planes armed, or were they not? Were they fired on or were they not? Neither faction will agree that the other side's evidence is true.

Analyzing propositions in terms of the five points at which conflicts of opinion will arise helps you to formulate the issues. This formulation helps you to identify and deal with the doubts and contrary opinions of the audience that constitute the barriers to persuasion. These barriers can be pierced—persuasion can take place—when the doubts are resolved and the opinions changed.

It is one thing to talk about persuading but it is another thing to do the job. How many speakers can resolve the doubts and meet the arguments of the audiences they face? The answer to this question is at the core of what makes public speaking a fascinating study.

## How Issues Are Used

### To Indicate the Lines of Argument

Analyzing the proposition lays out the groundwork for a speech. Finding the issues points the direction the line of argument must follow. For if you are to resolve the doubt and opposition in an audience, the central arguments in your speech, those which are best developed and best supported, should be the arguments which deal with the issues. A candidate for Student Council Treasurer may be an honest, brilliant, and trusted member of the college community. But if his fellow students doubt his ability to keep a good set of records, that doubt is the issue his supporters need to attack.

This emphasis on issues raises a question: Does a speaker always talk about issues? Does he ever use generally accepted ideas? In one sense you do always talk about issues, but in doing so you will use noncontroversial ideas in a very helpful way:

When you analyze a proposition, you discover points of agreement as well as areas of dispute and doubt. These points of agreement are the *waived matter* described on page 45. They serve as a common ground between you and your audience; they are the base upon which you support your position on the matters at issue.

During the campaign for Student Council Treasurer, the candidate's fellow students recognize him as a trusted person, an honest person, and a person with good ideas about student government. These acknowledgments are waived matter. His supporters can use them as arguments to help minimize the fact that he has not had the training in accounting which many of the students believe a treasurer needs. Waived matter should not be used to hide or avoid an issue. The issue is there: "Does the

Student Council Treasurer need to be trained in accounting?"
And the issue must be resolved. But by giving a more complete
picture of the contest, arguments built on waived matter help
to establish the probability that as treasurer a man might do a
better job than his opponent *even though the opponent is an
accounting major*. In this sense, even noncontroversial waived
matter should be emphasized *in relation to the issues*.

## To Group the Arguments

The practice of grouping the specific issues in a proposition
of policy under the general questions is used successfully by many
speakers. It is a good practice because it accomplishes several
things:

1. It avoids giving the audience the impression that you have a
   loose collection of scattered arguments.
2. It creates the idea that you have blocks of arguments and
   evidence, first in one area and then in another.
3. It makes transitions easier because similar issues are annexed
   to one another.
4. It gives your speaking a sense of thoroughness and adds
   credibility to your proposition.

## SUMMARY

In order to prove a proposition, a speaker must analyze it to
find the points at which his audience disagrees with his proposal.
These points of conflict are called issues.

To find the issues in propositions of policy, the propositions
are analyzed by drawing out of directly opposed arguments the
essential elements of clash and phrasing them as clearly stated
questions. The number of these questions is reduced by com-
bining issues that overlap, by eliminating waived matter, and
by eliminating issues which seem to be trivial or irrelevant. The

issues that make up the resulting list are grouped according to the general issues that embrace them. The general issues are three questions which apply to all propositions of policy and which the audience must be able to answer affirmatively before a proposition can be accepted as proved.

To find the issues in propositions of fact or value, the propositions are analyzed by defining the predicate term in the proposition. This definition is used as a criterion for determining whether available evidence warrants the judgment that the predicate term makes about the subject term.

Issues will arise at one or more of five loci:

1. The question whether a problem is serious enough to warrant a change in policy.
2. The acceptability of the criteria used to evaluate judgments of value and fact.
3. The relative importance of the criteria.
4. The judgment that is made when the criteria are applied to the available evidence.
5. The accuracy of the evidence itself.

The issues a speaker finds when he analyzes a proposition are used to help him find the lines of argument he should use in proving his proposition, and as a means of grouping his arguments for greater strength in either attack or defense.

## QUESTIONS

1. What is an issue?
2. When is an argument not an issue?
3. What three questions are the general issues used to test propositions of policy?
4. What is the use of the general issues?
5. How are propositions of fact and value analyzed?
6. What must be done first to resolve disagreements where abstract terms such as "good," "truth," or "peace" are used?
7. How are noncontroversial ideas used to argue issues?
8. For what two purposes are issues used?

## EXERCISE

1. What are the issues in the following controversy? The material is taken from an official pamphlet which the election authorities distributed to San Francisco voters before the 1961 municipal election. The opposing arguments are drafted by proponents and opponents of the measure. The statement that follows them was prepared by the League of Women Voters.

### Proposition I

The undersigned members of the Board of Supervisors of the City and County of San Francisco hereby submit to the qualified electors of the said City and County, at an election to be held therein, November 7, 1961, the following declaration of policy upon the ballot at said election, so that the electors can express their preference for or against said declaration voting "Yes" or "No" thereon, to wit:

*Shall the city and county institute proceedings to acquire the land and improvements commonly known as the Fox Theatre property as a site for musical, cultural, artistic, convention and other public assembly purposes?*

[Signatures of four Supervisors]

### Argument for Proposition I

Proposition I enables the purchase of the Fox Theatre property, bounded by Market, Polk, Hayes and Larkin Streets, for convention and other public assembly purposes, at the discretion of the San Francisco Board of Supervisors.

The Fox Theatre, which is located directly across Hayes Street from the Civic Auditorium, is a natural and essential expansion of the City's civic center convention and exhibition plant. The Fox Theatre will provide San Franciscans with a medium-sized public assembly facility urgently needed to make available necessary convention space during the Civic Auditorium remodeling already underway. It moreover fills the need for the medium-sized meeting facility which is becoming more and more important in attracting major conventions and has been adopted by other leading convention cities with which San Francisco must compete.

San Francisco's thriving convention business, which injects $37,-500,000 annually into our economy, representing according to Federal Reserve Bank estimates more than $900,000,000 in its annual flow through San Francisco trade channels, threatens to "level off" unless present facilities can be expanded.

Acquiring the Fox Theatre, along with the off-street parking ◈ this property provides, will enable San Francisco to increase its lucrative convention business in step with [the] increased number of hotel and motel rooms now being constructed to meet the rising competition from other cities.

The need for a supplementary auditorium at Civic Center has long been recognized. It was confirmed by professional planning specialists, including the Mayor's Technical Coordinating Committee on Civic Center Development. That Committee concurred with the findings of a 1958 survey by the Industrial Planning Associates in recommending that the Fox Theatre be acquired by the City and County as a part of the long-range program of Civic Center Development.

Reports by the City Engineer, the City Architect and the Superintendent of Building Inspection indicate the building is in good condition. The San Francisco Convention and Visitors Bureau states: "If the Fox Theatre is not purchased at this time, according to Director of Property, Philip Rezos, eventually a new facility of like capacity will be required by the City at a cost of over $14,000,-000 rather than the $1,050,000 which is the present price of the Fox."

The Fox Theatre has an unsurpassed location convenient to the theatres, hotels and other convention facilities. Besides helping to fill the void existing during the rehabilitation of the Civic Auditorium it will further help to create new convention business after the Civic Auditorium returns to full operation in 1965.

The use of the Theatre will permit two different conventions to meet simultaneously in the Civic Center, and in freeing the main arena of the Civic Auditorium of meetings, will permit the Civic Auditorium to be used for trade show exhibits and other events necessary to the modern convention while meetings are held in the Fox Theatre.

Acquisition of the Fox Theatre also will fill a need for medium-sized, local cultural, theatrical and other events to supplement convention use when not required for convention purposes, a growing problem now being faced by existing City facilities.

As a result of the Fox Theatre facility attracting more and larger conventions to San Francisco, the increase of outside money spent in our City by increased numbers of conventioneers will add many times the additional income from rentals of the Theatre, to the City's business, industry and payrolls.

The following, among many others, urge you to vote YES on Proposition I:

[Eight organizations listed.]

◈     This argument authorized for inclusion in the election pamphlet by [the four Supervisors listed above].

### Argument against Proposition I

The taxpayers of San Francisco are being asked to take the obsolete Fox Theater off its owner's hands. The excuse given is that the theater is needed as a "convention center."
Is it needed? What will it cost?
Read the facts that prove we do not need the Fox Theater.
The sale price has been variously estimated at anywhere from $750,000 to $1,750,000. Now it is reported at $1,100,000.
But that is just the start.
If the city buys the Fox, we taxpayers will lose $75,000 a year in tax revenues alone.
If the city buys the Fox, we taxpayers will also have to assume more than $125,000 in annual costs for rehabilitation, watchmen, and other services.
The initial investment gets the foot in the door—THEN, the taxpayers will be obligated for over $200,000 A YEAR IN COSTS.
What about the need? DON'T BE MISLED! San Francisco has no shortage of meeting space.
Mayor Christopher has said we do not need the Fox Theater, and the mayor is well acquainted with our tourist and convention business requirements.
Don't forget that two years ago we approved a $7 million bond issue to enlarge and rehabilitate the Civic Auditorium.
Don't forget that we have the Opera House, the Veterans War Memorial Building, the Masonic Temple, and many new convention accommodations in hotels recently built or now building.
Then why this sudden drive to foist the obsolete Fox Theater on to the taxpayers' backs? There are many other theaters available in San Francisco because, like the Fox, they have outlived their usefulness. If we buy the Fox won't we then be asked to buy some of these other outmoded movie palaces on the same pretense?
We agree with Mayor Christopher that the Fox Theater is not needed as a convention center.
The City of San Francisco has many other obligations far more important than taking obsolete structures off the hands of owners who understandably want to dispose of them. We can't afford to play Santa Claus to those owners.
For your own sake as a taxpayer, and as a matter of good business sense, Vote NO on the Fox Theater Purchase Proposition I.
This argument is sponsored by [four members of the Bond Screening Committee].

The arguments for and against the proposition were stated by the League of Women Voters as follows. Do any issues appear that the proponents and opponents did not raise?

FOR: The price is less than the value of the land. It could be ◈ financed by the hotel tax, and could be resold without loss if necessary. It would bring in $24,000 per year over maintenance costs. The building is in good condition, needing only elevators, stand pipes, and painting. There would be more space for exhibits in Brooks Hall and the Civic Auditorium if meeting space were available at the Fox. Medium-sized convention facilities are needed, especially while the Civic Auditorium is being remodeled next year. The office space in the building could house a small city department.

AGAINST: The Fox would not be a good investment; repairs and maintenance are sure to cost more than estimated. The source of funds for it is uncertain and may present serious legal problems or an added burden for taxpayers. Maximum use is not being made of present convention facilities. Loss of taxes ($75,506 for the theater, or $41,499 for the land if the theater is razed) is greater than any income that might result. Voters have no assurance of the amount of money that will be spent, since no dollar amount is indicated in the proposition.

# ANALYZING THE AUDIENCE

I. The nature of audience analysis
II. General attitudes of audiences
    A. Attitudes toward the speaker
    B. Attitudes toward the subject
    C. Attitudes toward the occasion
III. Specific attitudes of audiences
    A. Attitudes associated with sex
    B. Attitudes associated with age
    C. Attitudes associated with economic position
    D. Attitudes associated with social background
    E. Attitudes associated with affiliations
IV. Speech development determined by audience analysis
    A. The amount of material
    B. The kind of material
    C. The central tendency of the audience
    D. Cross pressures in the audience
    E. Premises for argument
    F. Language fitted to the audience
    G. Organization
    H. Motivation
V. Summary, questions, and exercises

# Chapter V

## ANALYZING THE AUDIENCE

A speaker could never inform a Russian audience about life in the United States if his listeners understood no English and he spoke no Russian. But using unfamiliar national tongues is not the only way in which people "speak different languages." Because of broad differences in the social and economic backgrounds of his listeners, an American speaker using English to address an American audience will in a sense talk a different language to every hearer. For example, members of the National Association of Manufacturers relate themselves in one way with the capitalist economic system, the members of the Socialist party in another. The phrase "capitalist system" triggers an entirely different set of responses for each.

To come as close as possible to talking the same language as his listeners, a speaker must have some insight into what the different responses of an audience may be. Gaining such insight requires the speaker to be conscious of the people he addresses and to be keenly aware of the things that have meaning and value for them. To understand people, he must study people, their psychology and their social behavior. Effective speakers are masters of this kind of audience analysis. They study men and social institutions to learn how people in general react to ideas and to language. They are students of art, of history, of literature, and, above all, of men.

# The Nature of Audience Analysis

The learning necessary to make you a skillful speaker began when you first became aware that you live in a complex, social world. Your work in college should broaden your general understanding of this complex world. But no one can tell you exactly how to translate general knowledge about people into specific understanding of how any given audience will respond. Neither can this chapter; but the discussion that follows will offer some suggestions about the general attitudes that audiences tend to have; it will consider some of the factors that help to determine the more specific attitudes of audiences; it will examine ways in which audience analysis influences the development of a speech. But you must discover for yourself what the members of your specific audience may think and believe and how your specific group of listeners will react.

# General Attitudes of Audiences

Every audience has three general attitudes that a speaker considers. These are the attitudes of the audience toward the speaker, toward his subject, and toward the occasion of the speech.

## ATTITUDES TOWARD THE SPEAKER

An objective understanding of the audience's attitudes toward himself is perhaps the most difficult for a speaker to attain. It is natural to think that others see him as he sees himself. He may be well qualified, honest and intelligent. But what he thinks he is or what he actually is may not be as important as what others consider him to be. He must examine his audience carefully to gain some insight into what they will think of him. In most cases the effectiveness of a speech will be increased by the realization on the part of the audience that the speaker is an expert. If you are a football player, a musician, or a campus leader, an audience may be likely to accept your information on sports, music, or student government. However, in some instances this expertness can stimulate audience resistance. Thus, if a football player asks for more aid to athletics, or if a musician wants a required course in music, or if a student leader calls for more participation in student-body activities, each of these views is to be expected and the speaker may be suspected of bias. In such instances, the speaker must be aware of possible negative reactions and develop his speech accordingly.

The football player might argue that if it were not for athletic scholarships many students would not be able to attend college. An audience made up of students seeking or holding athletic scholarships would find this argument valid. But a cross section of the student body might have an entirely different reaction. Their response would be: "Of course, he favors athletic scholarships because he gets one. But what about people like me? I'd like to have a scholarship too." The speaker would do much better if he were to recognize the possibility of such a response. He would not then argue that without scholarships many athletes would not be able to go to school, nor that scholarships are the only way to build a football team. Instead, he would choose arguments that reduce the implications of his own self-interest:

1. Tradition of athletics from Greek and Roman times.
2. Need for balanced curriculum: artistic, intellectual, physical.
3. Average student's degree is enhanced by being from a "known" school.

## ATTITUDES TOWARD THE SUBJECT

Audiences have general reactions to the subject of a speech. After a political campaign, listeners are frequently "tired of hearing about politics." Church groups may prefer not to be exposed to additional missionary drives, and in your speech class, a fourth talk on racial prejudice may be overworking a theme that was interesting in the first three. Each set of listeners must be analyzed to determine what their reactions are likely to be.

But what does the speaker do when what he wants his listeners

to know or believe seems to conflict with what they want to hear?
Change his subject and tell them what they want to hear? Certainly not. Too much of the platitudinous "God, Flag and
Mother" kind of speaking is already with us. And too many
speakers fail to realize that listeners don't really want to hear
this innocuous talk any more than they want to be told that they
are ignorant or wrong.

When the speaker feels that his listeners are not interested in
his subject but he thinks they ought to be, he bridges the gap
by building interest in his subject from the interests his listeners already have. Through his analysis of the audience, he discovers what their interests are and relates his ideas to these
interests. Thus, the speaker must know not only the audience's
attitude toward his subject but also its attitude toward many subjects. A group of business men may not be interested in religion,
but they could be interested in a subject which related business
law to the moral systems which religions teach. Are young people
interested in the problems of the aged? Perhaps not, but they
could be interested in the subject if it was related to their own
problems in understanding their grandparents in the difficult
adjustments of old age. It is almost true to say that a good speaker
can make any subject interesting if he analyzes his audience carefully.

## ATTITUDES TOWARD THE OCCASION

The occasion upon which a speech is given can either help
or hinder the response a speaker wants to win. When a geology
class is assembled to learn about earthquakes and fault lines, it is
not prepared to hear an appeal to support the Campus Fund.
The members of a Sociology class may be interested in hearing
about the recently inaugurated and highly publicized charity
drive; but they may not be, and the speaker should be prepared
for negative reactions.

If there is audience hostility, it does the speaker little good to
ignore it. Faced with negative reactions, he should treat them
honestly. He can acknowledge that his listeners are met for a
purpose other than to hear him speak. To overcome his disad-

vantage, he needs to build a speech associated with interests his audience has.

The attitude an audience has toward an occasion frequently can be used to strengthen the speech. If the occasion has some special meaning to the listeners, a speaker can associate his subject with the occasion to build interest. Holiday speeches invariably do this. The speaker at a Labor Day meeting may want to speak on world affairs but he will link his subject to the aspirations of the laboring man.

One of the most significant things a specific occasion does is to limit the scope of the audience's conception of itself. Two men sit side by side at a lodge meeting. Although one is a Democrat and the other is a Republican, they think of themselves, on this occasion, as lodge members. For a time they forget or at least submerge their political preferences. They see themselves as "brothers" and in this narrow sense they think alike. The audience's narrowed conception of itself helps to polarize the group and makes it easier for the speaker to analyze and adapt to his listeners. The religious convictions, political loyalties, and economic stations of the members, however, are still present although they may be latent. What a speaker says can awaken these latent associations in the audience to his own advantage or disadvantage.

## Specific Attitudes of Audiences

A speaker's understanding of the general attitudes any audience may have toward himself, his subject, and the occasion can give him clues to the ideas, knowledge, and feeling of the audience. But if he is to make a meaningful and useful analysis, he needs to know something about the *specific* attitudes of the audience. This is possible only if he knows something about the different kinds of values specific listeners have. While it is quite possible to over-generalize about the values which are found in audiences, some generalizations, if carefully drawn, can be quite helpful.

There are five basic factors to be considered: sex, age, economic position, social background, and specific affiliations.

## ATTITUDES ASSOCIATED WITH SEX

We would expect women to be moved by ideas that do not appeal to men, and vice-versa. An audience made up primarily of women will ordinarily be concerned with the home and children. Women will tend to be receptive to subjects they can associate with domestic problems. Men tend to be concerned about matters of job security and working conditions.

These examples reflect the usual stereotypes found in everyday life. To a significant extent, they are correct. But every classification has its limitations. An audience of women workers in a factory would very likely be much concerned about job security and working conditions, more so than men in a lodge meeting. There are factors other than sex which need to be considered and which tend to differentiate individuals and groups.

## ATTITUDES ASSOCIATED WITH AGE

Young people, it is said, tend to be flexible in their political and religious affiliations and are perhaps idealistic. As they increase in age, they tend to become concerned about the practical operation of ideas and to develop somewhat fixed attitudes toward religious and political affiliations. While these generalizations do not apply to all, they do provide a starting point for more specific analysis.

The age group of an audience may help a speaker anticipate reactions to specific subjects. A group of college freshmen and sophomores will usually be more skeptical of plans to increase the number of men drafted into military service than will an older group. Why? Because such a proposal affects them directly and inconveniently. Older people may be concerned if they have boys of draft age.

On a college campus shortly after World War II, a local community leader was arguing in favor of the draft. He argued in terms of national defense and pointed out fervently that he believed in the draft even though he knew his own boy would have to serve in the armed forces. His audience of young college students viewed this proposal as an attempt to restrict their freedom and also felt the man had no feelings for his own son.

## ATTITUDES ASSOCIATED WITH ECONOMIC POSITION

Many problems have implications for the listener's pocketbook. Proposals that involve an increase in taxes are usually less acceptable to those who must pay the taxes than they are to those who may avoid them. Also, proposals which will benefit specific groups economically, such as support for farm income, airline subsidies, tax preference for the oil and gas companies, will find acceptance among these groups more readily than among groups which do not benefit. In your local community or college, some of the same reactions can be seen. Athletes and students interested in athletics may strongly support an increase in the student-activities fees by which athletic programs are financed. Other students who have no lively interest in athletics may object to an increase in their student fees.

It is easy to put more emphasis on economic position than is justified. Many people have come to consider all reactions as economic. These "economic determinists" ignore the many other factors which determine attitudes. Because of a strong belief in education, an upper-income person without school-age children will frequently favor aid to education despite increased taxes. And so, while their economic position can tell you much about your listeners, it must be viewed as just one of the factors that influence their reactions.

## ATTITUDES ASSOCIATED WITH SOCIAL BACKGROUND

The past conditions of their lives, the way they grew up, the kinds of attitudes and values their parents had, make up the social background of audiences and have a significant effect on how they react to ideas. You can easily imagine that the views of one group might differ from the views of any other. Does an audience meet as a group of Polish-Americans? Of Nisei? Of Negroes? Of Southerners? Of Roman Catholics? Of Sons or Daughters of the American Revolution?

Most people find it impossible to escape their background completely. Even though a man may leave behind certain ties like the "old-fashioned" ideas of his parents, these ties still have the power to color his thoughts and to affect his responses. His own ideas have changed, but he still lives in the atmosphere of his background. The old ideas must at least be tolerated and the people who still hold them expect him to act in accordance with the value systems of the old background.

## ATTITUDES ASSOCIATED WITH AFFILIATIONS

While the analysis of sex, age, and economic-social backgrounds tells much about audiences, a knowledge of their affiliations will help to pinpoint analysis much more sharply. Knowing that an audience has a substantial percentage of American Legionnaires, Protestants, or Democrats can help a speaker judge its probable attitudes toward a subject. These specific affiliations do not tell all that one needs to know about a group, but as a part of total audience analysis, they give helpful clues. Organizations such as the American Legion have specific statements of principle which will help to guide a speaker in developing a topic. Chambers of Commerce, farm groups, and labor unions usually represent recognizable social and economic attitudes. Service clubs, such as Rotary, Kiwanis, and Lions all have projects which are important to them. Specific religious organizations— the Knights of Columbus, B'nai B'rith, the Men's Club of the First Baptist Church—have distinctive approaches to questions of faith and morals. Political clubs have their obvious partisan positions. Knowledge of the aims of these specific groups will help a speaker to do a better job of persuading their members.

A careful analysis of the audience in terms of the sex, age, economic and social backgrounds, and specific affiliations of its members, combined with a broad knowledge of people in general, and reinforced by an understanding of their thoughts and feelings, will give a speaker useful insights into the responses the audience may be expected to give.

## Speech Development Determined by Audience Analysis

It is rarely possible for a speaker to give an audience all the evidence and reasoning that support his position. He must find some basis on which to select the material. That basis is the audience. Audience analysis helps to determine eight elements of the content and development of a speech: (1) the amount of material to use; (2) the kind of material; (3) the central tendency of the audience; (4) cross pressures in the audience; (5) premises from which to reason; (6) language; (7) organization; and (8) motivation.

### THE AMOUNT OF MATERIAL

The amount of material needed to clarify or to prove a specific point within a speech is determined by the need of the audience. In a speech to inform, for example, you will need few specific details if you know that the audience can easily understand a given point. In persuasion, the keynote speaker at a political convention judges the amount of evidence he will need to support his arguments from knowing that the members of the convention will already agree with the position he upholds. When student-body funds are allocated to various campus activities, a lack of student interest in music may motivate the members of the student council to cut the budget for the opera program. A speaker who is aware of the student council's attitude will give a great deal of evidence when he goes before that group to ask more money for the opera program.

### THE KIND OF MATERIAL

As you prepare a speech, you will gather more information than you can use in one speech. The process of selecting the items that are best for your purpose will be based on the nature of your audience. You will choose quotations not only because they say exactly what you want them to say but also because the authorities you quote are respected by your audience. You will draw illustrations from experiences which are understandable to the group to which you speak. If you are speaking to freshmen students who have never had a chemistry course, you will need to adjust your talk on atomic energy to take account of this fact.

## THE CENTRAL TENDENCY OF THE AUDIENCE

From your knowledge of the composition of the audience look for some central tendency around which your listeners' attitudes can be grouped. Will they tend to be liberal or conservative on economic and social problems? Do they have strong religious convictions? Does the age of the group affect the kinds and amount of experience they have had? What is the proportion of men and women in the audience and what effect is this likely to have on the way they view the subject of your speech?

Naturally, this central tendency provides only a general picture of what an audience is like. You cannot, in one speech, take into consideration all the possible attitudes an audience may have. Prepare your speech to appeal to the bulk of the audience. *You cannot please everyone.*

## CROSS PRESSURES IN THE AUDIENCE

Although many audiences will have strong central tendencies on which a speaker can build an appeal, others will be under cross pressures. Whenever two or more central tendencies conflict in an audience at any one time, cross pressures exist.

Investigations of the American electorate in the 1952 presidential campaign revealed this example of cross pressures: While a majority of the American people had a strong emotional attachment to the Democratic party, there was present also strong dissatisfaction with conditions in the country. The Republican party resolved this cross pressure by nominating for the presidency a man who could convincingly argue that he could improve conditions in America but who was at the same time sufficiently nonpolitical to neutralize the strong emotional attachment of many people for the Democratic party. Many Democrats in 1952 were able to say, "Eisenhower is almost a Democrat. He really isn't a Republican at all."

A common example of cross pressure is furnished by the teenager whose parents have always emphasized the need to do well in school. The young man agrees with his parents, but he also needs the companionship of his own friends. When his friends want him to "go with the gang to the movies" on the night before a chemistry test, he is under cross pressure. If he can find a way to go to the movie and still get his studying done, the cross pressure will be resolved and he will go to the movie after all.

It is an important part of audience analysis to discover whatever cross pressures are in the audience. A speaker must then find evidence, argument, and motivation which will resolve them.

## Premises for Argument

Frequently, reasoning is based upon starting points or premises that speakers do not need to prove. Such unproved and sometimes even unmentioned premises are called assumptions. It is not necessary for a speaker to prove certain assumed premises because they are already accepted by his audience. A minister begins a sermon on the assumption that there is a God and that his congregation believes it. Frequently he assumes other theological principles which are accepted by his congregation. In most Christian churches, for example, he assumes that God is triune, but not so in the Unitarian church.

It is virtually impossible to argue without assumptions. If a speaker felt compelled to go back to first principles on every argument, he would both bore his listeners and waste valuable speaking time.

Look at such traditional documents as the Declaration of Independence and the Constitution. See there the excellent examples of premises stated without proof. Observe:

We the People of the United States, in Order to form a more perfect Union, establish Justice, insure domestic Tranquility, provide for the common defence, promote the general Welfare, and secure the Blessings of Liberty to ourselves and our Posterity, do ordain and establish this Constitution for the United States of America.

The writers of this document assume without submitting any proof that union is desirable, that justice ought to be established, that domestic tranquillity should be insured, that the general welfare is worth promoting, and that liberty is a blessing. What proof is necessary? Would *you* reject any one of these assumptions?

A speaker should know enough about the groups he addresses to be able to use arguments based on premises which his audience already believes. To know what premises will be acceptable to a given group, the speaker must determine what assumptions his audience holds and use them as premises for his arguments.

## LANGUAGE FITTED TO THE AUDIENCE

Language is affected, even determined, by such factors as time, place, sex, and circumstances. At a Presbyterian convention, a man does not use the same language he might at a convention of Lion's club members. In many significant ways, there are differences between the language of men and the language of women. Certainly the language of the educated person is different from the language of the uneducated. Adlai Stevenson was criticized in 1952 because he "talked over the heads of the American people." But Stevenson was not being criticized for not knowing the language. Most people lauded his language. The real criticism was of his audience analysis. The Democratic party countered with the charge that Mr. Stevenson's critics were underrating the American public. In this instance, analysis of the contemporary American political audience became an actual issue in the campaign.

## ORGANIZATION

Chapter XVIII (Speaking to Persuade) discusses the way in which the organization of the speech is determined by the nature of the audience you address. You will want to use different methods of organization depending on the extent to which the audience agrees or disagrees with what you say.

## MOTIVATION

The motivation you select should be one that is not only related to the needs of your audience but is also acceptable to its values. The experience of the supervisor of a group of electricians working on high-tension lines illustrates this point. The accident rate among the workmen was quite high and all attempts to frighten the men by telling them of the physical dangers of not grounding the line and of not wearing safety helmets failed. Even such crudely direct approaches as showing them the dead body of a friend who failed to heed the warnings were not successful.

The supervisor was completely frustrated until he realized that self-preservation was not an acceptable motivation for the men. To them, not wearing a safety helmet and not grounding the wire were signs of manliness. They were, in their own minds, strong and able people; others had made errors because of their weakness. The emotional motivation was changed. The ego of the men was utilized as a basis of persuasion. They were told that no one cared if they wanted to kill themselves but that only fools did what they were doing. The workman who violated the safety rules was ridiculed as silly or even worse. When the men identified themselves with this concept, the number of accidents decreased. The success of this second motivation was the result of a more realistic analysis of the audience.

## SUMMARY

To be effective, a speaker must adapt his speech to his listeners. He must know their ideas before he prepares his speech. The process of audience analysis, through which the speaker gains his knowledge of his listeners, is one which demands continued study and observation of people. There are no infallible rules for knowing how audiences will respond. However, some clues to the nature of the audience can be found.

A speaker must determine the kinds of attitudes an audience has toward him, toward his subject, and toward the occasion of his speech. There are, moreover, specific factors which the speaker can use to gain insight into the ideas and attitudes of his listeners. He needs to know the make-up of the audience in terms of its sex, age, economic position, social background, and affiliations.

Once the speaker has made his analysis of the audience, he can use it in a number of ways to strengthen his speech. His analysis will help him choose the amount and kind of material he should use. He can estimate what the central tendency of audience attitude is, or, in cases where there are conflicting central tendencies, he can determine what cross pressures are operating. The speaker uses the information he gains from analyzing the audience to determine what premises he can assume without the need for proof. His language and the organization of his speech will be influenced by what he knows about the audience. He uses his analysis of the audience to help him select the best motivation for the speech.

## QUESTIONS

1. What general attitude of an audience is the most difficult for a speaker to assess?

2. Your class being your audience, which of the five factors of audience analysis do you consider most important? Least?

3. How do cross-pressures affect audience response?

4. How is argument affected by the assumptions of an audience?

5. If you say that someone "talks over the heads of his listeners" do you mean his language is poor? If you do, then in what way?

6. How might the motivation of a teen-ager for safe driving be different from those of his parents?

# EXERCISES

1. Write a brief paper (no more than three double-spaced typewritten pages) in which you explain what you need to know about one of your parents or a brother or sister before you ask a favor. You will probably find it easier to write this paper if you select a specific favor to ask. Your purpose in this paper is to make an "audience" analysis of that one person, so do not write about the techniques you would use to get the favor. For instance, what do you need to know about your father's ideas and attitudes in order to successfully ask him to let you use the car for a Saturday-night date?

2. Select any one of the five factors which determine the specific attitudes of an audience. Also select for consideration some specific question of current news interest. How do you think the attitudes of any two groups of people within the classification (for example: men and women, teenagers and middle-aged people, well-to-do people and poor people, Negroes and Caucasians) would differ *generally* on the question? What limitations do you see in this generalization? If you believe that on the question you have chosen there are no differences, explain why you believe so.

3. Make a careful and honest assessment of yourself, as "audience" for a speaker. What do people who have known you think about your knowledge and beliefs?

# SUPPORTING MATERIAL: TYPES AND USES

    **I. Clarity and interest**
    **II. Types of Supporting Material**
        **A. Definition**
            1. Logical definition
            2. Rhetorical definition
        **B. Facts**
            1. Examples
                a. Real examples
                b. Hypothetical examples
                c. Extended examples
                d. Using examples for clarity and interest
                e. Using examples to prove
            2. Statistics
                a. Using statistics for clarity and interest
                b. Using statistics to prove
        **C. Opinions about facts: testimony**
            1. Using testimony
            2. Evaluating testimony
        **D. Comparison and contrast**
    **III. Acceptability of supporting material**
        **A. To the speaker**
        **B. To the audience**
    **IV. Summary, exercises, and questions**

# Chapter VI

## SUPPORTING MATERIAL:
## TYPES AND USES

In any serious effort to communicate, a speaker must select carefully the materials which will support and illustrate his ideas. Since he will have (or should have) far more as the result of his research, he uses only those specific items which will convey his ideas to his audience.

In every kind of speaking—to entertain, to inform, to persuade, to explore—the kinds of materials used are of the same sort. As the purpose in speaking differs, however, and speakers work toward different general ends, they make different uses of the material. That is, they adapt their materials to the specific end they want to attain. But no matter what the end, and no matter what materials speakers use, if they are to be effectively communicative, the materials they choose must meet the requirements of clarity and interest.

### Clarity and Interest

A speaker's analysis of his audience will help him decide which of his materials he should use to achieve the two necessary qualities of clarity and interest. Clarity without interest will produce a speech that is dull and therefore difficult to listen to. Actuarial tables, for example, can be eminently clear, but they do not make good listening. On the other hand, there is harm in using materials which may be interesting in themselves, but which add nothing necessary to the clarification of the ideas.

The ideas in a speech are reflections of the experiences of the speaker (these include his research and knowledge). But an audience understands the ideas in terms of its own experience. Language is interpreted by a hearer on the basis of his experience with the concepts and objects to which the language refers. To provide clarity and interest, a speaker communicates his ideas in language that makes it easy for an audience to visualize the concepts and the objects the speaker is discussing. Abstractions must be made concrete; generalities must be made specific; what is obscure must be made clear. The speaker uses concrete, specific, and vivid details to help his listeners visualize his ideas in terms of their own experience. These details are called supporting material.

## Types of Supporting Material

Supporting materials are of four kinds: *Definitions* are used to clarify words or concepts whose meanings are unfamiliar or obscure. *Facts* are details found in the form of examples and statistics. Opinion about facts is the *testimony* of others. *Comparison and contrast* provide a relationship between the known and the unknown. Each of these helps to clarify and provide interest for your ideas.

### DEFINITION

When a druggist fills a prescription, he labels his bottle of medicine carefully so that there may be no confusion about the contents or the dosage. In a similar sense, language provides labels for ideas. The labels put on ideas, like the labels on bottles of medicine, should be instantly recognizable, clear, and precise. But language is not always easy to use in speaking about complex or abstract ideas. "Democracy," "communism," "union shop" are not "seen" in the same sense as "aspirin" or "Vitamin C." When a speaker uses words like "aspirin" or "Vitamin C," a listener recognizes with immediate clarity exactly what the speaker is talking about even though he may not have full insight into the chemical components of the concrete things named. "Democracy," "communism," and "union shop," however, are abstract terms. These labels have a greater variety of meanings than do those of more concrete objects. Speakers often use language as if the labels for such abstractions were understood as easily and universally as the labels put on concrete things. But too often listeners are confused because they do not understand the labels. Therefore, an abstract, unfamiliar, or obscure term will need to be defined.

No amount of effort at clear definition will make it certain that doubtful words have precisely the same meaning for every listener. Universal understanding is virtually impossible, but fortunately it is also unnecessary. Ideas can be communicated adequately in spite of the inherent ambiguity of language. Of course, the closer a speaker and his audience come to a mutual understanding of language, the better the communication will be.

The basic requirements of a good definition are two: (1) it will give meaning to the term defined and, (2) it will limit or restrict the meaning of the term in order to avoid ambiguity. Effective definitions must not only fulfill these two requirements, but they must also be within the scope of the listener's experience: his willingness to accept them and his ability to understand.

***Logical definition.*** There are many different methods of definition, but the one that best fulfills these two requirements is definition by classification, so-called *logical* definition. In order to supply meaning to a term, logical definition puts the thing defined into a class with which the listener is already familiar. Then, to restrict the meaning and eliminate ambiguity, the definition distinguishes the thing defined from all other members of that class. To the baseball player, a "Texas Leaguer" is a safe hit on a short fly ball which falls to the ground between the infielders and the outfielders. It belongs to the class of safe hits, but is differentiated from other safe hits by the facts that (1) it is a short fly ball, and (2) it hits the ground between the infielders and outfielders.

***Rhetorical Definition.*** Whereas definition by classification is called logical, definition by certain other methods may be termed *rhetorical.* Strictly speaking, these methods do not actually define terms, but they are instrumental in helping hearers to understand them.

*Examples, descriptions,* and *figures of speech* are illustrations of rhetorical definition. While they do not define, they help to explain and thus are useful. A speaker can use definition by *example* to explain his use of the term "integrity."

> The characteristic of integrity was what made Woodrow Wilson tour the country in defense of the League of Nations, an idea he believed in, even at the cost of his health. He might have stayed home and said, "There is nothing more I can do." Edmund Burke retained his integrity by denouncing the excesses of the French Revolution over the objections of his friends, even though it meant he must leave the party he had struggled to build. In 1952, Adlai Stevenson refused to strengthen his political position at the expense of his convictions when he declined to dissociate himself from the policies of Secretary of State Dean Acheson.

To describe a gambrel roof by telling what it looks like does not define the term, no matter how many details are elaborated, but the *description* may help to clarify a hearer's understanding.

Such *figures of speech* as "the world is a stage" or "the devil is a roaring lion" do not define the world or the devil; nevertheless, to a certain extent they help a listener to visualize the world and the devil.

*Comparison and contrast* are other methods, or aspects of a single method, of rhetorical definition. In these, a speaker tries to show the meaning of a term either by likening it to something or by differentiating it from something with which his listeners are already familiar:

> Writing is like speaking in that its major purpose is to communicate an idea.
> The union shop is not exactly like the closed shop. A man can get a job at a union shop before he joins the union, but he must already belong to a union before he can be employed in a closed shop.

Strategy makes plans; tactics puts them into operation.

Explaining the *usage, etymology,* or *history* of a term is also rhetorical definition. A dictionary may report the *usage* of a term:

"EXPEDIENT, *adj.* Tending to promote some proposed or desired object."

It may also report the *etymology* of a word or the *history* of its development. The meaning of the word "persuasion" may be clarified by showing that it comes from the Latin phrase *per suasionem,* which means "through sweetness." To the *etymology* of the word may be added something of its *history:* The tribes of Europe, who found the declensions of the Latin language difficult and awkward, dropped off endings and used words in their root forms. Thus the phrase *per suasionem* lost its *em* ending and became the single word "persuasion." The concept of sweetness is still an important connotation of the term. The dictionary's report of usage makes no precise logical definition of a term; neither does the etymology of a word or the history of its development. By telling these, though, a speaker may convey enough of the term's meaning to make it understood.

An *operational definition* tells what something does, how it operates. It will frequently be the clearest of all rhetorical definitions because it can give an exact picture of how the thing being defined acts.

A ship floats on water and transports men and goods from one shore to another.

Freedom gives one the right to do anything he wishes so long as he does not harm another or limit another's rights.

In representative government, the people elect men and women to act for them in carrying out their wishes.

One brief word of caution is necessary about the use of definitions. While audience analysis may reveal that many of your listeners do not understand a word, there may be in the audience many who already know what it means. So, avoid phrases such as, "I know that you don't understand what this term means so let me define it for you." If your listeners do not know what the term means, you scarcely need to tell them that they don't know. It is far better to put the responsibility on yourself: "To make myself clear, let me point out that by ——, I mean ——."

## FACTS: EXAMPLES

Facts are objective data gathered by experience and observation. These are presented to an audience by a speaker in two forms: *examples* and *statistics*.

If you want to become a truly effective speaker, learn to use examples well. Think of the interesting speakers you have heard, whether on a public platform or in your own living room. Remember the many examples they used to illustrate the subjects they discussed.

Examples may be either real or hypothetical, brief or extended in length.

***Real examples.*** An example is an account of an incident or occurrence that a speaker relates to illustrate a point, or an object or condition that he cites. A real example is an incident that has actually occurred or an object that actually exists. "A good example of a great T-formation team was the old Chicago Bears." "St. Stephen's Church is a good example of what I mean by modern church architecture." "The Ford, Plymouth, and Chevrolet are low-priced cars."

***Hypothetical examples.*** If an example describes an incident that did not actually occur, but might, the example is hypothetical. A speaker wanted to illustrate the idea that optimism can sometimes be foolish. He told the story of a man who was gaily whistling as he drove down a country road one day and met a neighbor.

"Bill," said the neighbor, "what makes you so happy today?"

"I'm just coming back from town where I sold a hog for $100."

"That's wonderful, Bill, that's wonderful. What did the hog cost you?"

"Just $50.00."

"And how long did you keep him?"

"Just a year."

"And how much corn did you feed him?"

"Just $50.00 worth."

"Well, Bill," continued the neighbor, "you didn't make much money on that hog, did you?"

"No," said Bill, still smiling. "I didn't make much money but I had the use of the hog for a year."

Except for the fact that it recounts an incident that did not occur, a hypothetical example is no different from an example that is real.

*Extended examples.* On occasion, a speaker will want to develop an example at somewhat greater length and in more detail than is possible in the brief form the example ordinarily takes. Such illustrations are called extended examples and may be either hypothetical or real. In Washington, D.C., on September 23, 1944, President Franklin Delano Roosevelt addressed the Brotherhood of Teamsters. It was the opening political speech of his fourth-term campaign. In the following portion of that speech, President Roosevelt leaves no doubt that he is using an example to show the attitude of the Republican party toward labor:

I got quite a laugh, for example—and I am sure that you did —when I read this plank in the Republican platform adopted at their national convention in Chicago last July:

"The Republican party accepts the purpose of the National Labor Relations Act, the Wage and Hour Act, the Social Security Act, and all other Federal statutes designed to promote and protect the welfare of American working men and women, and we promise a fair and just administration of these laws."

Many of the Republican leaders and Congressmen and candidates, who shouted enthusiastic approval of that plank in that convention hall, would not even recognize these progressive laws if they met them in broad daylight.

Indeed, they have personally spent years of effort and energy —and much money—in fighting every one of those laws in the Congress, in the press and in the courts, ever since this Administration began to advocate them and enact them into legislation.

That is a fair example of their insincerity and their inconsistency.

*Using examples for clarity and interest.*    There are some rules for using examples which can well be remembered by a speaker:

(a) Use extended examples only when the point to be described is an essential one. For minor points, brief examples are sufficient.

(b) Use the best example you can find for the particular idea you are discussing. Unless examples are carefully chosen, there is a danger that they will not clearly exemplify the point a speaker is making. The offering of an example which fails to illustrate his point precisely forces a speaker to say, "This isn't exactly what I mean, but . . ." The listener is thrown off the track and, after a few such instances, he may well give up listening.

(c) Be sure that the necessary value characterizations are given with the example: The Chicago Bears are not just *any* T-formation team; they are a "great" one, while the Reseda High School Regents are a "typical high-school" T-formation team.

(d) If necessary, use more than one short example for a specific point. A single example might enlighten part of the audience and not the rest, or may only partly enlighten the audience as a whole. A greater number and variety of examples will often clarify or prove when one example might fail.

(e) Use real examples whenever it is possible; but when it is not, use hypothetical ones. If no real example of how to use your brakes on a slippery pavement is available you can say, "Suppose you were coming down Ventura Boulevard at about twenty-five miles an hour in a heavy rain when a truck pulled out of Balboa Boulevard. Here's what might happen. . . ." Though your hearer never experienced this event, he can visualize it and can profit by the description. This hypothetical example has the characteristics of the real example: the experience on Ventura Boulevard is not real but hearers recognize the event and have had similar experiences or heard of similar experiences which are enough to make it seem real.

***Using examples to prove.***    When a speaker uses examples to prove a point in a speech, he must not only choose illustrations for their value in achieving clarity and interest, but he must also select instances that meet three further criteria. If the answer to all three of the following questions is Yes, the examples may be considered acceptable:

*Are the examples representative?* Examples must be typical, not exceptions to the rule. A father may be generous with his son to the point of indulgence. He may give the boy everything he needs or wants. But let Dad say No when Bob wants the car some night in the middle of the week and what does he hear? "Aw, Dad, you never let me have any fun." The boy singles out what is perhaps the only atypical example in an otherwise clear pattern of behavior as the basis for an unfounded generalization. A specific instance must give a true picture of the situation it illustrates if it is to be effective as a means of proof.

*Are the examples sufficient in number to give clear support of the point the speaker is making?* The number of instances that will be necessary is not the same in every case. One may be enough: the first sunburn you get on a cloudy day will be quite enough to establish the generalization that exposure to the sun is dangerous even on a cloudy day. On the other hand, it took quite a number of treacherous acts by the Communists to demonstrate that they are not to be trusted.

*Are negative instances accounted for?* It is not reasonable to expect to establish belief in an idea if there is substantial evidence to the contrary. A wealthy man may on many occasions show civic pride and social responsibility, and a speaker might try to characterize him as a good and philanthropic citizen. The speaker would not be notably successful if his audience knew the man's fortune was made in legal but morally doubtful operations in slum-area real estate.

## FACTS: STATISTICS

Statistics are figures a speaker uses to clarify an idea or to prove a proposition. Speaking to the California Council of Geography Teachers at San Jose, California, on May 7, 1960, the Stanford University geographer C. Langdon White supported the proposition that industrial development should not be imposed too rapidly on predominantly agricultural Latin America. He used statistics to explain certain aspects of food supply in Latin America:

Considering that agriculture predominates over most of Latin America, it is rather shocking to learn that with the exception of Argentina, Uruguay, Cuba, and Chile the diets of most of the inhabitants are inadequate on all counts. The average caloric intake is about 2,400, varying from around 1,900 in Peru to 3,200 in Argentina. While the total agricultural production in 1958–1959 exceeded the previous year by 3.5 per cent, the population is growing so rapidly that the per capita increase is only about 1 per cent. . . . It is believed that even if the amount of food were to be increased by 25 per cent, it would bring the diet barely above the minimum needed for health.*

In a sense, statistics are often collections of examples. When White described the average caloric intake as "varying from around 1,900 in Peru to 3,200 in Argentina," he had in effect compacted examples of the diet-measure from many inhabitants of these countries.

*Using statistics for clarity and interest.*    When statistics employ large numbers (roughly four or more digits), it is wise to round them off. For instance, the 1950 population of Chicago, Illinois, was 3,620,962 but if you wanted to use this in a speech you would probably say, "In 1950 the population of Chicago was a little over three and one-half million." Even though 120,962 is a substantial number of people, "three and one-half million" is accurate enough for most purposes and much easier for the listener to remember.

* *Vital Speeches of the Day*, August 1, 1960. Reprinted by permission of the editors of *Vital Speeches*.

After statistics have been rounded off, they can be made still more meaningful by comparison. The round figure of three and one-half million is easier to comprehend if it is compared: "That's approximately five times the size of our own city of Pittsburgh." Percentages, fractions, and proportions all help to put the compacted examples we call statistics into a clear relationship with other facts. Statistics, then, can add clarity and interest if you round them off and, by using comparison, show their relationship to other ideas.

*Using statistics to prove.* When statistical data are used as illustrations to clarify an idea, it is important, of course, that they be accurate and meaningful as well as interesting and clear. When figures of this kind, however, are used as evidence to support a proposition, it is even more important that they be examined carefully. Ask these questions about the statistics you use:

*Are the data current?* The date of compilation is one of the first things to ask about statistical information. Recency is of little concern, of course, in matters that change slowly or slightly if at all. A statement of the number of times a human heart beats per minute need not be doubted today just because the subject was studied years ago. The infant-mortality rate in American hospitals does not change rapidly enough to demand new study every day. If, however, you see a report on the number of jet fighter planes Russia is supposed to have, you would want to know when the count was made. Soviet air power is not static. A report of this kind suggests a second question to ask about statistics.

*How reliable is the source of the statistical data?* Completely apart from any interpretation put upon figures—the validity of any comparison between, let us say, the air powers of the United States and Russia—accurate reporting depends upon the reliability of sources. You must ask: Who made the statistical study? Did the information come from Soviet sources which may be intentionally misleading?

Certain governmental agencies such as the Bureau of Labor Statistics are generally accepted as a source of honest reports. The Brookings Institute is a private research group which has earned general acceptance. But, as any television viewer can tell you, many so-called independent agencies are nothing more than sources of advertising copy.

*Do the statistics measure what they appear to measure?* This question asks about the reliability of any interpretation of the statistics themselves. It would be doubtful to conclude that one-fourth of the student body of an entire college is Italian because two of the eight students in an advanced class in the Modern Language department happen to have been born in Rome. This is an insufficient sampling.

Suppose, moreover, that the average age of the same eight students is thirty years. This measure of the sample is probably a poor measure of the age of the students in the whole college, and it can be misleading in reference to the class itself. The two Italian students may be a man and his wife who came to this country after the man had retired from business and both may be sixty-five years old. If four of the other students in the class are eighteen and two are nineteen, this distribution makes the *average* age of the class thirty, but no one in the class comes within ten years of the average.

Finally, it would be wise to ask how the word "average" is used: Does it refer to the mean, the median, or the mode? The *mean* is a simple arithmetical average. To find it, add together the quantity of each item in a series and divide by the number of items. The *mode* is the figure which appears most frequently in a series. The *median* is the point above and below which half of the items fall. In the example cited above, the mean age of the students is thirty, the mode is eighteen, and the median is between eighteen and nineteen. In other words, statistical data are subject to scrutiny and interpretation. The old saying that figures don't lie is itself a generalization that bears investigation.

## Opinions about Facts: Testimony

Often the material a speaker has gathered reflects some judgment on the part of its source and comes to him as an interpretation of the data involved. These interpretations are called *testimony* and are *opinions* about *facts*.

***Using testimony.*** Using testimony in a speech makes it possible for you to tap the resources of generations of thought and expression. All that mankind has written and said becomes a vast reservoir from which you can draw the authoritative testimony of expert witnesses. You add clarity and interest to your ideas and strength to your propositions when you associate your attitudes and opinions with the thoughts and feelings of men your audiences know, respect, and admire.

The privilege of using testimony in a speech is one that brings certain obligations. Honesty demands that you identify ideas and language that you have taken from someone else. Completely apart from the added strength that the citation of an authoritative source adds to your speech, any hint of plagiarism is to be avoided.

Putting directly quoted testimony into a speech may bring some awkward moments. To avoid these, it is generally wise not to use the words "quote" and "unquote" to identify the beginning and end of a direct quotation. Instead, identify the source of your material as thoroughly as honesty demands, then let your voice (through pause, change in tempo, or other means) indicate which words are yours and which belong to your source.

Your use of testimony need not be in the form of a direct quotation, that is, word for word. It can be presented in your words with an indication that the explanation or comparison has some respected person as its source. If the explanation of an authority is particularly clear, you may want to quote it *verbatim,* but, in general, putting the idea into your own words will keep it on the level of language used in your speech.

Regardless of the form, testimony is always opinion *about* facts, not fact itself. Consequently, the best use of testimony will reveal how the authority cited arrived at his conclusion. Testimony which merely states an opinion asks a listener to accept the conclusion simply because he trusts the authority. It is far stronger to support this trust with the facts and reasons behind the judgment.

***Evaluating testimony.*** Before you decide to use a piece of testimony, you should ask yourself two questions about it:

*Is the authority qualified?* The background, training, and experience of the person whose opinions you use for evidence should put him in a position to know what he is talking about. To be truly qualified, he should be speaking in his field of competence. A theologian, for example, is by no means necessarily an authority in the field of nuclear biology. The newsboy on the corner is not necessarily an authority on current history.

*Is the authority objective?* It is reasonable to question the objectivity of any person in a matter that concerns himself. You may be thoroughly convinced that the United States is the best country in the world. But what if you were to ask a British audience to believe it because John F. Kennedy says so? The response would be, "But he's your President! What would you expect him to say?" Opinions you quote as supporting material should come from persons who will not be accused of bias in the matter at hand.

## COMPARISON AND CONTRAST

While they can be treated separately, *comparison* and *contrast* are in essence the same process. Comparisons show how things are *like* other things; contrasts show how things are *unlike*

In comparison, the speaker chooses something familiar to the audience and likens it to the unknown factor he wishes to explain. One student speaker, in explaining the principle of radar, compared it to bouncing a ball off a garage door in that the farther away from the garage the player gets, the longer it takes the ball to bounce and return. If he could measure the amount of time and the speed of the ball, he could determine the distance to the door. He then went on to say that ball-bouncing is roughly comparable to the way radar works. Radio waves, whose speed is known, are thrown against an object and the length of time the reflected wave takes to return indicates the distance of the object from the sender.

Contrast is used to show differences. An audience may not be clear on the difference between radar and sonar. After explaining the basic nature of radar by comparing a radio wave with the ball bounced off the garage door, a speaker can explain sonar by noting that, while radar employs radio waves, sonar employs sound waves.

## Acceptability of Supporting Material

### TO THE SPEAKER

A speaker necessarily asks whether speech material is acceptable to himself before he asks whether it is acceptable to his audience. A socially responsible speaker uses supporting material only if it is correct and truthful. A speaker who falsifies evidence, who deliberately deceives to "prove" a proposition, seriously perverts the whole function of speech. For literally thousands of years, high moral standards have been recognized as the mark of an intelligent man discussing social problems.

In most cases, however, the truthfulness of a speaker can be assumed. It may normally be taken for granted that when a speech is built of faulty materials they have been used through honest error. The error may arise because the material is insufficient, because it comes from an inadequate number of sources, because it is incorrectly recorded or interpreted, or because the sources themselves are at fault. In any case, the results will appear as poor definitions, insufficient examples, inaccurate statistics, inadequate testimony. For these reasons, a speaker must rigorously examine his supporting materials before he decides to use them.

### TO THE AUDIENCE

Regardless of its accuracy, however, a speaker's material will be of little value unless it is *acceptable to the audience.* Acceptability is not a logical characteristic; it is psychological. Even purely objective data appearing in the *Democratic Digest* might draw the raised eyebrow of disbelief from a vigorous member of the Young Republican Club. There are probably few non-Communist Hungarians willing to accept much of anything that Nikita Khrushchev says. The *American Mercury* of July, 1957,

refers to *The Reporter* as a "Leftist magazine," yet articles and
editorials in *The Reporter* are looked upon by many intelligent
people as accurate appraisals of the political scene. A loyal
reader of either magazine might refuse to accept a statement
from the other. As a speaker looks over all his possible material,
he must choose that which will be acceptable to his audience.
Here are a few rules of thumb:

*Public position does not necessarily indicate acceptability.* The
President of the United States, a Senator, a Methodist bishop, a
union president, and a school principal are authorities only to
those who accept them as such. A speaker cannot successfully employ them as his authorities unless he can be reasonably confident that his audience will accept them.

*Titles like "economist," "psychologist," or "historian" do not
automatically make a man's views acceptable.* Even among authorities who deserve respect, there are often large areas of disagreement. In such situations, an audience must necessarily refuse to accept the testimony of some authorities, however imposing their titles.

Moreover, it becomes a problem to know who is an authority.
The difficulty is compounded by the fact that would-be authorities frequently appropriate titles as a means of getting credence
for their ideas. Audiences often, therefore, distrust titles and
refuse to accept the views of legitimate and expert authorities.

A speaker needs to analyze his audience carefully so as not to
offer testimony that his listeners may refuse to accept.

*Published material is not automatically acceptable.* Perhaps
because so much of education centers in printed materials, some
people assume that those things which are printed are true. They
may extend this credence to what they see in motion pictures,
television, and radio. A speaker should not make this mistake,
nor assume that his audience will accept published material as
correct. People of any alertness will not, for they know that
printed and broadcast matter, and motion pictures, are quite
normally designed to convey certain attitudes to readers, hearers,
and viewers. In short, it is biased—perhaps quite candidly. A
book may have much useful and objective material, but it is
written by a person who has a philosophy which he cannot, and

should not, keep from his book. A speaker, therefore, needs to find the bias of any source of supporting material before presenting it to his audience; the audience may find the material acceptable if it can take the biases into account and make allowances for them.

*The speaker must estimate correctly the amount of material the audience will accept or demand.* In any speech situation, the amount of information necessary either to clarify or to prove is determined by the expectations of listeners. For some audiences, there is little need to clarify or to prove basic points. Issues that have to be discussed at length for one group can be merely stated to another. A speaker must always judge how much material he will need to satisfy his audience, but he should always have more information than he needs. Thus supplied, he is better prepared to adapt his use of material to any audience situation that may arise.

## SUMMARY

Effective speaking is interesting and clear. The supporting materials a speaker uses supply clarity and interest by helping an audience visualize ideas concretely and specifically. In all speaking (to entertain, to inform, to persuade, or to explore), the supporting materials are of four types: (1) definition; (2) factual data in the form of examples and statistics; (3) testimony, and (4) comparison and contrast.

The materials selected for a speech should be suited to the speaker's general end; they should be accurate; they should be of such quality and quantity that they satisfy the expectations of the audience.

## QUESTIONS

1. What are the two major requirements which speech materials must meet?

2. Why do some words require definition while others do not?

3. What are the basic requirements of a good definition?

4. What is a logical definition?

5. Explain three kinds of rhetorical definitions.

6. Differentiate between real and hypothetical examples.

7. Discuss the four rules of thumb for evaluating the acceptability of material to an audience.

8. What three questions are asked as tests of examples which are used to prove?

9. Explain how statistics can be made clear and interesting.

10. How should a speaker test the statistics he uses?

11. What value does testimony have in a speech?

12. What two questions should be asked in evaluating testimony?

13. Explain comparison and contrast.

## EXERCISES

1. Develop a one-point speech in which you support that one point with at least three different types of supporting material.
2. From one of the other classes you are enrolled in, select a term you had never heard of before. Define that term in a brief logical definition and by three different rhetorical methods of definition. Decide which of the four methods has given the clearest explanation of the term. Decide which method was the least clear. Why do you think the one method is better than the other for defining this term?
3. Make a survey of opinion among some group of students on campus. For instance, what do the men at the Phi Kappa Tau fraternity house think about rock and roll? What generalization can you make from the statistics?
4. Develop three hypothetical examples which have "the characteristics of a real example." Indicate the point they would be used to support.
5. In *Vital Speeches of the Day* or in *Representative American Speeches* find speeches that illustrate the use of:

operational definition          statistics
extended example               comparison and contrast
            testimony (direct and indirect quotations)

## SUPPORTING MATERIAL: SOURCES

I. Personal experience
II. Secondary experience
   A. Conversations and interviews
   B. Radio, television, lectures
   C. The library
      1. The card catalog
      2. Special reference tools
         a. For basic facts and statistics
         b. For brief authoritative articles
         c. For more extensively developed items of information
         d. For biography
         e. For dates
         f. For quotations
III. Methods of recording materials
IV. Summary, questions, and exercises

*Chapter* **VII**

## SUPPORTING MATERIAL: SOURCES

One of the really great offenses a speaker can commit against an audience is to be inadequately informed about the subject of a speech. No matter what the subject, audience, or occasion, a speaker, by appearing before a group, professes to have something to say. Unless he knows what he is talking about, he can claim little right to be heard. To help earn this right, he must supply himself with an abundance of good supporting material.

Making an audience identify its thoughts, feelings, attitudes, and beliefs with the purpose of a speech is rarely a simple task. A mature speaker and a person of good judgment is, therefore, not one who confines himself to such support as a single article in the *Reader's Digest* or the report of a speech already made by someone else. A resourceful speaker will not leave any avenue untraveled in his search for clear and interesting material. In the preceding chapter we have considered the kinds of material that are useful to a speaker, and discussed the way in which they are used. In this chapter, we will examine some of the more useful sources of this material, and the tools for discovering it.

### Personal Experience

No other person can look back to precisely the same set of experiences you have had. Your life, the things you have done, and the things that have happened to you are unique when they are viewed as a whole. This uniqueness in your own personal experience has important implications for your speaking. First, there are some things that you know more about than anyone else. This special knowledge alone qualifies you to speak authoritatively about some subjects. A second consideration, however, qualifies the usefulness of your unique knowledge: not merely have no two persons had identical experiences; indeed, very few of your experiences have been shared by everyone. Consequently, that which is most valuable in your experience, its uniqueness, is also the most difficult to communicate. For successful communication demands a common ground of shared experience in order to bring about identification between speaker and audience. Though you may, for example, know more about automobiles, teen-age language habits, or ice hockey than any member of your audience, you can use your own personal experiences in communicating this knowledge to others only if you help your audience to interpret these experiences in the light of their own personal and unique backgrounds.

A good speaker is one who senses readily which of his own experiences are common to other people. When he draws on these common experiences and interprets them intelligently, he achieves clarity and creates interest through this common bond. The speaker who recognizes both the advantages and the limitations of personal experience as a source of supporting material can use this kind of material to bring clarity and interest to what he says. The speaker can go back into his own past and select material that makes it possible for him to explain his ideas with the accuracy and precision of immediate knowledge. A speaker who draws on his own experience can select material that helps an audience to perceive his ideas in concrete form. The man who has worked on an assembly line has absorbed countless minute details that could never come to him secondhand. Out of the vividness of his own recollection he can draw material that would not be available to him from the most meticulous research.

## Secondary Experience

The knowledge gained from examining what others have thought and done can be called secondary experience. Such in-

formation is necessary because frequently people must speak on
subjects with which they do not have direct personal experience.
Many have not been and can not be Negroes, Jews, Catholics,
forest rangers, United States senators, or social workers. Consequently, personal experience must be supplemented by examining the experience of others.

When a speaker does not find in his own background some
personal experience to lend vividness to his ideas, he draws from
what someone else has written or said an experience that *could*
have happened to anyone, including every member of his audience. This kind of supporting material brings clarity to the
speaker's ideas because it brings them within the comprehension
of the listener. It adds interest to the speech because it has the
immediacy of direct, personal experience.

Suppose a speaker were illustrating the idea that differences in
socio-economic status breed hostility. Perhaps he has no direct
personal knowledge to draw from, but he has read the report of
an experienced social worker which contains many examples to
support the proposition he defends. He might then say something like this:

> Henry Starbuck has worked for twenty-five years in
> various social agencies of Cook County, Illinois. He
> tells of a student at Lake Forest College who worked
> summers in a canning factory on the south side of Chi-
> cago. For about two weeks the student got along very
> well with the men and women who worked there. One
> day he happened to mention that he was looking for-
> ward to going back to college in the fall. After this
> chance remark, few of the workers except the super-
> visor would talk to him. Starbuck points out that this
> is a typical experience and shows the attitude of people
> in lower socio-economic brackets toward the middle
> class.

Being dependent upon others for information, however, is always a potential danger. Some of the difficulties of audience acceptance that arise in using secondary experience as speech material have been discussed in the preceding chapter. The further
point is to be made here that even when a speaker chooses his
speech materials carefully, the definitions, examples, statistics,

and testimony he gathers from sources outside his own experience are always subject to bias. No matter how meticulous the
speaker himself may be in trying to maintain an objective attitude toward his subject (and this he will seldom be able to do),
the external sources he consults are as susceptible as he to
personal bias.

It is extremely doubtful that all bias can be removed from any
extended discourse. The very fact that a speaker *selects* the
material he uses, elects to use one datum and to dispense with
another, automatically builds into a speech an inescapable bias.
Even reports appearing in the news magazines and newspapers,
theoretically intended to present an objective statement of news-
worthy events, often demonstrate the editorial bias of the
publication in which they appear. The evil in bias lies not in
its being present but in its not being recognized. In order to
detect the bias that will almost necessarily be present in the
writing and speaking of one who is concerned with what he says,
a thoughtful person will study many sources of information.

Beyond the need to be on the lookout for the bias of any
source of information a speaker consults, using the experiences
and ideas of others for speech material requires the speaker to
evaluate what he hears and reads. He must learn to listen and
read with maturity and judgment. To be ill-informed may be
even worse than to be uninformed.

When they are thoughtfully evaluated and properly used,
secondary materials will form a good basis for helping a listener
to identify himself with the ideas of a speaker. Remembering
that secondary experience must have the vividness and the immediacy of direct personal experience, let's look now at some
of the ways in which this kind of supporting material can be
found.

## CONVERSATIONS AND INTERVIEWS

The conversations you have with friends will frequently provide material for a speech. Even the ideas with which you disagree can be useful; they may be examples of concepts prevalent
in our society.

Frequently you will know of some expert, perhaps a faculty member or someone in the business community, who can help you to understand a more complex subject. You may be surprised to discover how willing people are to help you. Remember, their fields of specialization are important to them and they are usually pleased to know that they are of interest to others. Faculty members, for instance, feel a bit flattered when students ask for help in finding materials.

When you solicit information from others, however, it is wise to be sure you know what you want to ask. Begin thinking seriously about your subject some time in advance. Do some reading before you approach the person you want to interview. Arrange for an appointment convenient to him. Tell him what you will need to know, and the limits of the subject you intend to speak about. Give him time to think about your questions. Then, when you have the interivew, be prepared to ask specific questions. These will form the framework of the interview. You can expect to be disappointed with an interview which begins like this: "What can you tell me about electronics? I gotta give a speech tomorrow."

## RADIO, TELEVISION, LECTURES

Radio and television programs can be valuable sources of speech material. You will find, however, that gathering useful data from broadcasts is more difficult than gathering them from an interview. The major problem, of course, is that you can't ask questions. Accordingly you must be more careful in listening and in taking any notes you may want to keep for future reference.

In many instances, radio and television programs offer data that would otherwise be unavailable. It is not likely that a college student could approach the President, for instance, and ask him for his views on the relations of this country with the Soviet Union, or federal aid to education, or government support of a program of medical care for aged citizens. Yet the President's views are often communicated to the nation at large over radio and television. Some statements made under these circumstances will not appear in print, since many newspapers do not report the complete text of speeches broadcast on radio or television.

To make the most of an opportunity to gather speech materials from broadcasts requires much the same kind of preplanning that is done for interviews. You may discover that the Egyptian ambassador is appearing on a public-affairs broadcast. Because you are preparing a speech in which the background of Arab-Israeli conflict is pertinent, you will plan to listen. If you have done some early planning in your speech, you will know the kinds of things to listen for.

Public lectures, not broadcast, are information sources less often available than broadcasts, but their content is often especially valuable. Even college lectures may supply excellent speech material.

Note taking is an important skill to acquire. Anyone who can write can take notes of one sort or another. Taking good notes requires not only the ability to listen well, but it also demands some general background in the subject at hand. Otherwise, it is difficult to make a proper distinction between what is essential and what is not. Indiscriminately made notes are either unnecessarily voluminous because they are filled with unimportant data, or they are too sketchy because the note taker fails to put down important facts.

A practice that is helpful in taking notes is to keep paper and a pencil near at hand. Some people carry a notebook with them at all times so that they can jot down ideas as they occur. In this way, otherwise vagrant and fleeting thoughts, references, examples, and quotations can be captured and preserved.

## THE LIBRARY

By far the richest source of speech materials (indeed, of knowledge of all kinds) is a well-supplied library. Yet for many students a library is like a lost gold mine of fabulous wealth. They want the gold and are willing to work to dig it out, but they can't find the lode. A few nuggets fall into their hands by chance, but the real riches are never uncovered.

Each library has a systematic method of cataloguing and arranging materials, and these methods must become familiar to the one who uses the library. If you do not understand the card catalog, the use of indexes, or the numbering system in your library, ask a librarian to explain them to you. He will be glad to help. Remember that a librarian is much more than a person who charges out books and collects fines when they are overdue. He is in a very real sense a teacher and is professionally trained for his job. He will be glad to help you find specific pieces of information and to help you familiarize yourself with the resources of the library.

We make some general suggestions about how to find speech materials in the library. It would be virtually impossible to list every available source but we can provide a functional classification of basic materials.

*The card catalog.*　　Much of the material you will use in making speeches will be found in books. The card catalog is a device for locating these books. It is an alphabetically arranged collection of cards listing such bibliographical data as title, author, publisher, date of publication, and other pertinent data. Every book is entered in the catalog with an author card. All but the most general are represented by a title card as well, and these cards will be alphabetically arranged. For nonfiction books, one or more subject entries will also be found. Figures VII-1 to VII-5 are samples of several different kinds of card-catalog entries.

When you use the card catalog and cannot immediately find what you want, look for additional cross-references. If you wanted to explain why President Roosevelt kept the atomic bomb a secret from Vice President Truman, you might look not only under such obvious headings as "Franklin D. Roosevelt," "Harry S. Truman," and "atomic bomb," but under such others as "World War—1939–1945," and "U.S.—Politics and Government."

*Special reference tools.*　　In addition to the general book collection, a library contains many other sources of information. Among these are standard reference works, magazines, newspapers, pamphlets, and government documents. You will prob-

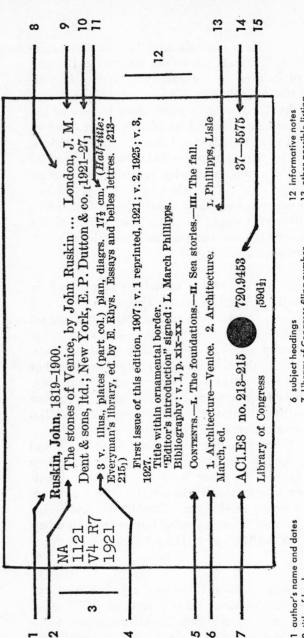

1 author's name and dates
2 title of book
3 library call number
4 number of volumes or pages, and kind of illustrations
5 contents note
6 subject headings
7 Library of Congress filing number
8 city of publication
9 name(s) of publisher(s)
10 date(s) of publication
11 height of book
12 informative notes
13 other possible listing
14 Library of Congress Catalog Card Number
15 Dewey Decimal System filing number

FIGURE VII-1. A LIBRARY CATALOG CARD, PRINTED FOR LIBRARIES BY THE LIBRARY OF CONGRESS. LIBRARIES OFTEN ADD INFORMATION TO THESE CARDS AND FILE THEM UNDER OTHER HEADINGS THAN THE AUTHOR'S NAME, AS IS EXPLAINED IN OTHER ILLUSTRATIONS. THE CALL NUMBER IS ADDED BY THE LIBRARY, ACCORDING TO ITS OWN SYSTEM. WHEN FILED IN THE CARD CATALOG AT THE AUTHOR'S NAME, AS *Ruskin* HERE, THIS IS THE "AUTHOR CARD" OR THE "MAIN ENTRY CARD."

Retention as a function of the
method of measurement

BF  **Postman, Leo Jeseph.**
21       Retention as a function of the method of measurement, by
C2     Leo Postman and Lucy Rau.  Berkeley, University of Cali-
v.8    fornia Press, 1957.
no.3     217–270 p.  diagrs., tables.  24 cm.  (University of California publi-
        cations in psychology, v. 8, no. 3)

        Bibliography: p. 269–270.

        1. Memory.  i. Rau, Lucy, 1930–     joint author.  ii. Title.
      (Series: California.  University.  University of California publica-
      tions in psychology, v. 8, no. 3)

      BF21.C2  vol. 8, no. 3        154.32              A 57–9951

      California.  Univ. Libr
      for Library of Congress            ₍5₎†

FIGURE VII–2. A "TITLE CARD," FOR LIBRARY USERS SEEKING
A BOOK BY ITS TITLE, AS SOME DO WHEN THEY DO NOT KNOW
THE AUTHOR'S NAME. HERE THE TITLE HAS BEEN TYPED ABOVE
THE NAME OF THE AUTHOR; IN SOME LIBRARIES THE TITLE IS
MERELY UNDERSCORED, PERHAPS IN COLORED INK. IN EITHER
CASE THE CARD IS FILED IN ALPHABETICAL POSITION BY TITLE
RATHER THAN BY AUTHOR—THIS CARD WOULD BE AT *Reten-
tion,* NOT AT *Postman.*

ably find yourself using these sources in preparing speeches at
least as much as you use the general book collection but you may
know less about them and their indexes than you do about using
the card catalog for finding information in books. For this reason we have devised six main categories of information which
student speakers usually need, and have provided brief explana-
tions of where and how such information is most likely to be
found.

I. FOR BASIC FACTS AND STATISTICS.    The *World Almanac,* the
*Information Please Almanac* and a number of other such volumes give a vast amount of specific information. The *Statistical
Abstract of the United States* provides quantitative summary
statistics (usually covering 15 to 20 years) on the political, social
and industrial organization of the United States. The *States-
man's Yearbook* gives statistics and facts on matters which con-

FIGURE VII–3. A "JOINT-AUTHOR" CARD. THIS CARD IS FILED
IN THE CATALOG AT *Rau*. THE NAME OF THE JOINT AUTHOR
MAY BE TYPED AT THE HEAD OF THE CARD AS HERE, OR MAY BE
MERELY UNDERSCORED. ANOTHER CARD, FILED AT *Postman*, IS
THE "AUTHOR CARD" OR "MAIN ENTRY CARD." CARDS MAY BE
PREPARED SIMILARLY, USING INFORMATION ON THE CARD (SEE THE
ARROW), FOR FILING BY THE NAME OF TRANSLATORS, EDITORS,
OR OTHERS, IN ADDITION TO THE "AUTHOR CARD."

cern the government. *Facts on File* is a weekly synopsis of world
events which, with its index, becomes a ready reference for a
variety of information. The *Congressional Quarterly* gives a
synopsis of federal legislation and the voting records of senators
and representatives.

II. FOR BRIEF AUTHORITATIVE ARTICLES.    For an introductory
discussion of a subject, you should go first to an encyclopedia.
General encyclopedias such as the *Britannica* and the *Americana*
give information on all phases of human knowledge and their
articles usually include bibliographies to suggest further study.
The *Britannica* is widely considered the best general reference
in the humanities while the *Americana* is thought to be stronger
in the areas of science and technology.

Specialized encyclopedias are available for more thorough
treatment of a subject. To list a representative group we may

Memory

**Postman, Leo Jeseph.**
BF          Retention as a function of the method of measurement, by
21          Leo Postman and Lucy Rau. Berkeley, University of Cali-
C2          fornia Press, 1957.
v.8
            217–270 p.  diagrs., tables.  24 cm.  (University of California publi-
no.3        cations in psychology, v. 8, no. 3)

            Bibliography : p. 269–270.

            ⟶   1. Memory.   I. Rau, Lucy, 1930–   joint author.  II. Title.
            (Series: California.  University.  University of California publica-
            tions in psychology, v. 8, no. 3)

            BF21.C2   vol. 8, no. 3        154.32            A 57–9951

            California.  Univ. Libr
            for Library of Congress            ₎5₎†

FIGURE VII–4. A "SUBJECT-ENTRY" CARD, USEFUL TO A LI-
BRARY USER WHO KNOWS THE SUBJECT IN WHICH HE WISHES TO
INQUIRE, BUT NOT THE NAMES OF AUTHORS OR TITLES OF BOOKS
IN THE SUBJECT. THIS CARD IS FILED AT *Memory;* THE "MAIN
ENTRY" OR "AUTHOR" CARD IS FILED AT *Postman.* THE SUBJECT
ENTRY IS TYPED OR WRITTEN ABOVE THE NAME OF THE AUTHOR,
SOMETIMES IN RED. IT IS TAKEN FROM THE CARD; NOTE THE
ARROW.

mention encyclopedias of *The Social Sciences, Religion and
Ethics, World History, Banking and Finance, The Arts and
Sports.* Van Nostrand's *Scientific Encyclopedia,* Grove's *Diction-
ary of Music and Musicians,* and the *Dictionary of American
History* supply information in the specific areas their titles
name.

III. FOR MORE EXTENSIVELY DEVELOPED ITEMS OF INFORMATION.
Magazines will probably be your greatest source of current information. The most common index of such material is the *Reader's Guide to Periodical Literature.* It indexes a large number of
popular periodicals from 1900 to the present. Its entries are arranged in much the same fashion as the card catalog.

Except for the card catalog, the *Reader's Guide* is probably
the most used index in the library, but its limitations are too
frequently overlooked. Because it indexes only popular maga-

California, University.
   University of California publications in
BF   **Postman, Leo Joseph.** psychology, v.8, no.3
21       Retention as a function of the method of measurement, by
C2     Leo Postman and Lucy Rau.  Berkeley, University of Cali-
v.8    fornia Press, 1957.
no.3
        217–270 p.  diagrs., tables.  24 cm.  (University of California publi-
        cations in psychology, v. 8, no. 3)

        Bibliography : p. 269–270.

        1. Memory.    I. Rau, Lucy, 1930–    joint author.  II. Title.
        (Series: California.  University.  University of California publica-
        tions in psychology, v. 8, no. 3)

        BF21.C2  vol. 8, no. 3        154.32            A 57–9951

        California.  Univ.  Libr.
        for Library of Congress              [5]†

FIGURE VII–5. A "SERIES-ENTRY" CARD. THE SERIES ENTRY IS
A FILING DEVICE USED TO BRING ALL WORKS WHICH BELONG TO A
SERIES TOGETHER UNDER THE NAME OF THAT SERIES AS A HEAD-
ING. THIS CARD IS FILED AT *California.* THE "AUTHOR" OR
"MAIN ENTRY" CARD IS FILED AT *Postman.* THE SERIES HEAD-
ING IS ADDED BY THE LIBRARY FROM INFORMATION ON THE
CARD; SEE THE ARROW.

zines, it is of limited usefulness in investigating more specialized
topics. There are too many specialized indexes to permit a complete enumeration here but we will list some that should prove
useful. The *International Index to Periodicals* catalogs the contents of some 170 scholarly periodicals, most of them published
in the United States. It is most useful in the study of the social
sciences. The *Applied Science and Technology Index* (formerly
part of the *Industrial Arts Index*) lists articles on business administration, public administration, and economics. The *Public
Affairs Information Service* indexes a wide variety of books, periodicals, public documents, and mimeographed material in government, sociology, and business. The *Agricultural Index,* the
*Education Index,* the *Art Index,* and the *Music Index* catalog
periodical literature in their special fields.

    The *New York Times* through its index is an especially useful
source of information on current events. This paper prints com-

plete texts of speeches and documents of public interest. Its treatment of news items is ordinarily more extensive than that found in other newspapers and in the news magazines. Most libraries subscribe to the paper and keep it on microfilm. The *New York Times Index* locates specific items in the paper and is an excellent reference tool.

IV. FOR BIOGRAPHY.    *Current Biography* is a publication which gives short useful biographies of living persons. A wide variety of *Who's Who* books give brief biographical sketches. *Webster's Biographical Dictionary* contains very brief biographies of a great number of distinguished persons of all countries and all times. The *Dictionary of American Biography* sketches the lives of prominent Americans and the *Dictionary of National Biography* includes data on the lives of notable Englishmen. Moreover, all of the specialized encyclopedias mentioned earlier contain biographical studies.

The *Biographic Index* is helpful in locating more extended biographies. It is cross-referenced according to the profession or occupation as well as the name of the personages listed and it indexes biographical periodical articles as well as books.

V. FOR DATES.    Dictionaries will supply many of the dates you will need. The *World Almanac* has a chronological listing of the events of the year previous to its publication. The *New York Times Index* provides the dates of events reported in the news-papers.

VI. FOR QUOTATIONS.    John Bartlett's *Familiar Quotations* is the best known source of short quotations. It is arranged chron-ologically by authors and has a fine index of topics as well. An-other source of quotations, Burton E. Stevenson's *Home Book of Quotations,* contains a larger number of entries than Bartlett's book. It is arranged by topics.

## Methods of Recording Materials

The information you wish to consider for your speech should be collected on cards or slips of paper, about 4 × 6 inches. It is

Basic principles of conservation
Clinton Rossiter
The conservative says that man is a composite of good and evil. He is not perfect
nor perfectible. No matter what he does he
can never throw off such qualities as
irrationality and selfishness.

Clinton Rossiter, Conservatism in
America, 1955, p. 21.

FIGURE VII–6. A NOTE CARD TO RECORD AN AUTHOR'S IDEA IN
WORDS OTHER THAN HIS.

perfectly satisfactory to cut 8½ × 11 sheets of paper into four
pieces and use these, or you can buy cards at any bookstore. Four
items of information should be entered on these cards: (1) a
label to identify the material; (2) the author; (3) the information
you wish to use, and (4) the necessary bibliographical data. If
you prepare note cards carefully, you will need to check the
original source only once.

Three useful kinds of cards are illustrated by examples as
Figures VII–6, VII–7, and VII–8.

Because the information you gather from all the sources we
have listed may eventually find its way into the outline of your
speech, you will want to make it as easy as possible to handle.
Putting each item on a separate card makes it easy to rearrange
the sequence of cards without excessive rewriting or checking
back to your notes. When the rough draft of your outline has
been prepared, you can decide where the data on each card
properly fit into the outline. When you use note cards in this
manner, much of the work in preparing an outline is done automatically, painlessly, and with ease.

*Natural tendency of our economic life is to combination* - Justice Oliver Wendell Holmes
"It is plain from the slightest consideration of practical affairs, or the most superficial reading of industrial history, that free competition means combination, and that the organization of the world, now going on so fast, means an ever increasing might and scope of combination. It seems to me futile to set our faces against this tendency. (over)

Whether beneficial on the whole, as I think it, or detrimental, it is inevitable, unless the fundamental axioms of society, and even the fundamental conditions of life, are to be changed."

Catherine Drinker Bowen, *Yankee from Olympus*, 1945, p. 330.

FIGURE VII–7. A NOTE CARD RECORDING THE EXACT WORDS OF THE SOURCE MATERIAL.

*Population of the world by continents, Statistical Office of the United Nations, Mid-year, 1959*

| | | |
|---|---|---|
| Africa | 236 | million |
| America, North | 261 | " |
| America, South | 137 | " |
| Asia | 1,624 | " (without U S S R) |
| Europe | 421 | " ( " " and Eur. Turkey) |
| Oceania | 16.1 | " ( " Hawaii ) |
| U S S R | 210.5 | " |
| Total | 2,905.6 | " |

*World Almanac, 1961, p. 466*

FIGURE VII–8. A NOTE CARD RECORDING FACTUAL DATA FROM THE *World Almanac,* A SECONDARY SOURCE. THE PRIMARY SOURCE IS ALSO RECORDED: STATISTICAL OFFICE OF THE UNITED NATIONS. THE INFORMATION ON THIS CARD IS PART OF A TABLE PRINTED IN THE *World Almanac.*

## SUMMARY

The supporting materials for a speech are found in one or the other of two main sources of information: personal experience, or the experience of others. The latter, also called secondary experience, comes partly from talking with others in conversations and interviews, and from listening to lectures or to programs on radio or television. By far the most fruitful source of secondary speech material is the vast collection of data to be found in any good library. The card catalog, a great variety of published indexes, and a large number of standard reference works, both general and special, offer an almost unlimited supply of valuable material.

The items of information that you gather are entered on cards for ease of handling. From these, they may be transferred to the final outline of your speech. With the kind of material that will come to hand when you look diligently and prepare conscientiously, you can make sure that your speeches will show you know what you are talking about. Then you can claim the right to speak and can expect the respectful attention of an audience.

## QUESTIONS

1. What is the value of your own experience as a source for supporting material?

2. What is secondary experience?

3. Can a speaker give an unbiased speech?

4. Explain how to go about setting up and conducting an interview.

5. On what basis are books classified in a card catalog?

6. Where would you go to learn basic facts and statistics?

7. What is the value of an encyclopedia?

8. Where are magazines indexed?

9. Draw up a sample note card which records an idea.

## EXERCISES

1. Develop a three- to five-minute speech in which the supporting materials are based on personal experience.

2. Develop a three- to five-minute speech in which the supporting materials have been collected in interviews.

3. Answer the following questions using the sources available in the library:

   (a) Who is the author of a novel titled *Gideon Planish?*
   (b) What are the title, publisher, and date of publication of a book by Giles W. Gray and Claude M. Wise?
   (c) What was the date on which the Soviet Union orbited Sputnik Number 1?
   (d) What was Mickey Mantle's batting average in 1958?
   (e) What is Neo-Orthodox Christianity?
   (f) Whom did Bernard Baruch support for the presidency in 1952?
   (g) Where did Richard Neutra get his undergraduate education?

# OUTLINING

I. The purpose of the outline
II. Types of outlines
    A. The complete-idea outline
        1. The brief
        2. The rhetorical outline
    B. The topic outline
III. Techniques of outlining
    A. Parts of the outline
        1. Introduction
        2. Body
        3. Conclusion
    B. Subordination and co-ordination
        1. Subordinate ideas
        2. Co-ordinate ideas
        3. Symbols of subordination and co-ordination
    C. Number of headings
    D. Checking the outline
        1. Logical consistency
        2. Formal correctness
        3. Content completeness of informative outlines
IV. Important technical principles
    A. Each heading a statement
    B. Each heading a single idea
    C. No more than one symbol for any one heading
    D. Headings discrete
    E. At least two co-ordinate headings at each level of subordination
V. Revising the outline
VI. Summary, questions, and exercises

*Chapter* **VIII**

## OUTLINING

Though a speaker gets his ideas and his information as he comes upon them, his audience insists on receiving them in coherent and orderly sequence and form. The speaker may have had five days to gather his material and prepare a speech that must reach his audience in five minutes. Only through orderly and coherent presentation can this efficient communication be achieved. And for achieving order and coherence, a valuable method is to outline the speech. Indeed, by using an outline to guide his preparation, a speaker can make this process orderly and efficient, save much time for himself, and improve his speech.

## The Purpose of the Outline

The basic function of an outline is to make clear to the speaker's eye and to his mind the logical relationships among the various ideas the outline contains. It makes an intelligent division of the materials into suitable groups of ideas and shows the logical connections among them. It is the speaker's blueprint for his speech.

In addition to helping the speaker think, the outline is helpful in the act of delivery. If the ideas he wants to communicate are carefully arranged in advance, if he has a plan of what he intends to say, the speaker will almost necessarily be effective. The outline helps him to say all that he intends to say, and at the same time helps him to refrain from saying too much.

117

## Types of Outlines

Almost any group of ideas can be jotted down on paper and called an outline. Such a *scratch* outline might be helpful in beginning to think about a topic but it would serve only poorly as a final means of organizing ideas. Instead, there are two other types of outline which are more useful than the scratch outline at all stages of preparation and in the delivery of the speech.

In the first of these, the *complete-idea* outline, the contents of the outline are fully developed. The complete-idea outline appears in two forms: (1) each idea is stated as a grammatically complete sentence; (2) the full sense of each idea is expressed in a brief telegraphic style.

A second type, the *topic* or phrase outline, is written in topic phrases instead of in complete ideas.

Each of these two forms has its uses. The complete-idea outline is better adapted to a speaking situation that demands close attention to specific statistics, verbatim quotations, and exact language, as in a formal, detailed report. The topic outline allows a speaker greater flexibility in detail and language, and is useful in most of the informal speaking situations he meets. In general, the more formal a situation, and the more complex the material, and the more exact the language required, then the more valuable the complete-idea outline will be. The more informal the situation and the more flexible the material, then the better the topic outline will serve.

### THE COMPLETE-IDEA OUTLINE

Depending on a speaker's purpose and needs, a complete-idea outline will appear in one or the other of two forms: a *brief* or a *rhetorical outline.*

***The brief.*** The most elaborate of all outline forms, the most thorough in its preparation and the most inclusive in its content, is called, paradoxically, a *brief*. The brief is an argumentative outline, and contains *all* of the arguments that a speaker can discover both *for* and *against* a proposition. It takes its name from the compilation of arguments presented to a court by an attorney. Ideally, the brief is a complete storehouse of arguments on both sides of a debatable proposition. Each item in a brief is a complete sentence.

The usefulness of a brief is apparent, especially in situations like debate where speakers are likely to be confronted with many of the opposing arguments included in the brief. Moreover, preparing a brief helps to assure complete analysis of a proposition. Despite its usefulness in analysis, however, and despite its value as a storehouse of detailed information on both sides of a controversy, the length of a brief makes it unsatisfactory as an outline for a persuasive speech. A speaker who is to argue for or against a proposition will select from the brief only those materials which will be useful to him in proving his case and organize them into an outline he can use. Indeed, the brief itself need not ever exist. When he has finished his analysis of a proposition, however, a speaker has examined the materials he would use if a brief were to be made. The materials selected for use in a speech are put into either a rhetorical or a topical outline.

*The rhetorical outline.* The rhetorical outline has the same general structure as the longer, more detailed brief and, like the brief, it is also prepared in complete-idea form. However, it is unlike the brief in one essential respect: instead of being a compilation of all the available information on a given subject, it contains only those materials and ideas which a speaker feels will be needed to accomplish his purpose in a specific speaking situation.

## THE TOPIC OUTLINE

The logical structure of the topic outline is identical with that of the complete-idea rhetorical outline. The essential difference is that instead of presenting complete ideas throughout, the topic outline employs phrases intended to help identify the idea that belongs in a given heading.

| *Rhetorical Outline* | *Topic Outline* |
|---|---|
| I. Slums are a serious problem in American cities. | I. Slums in American cities |
| A. Decay has occurred in major American cities. | A. Decay |
| 1. Areas of more than 40 years of age have been allowed to become decay spots. | 1. Spots 40 years old |
| 2. 27% of nonfarm homes do not meet federal standards of structure and sanitation. | 2. 27% unsound, unsanitary |
| B. There is an insufficient number of dwellings for the population. | B. Insufficient dwellings |
| 1. More than 1.5 persons per room is considered by sociologists to be overcrowding. | 1. Overcrowding at 1.5 per room |
| 2. Of America's dwelling places, 6% house more than 1.5 persons per room. | 2. 6% hold more than 1.5 |
| C. Slum areas create financial problems, as exemplified by the 15% of the population of Los Angeles who live in slum areas. | C. Financial problems: example, Los Angeles 15% live in slums |
| 1. They contribute less than 3% of the city's tax income. | 1. Less than 3% of tax income |
| 2. They consume 33% of the city Health Department's budget. | 2. 33% of Health Dept. budget |
| 3. They require more than 33% of the city's law enforcement budget. | 3. More than 33% of law-enforcement budget |
| II. . . . [and so on] | II. . . . [and so on] |

A student speaker, advocating passage of a federal slum-clearance bill, was demonstrating the seriousness of the problem. Let us use one section of his speech to compare the complete-idea outline with the topic outline.

The example on the left is a well-developed rhetorical outline that clearly communicates the intention of the speaker. In its entirety, such an outline will reconstruct for a reader the substance of the speech, even if he were not to hear it delivered. The topic outline, on the other hand, is of little use to anyone except the speaker himself.

## Techniques of Outlining

### Parts of the Outline: Introduction, Body, Conclusion

Speeches, and outlines for speeches, have three essential parts: introduction, body, and conclusion. A speaker uses each of these parts for its appropriate function.

Though people hear a speaker, they do not inevitably listen to him. But since no speaker can be effective until hearers begin listening, his first job is to make them listen. The devices he uses to catch their attention and arouse their interest, the things he says to make them listen, are included in the first part of the speech and of the outline. Included also are the subject sentence he uses to indicate his purpose in speaking, and any necessary background material. These elements that together make up the first part of the outline are called the *introduction*. After his introduction, the speaker develops his specific purpose in the *body* of the speech. Here he either informs, persuades, or entertains the audience in accordance with his purpose. Finally, he rounds out the speech in the *conclusion*. The following example illustrates the general format of the outline and its parts:

INTRODUCTION
I. Attention and interest material
II. Subject sentence of the speech
III. Background material if necessary

BODY

I. First main point
II. Second main point
III. Third main point
[And so on]

CONCLUSION

I. Brief summary of the main points
II. Restatement of the subject sentence
III. Remarks that will bring the speech to a graceful close

## SUBORDINATION AND CO-ORDINATION

The symbol (I, II, 1, 2, A, B, a, b, or the like) that marks each main head and subhead shows the relationship of that heading to others in the outline. The symbol used, and also the degree to which a statement in an outline is indented, indicate the superior, subordinate, or co-ordinate rank of the statement.

***Subordinate ideas.*** If one idea is derived from another, or is dependent upon another, or is used to support another, it is said to be *subordinate* to the other.

I. A main head is superior to its subheads.
   A. Subheads are subordinate to their main heads.

The indenting of the subhead and the use of a different symbol series indicates the subordination to the eye. In the outline, subordinate heads *always follow* the main head.

*Wrong:* I. Evidence or supporting material, (therefore)
             A. Main idea

*Right:*  I. Main idea (because)
             A. Evidence or supporting material

This same principle holds true at no matter what level of subordination you are outlining. If, for example, the subhead in the illustration just above were itself in need of further explanation or support, the material used to support it would be placed after

A, indented from it, and given a different symbol series to indicate subordination:

> I. First main head
>    A. Support or explanation for I
>       1. Support or explanation for A

For persuasive effect the speaker may wish to develop an idea by presenting first the subheads and then the main head. First, realize that the conventional procedure is far more often used. The danger in the evidence-first plan of outlining, that the speaker may become lost in detail and cause the audience to overlook the main head, cautions against using it without good reason.

However, if a speaker decides to arrange one point in this way he will not materially change from the conventional outline. A change in outline form might be confusing to the eye. Note in the following example the confusion when only a change in a letter, not any change in symbol form or indentation, marks the break from one main idea to another.

> I. First main head
>    A. Support for I
>    B. Further support for I
>    A. Support for II
>    B. Further support for II
> II. Second main head
> III. Third main head

The outline is clearer and easier to control if the speaker keeps it in conventional form and adds an arrow to the margin of the paper to remind him that the sequence of delivery is reversed.

> I. First main head
>    A. Support for I
>    B. Further support for I
> II. Second main head
>    A. Support for II
>    B. Further support for II
> III. Third main head

***Co-ordinate ideas.***    If ideas are of equal weight or importance, or if they support the same larger heading, they are said to
be co-ordinate. To illustrate:

> I. First main head
>     A. Support or explanation for I
>         1. Support or explanation for A
>         2. Further support or explanation for A
>     B. Further support or explanation for I
>         1. Support or explanation for B
>         2. Further support or explanation for B
> II. Second main head
>     [And so on]

In the outline illustrations just above, A and B are co-ordinate
divisions. Statements 1 and 2 under A are in turn co-ordinate
with each other, and by the same token, 1 and 2 under B are
co-ordinate with each other. In every instance, all of the co-
ordinate ideas under the same heading are given an equal degree
of indentation and are labeled with consecutive symbols of the
same type.

***Symbols of subordination and co-ordination.***    The symbols
used to show subordination and co-ordination are purely arbitrary, but custom has established a fairly general usage. Main
heads are designated with Roman numerals, first-level subheads
with capital letters; then follow Arabic numerals and lower-case
letters in that order for further subordination. If still further
levels of subordination are required, repeat the Arabic numbers
and lower-case letters, enclosed in parentheses rather than followed by periods. It is doubtful that you will go much beyond
this level of subordination; but if you do, any intelligible system
of symbols is perfectly satisfactory, provided they are consistent
for all of the ideas in a co-ordinated series, and provided they
distinguish subordinate from co-ordinate ideas. The sequence
may be as follows:

> I. First main heading
>     A. Clarification or proof of I

      1. Clarification or proof of A
         a. Clarification or proof of 1
            (1) Clarification or proof of a
               (a) Clarification or proof of (1)
               (b) Further clarification or proof of (1)
            (2) Further clarification or proof of a
         b. Further clarification or proof of 1
      2. Further clarification or proof of A
    B. Further clarification or proof of I
  II. Second main heading
    [And so on]

## NUMBER OF HEADINGS

The process of arranging the materials of a speech into a series of main heads and subheads that show proper co-ordination and subordination, will raise the question as to how many headings may be used at any given level of subordination. There is no definite answer beyond saying that the number of headings depends entirely upon what a speaker thinks will accomplish his purpose. For the main heads this number will usually be somewhere between two and five. It is quite possible, however, for a very brief speech to develop a single main head to explain one aspect of a subject in informative speaking, or to develop a single argument in persuasive speaking. Using more than five main headings will ordinarily make it difficult for an audience to remember very many details of what the speaker has said.

## CHECKING THE OUTLINE

As the outline develops, it should be checked for logical consistency and formal correctness.

***Logical consistency.*** Since the major purpose of outlining materials is to blueprint a speech and to put order into ideas, logical consistency is an absolute requirement for the outline itself. It is met by making sure that the co-ordination and subordination indicated by the outline are present in the ideas themselves. Suppose, for example, that a speaker arguing for the creation of a metropolitan transit authority were to organize a section of his outline thus:

    I. Residents of Los Angeles are facing a crisis in transportation.

       A. Responsible and informed citizens agree something must be done.

          1. . . . . . . . . . .

          2. . . . . . . . . . .

          3. . . . . . . . . . .

       B. Traffic congestion is at a breakdown point.

          1. . . . . . . . . . .

             a. . . . . . . . . . .

             b. . . . . . . . . . .

          2. Approximately 600,000 automobiles enter and leave the downtown area of Los Angeles every 24 hours.

             a. Most cars carry only one person: the average is 1.4 persons per car.

             b. More than half come and go between 7 and 9 a.m. and 4 and 6 p.m.

             c. Rush-hour traffic is mainly one-way.

                (1) Morning traffic mostly inbound

                (2) Evening traffic mostly outbound

             d. Cars are expensive to operate.

This organization would have told us that d is subordinate to 2 and that idea d helps to support or clarify idea 2. Clearly, though, the idea that cars are expensive to operate has no direct connection with the idea that a number of automobiles enter and leave downtown Los Angeles every day. Nor does the idea that driving a car is expensive help to show the truth of the idea B that traffic congestion is at a breakdown point. In no logical sense, then, is d subordinate to either 2 or B. Instead, the idea that cars are expensive to operate is much more directly connected with the idea in the main head I. Its logical purpose in the speech is to help show the urgency and magnitude of the problem itself. Its place in the outline should correspond. Since it has the same purpose as A (crisis confronting residents) and

B (traffic congestion), subhead d under 2 is really co-ordinate with A and B and should become C in the outline.

The corrected outline would then look like this:

    I. Residents of Los Angeles are facing a crisis in transportation.
        A. Responsible and informed citizens agree something must be done.
            1. . . . . . . . . . .
            2. . . . . . . . . . .
            3. . . . . . . . . .
        B. Traffic congestion is at a breakdown point.
            1. . . . . . . . . .
                a. . . . . . . . . . . .
                b. . . . . . . . . . .
            2. . . . . . . . . .
                a. . . . . . . . . . .
                b. . . . . . . . . . .
                c. . . . . . . . . . . .
                    (1) . . . . . . . . . . .
                    (2) . . . . . . . . . . .
        C. Cars are expensive to operate.

***Formal correctness.***    Many of the problems of logical consistency can be eliminated in the process of making the speech outline formally correct; they can be, that is, if the techniques of outlining are properly used. And the formal correctness of all speech outlines can be checked effectively by a simple and mechanical method.

To see how, begin by observing and reviewing the organization of the persuasive speech. The purpose of the speech is to build acceptance of a proposition. In the outline, main ideas are listed as main heads and are followed by supporting subheads. Main heads (I, II, and so on) are subordinate to the proposition itself. All co-ordinate divisions of the outline, taken together, should prove the heading to which they are in common subordinate. To illustrate:

The speaker's proposition should be accepted *for*
    I. The first main argument supports it. [The first main argument I is true] *for*

    A. The first subhead supports I. [The first subhead
       A in turn is true] *for*
       1. This piece of evidence supports A, *and* [A
         is true also because]
       2. This piece of evidence likewise supports A,
         *and* [I is true also because]
    B. The second subhead supports I. [The second
       subhead B in turn is true] *for*
       1. This piece of evidence supports B, *and* [B
         is true also because]
       2. This piece of evidence likewise supports B,
         *and* [the speaker's proposition is true also
         because]
  II. The second main argument supports it. [The sec-
    ond main argument II is true] *for*
    [And so on]

To check the outline of a persuasive speech, add the word
*for* to the end of each statement in the outline *which is followed
immediately by a subordinate point.* Add the word *and* to the
end of each statement in the outline *which is followed immediately by a co-ordinate point or by a larger heading.* The skeleton
looks like this:

    The proposition should be accepted *for*
    I. Helps to prove the proposition *for*
      A. Helps to prove I            *for*
        1. Helps to prove A        *and*
        2. Also helps to prove A    *and*
      B. Helps to prove I             *for*
        1. Helps to prove B         *and*
        2. Also helps to prove B    *and*
    II. Helps to prove the proposition *for*
    [And so on]

This word *for* signifies the various expressions associated with
the logical relation of subordinate points to their superior head.
If *for* seems incongruous when it is applied as a test, apply one
of these other expressions: *because, for instance, in the same way
that, as is shown by, as authorities agree.*

Checking a brief or a rhetorical outline by this *for-and* scheme is relatively simple. If the outline is in topical form, the complete ideas must be imagined.

The outline of an informative speech can be tested for formal correctness by mentally adding in front of subordinate points such connective phrases as *for example* and *that is to say*. In co-ordinate positions use such words as *moreover, furthermore, in addition.*

**Content completeness of informative outlines.**     The outline of an informative speech can also be tested by a system of adding ideas. The co-ordinate headings taken together should add up to no more and no less than their superior head. Consider the following:

*Specific Purpose*
  I. . . . . . . . . . .
      A. . . . . . . . . .
      B. . . . . . . . . .
         1. . . . . . . . . .
         2. . . . . . . . .
 II. . . . . . . . . . .
      A. . . . . . . . . .
      B. . . . . . . . . .

$$I.B.1. + I.B.2. = I.B$$
$$I.A + I.B = I$$
$$II.A + II.B = II$$
$$I + II = \text{Specific purpose}$$

The following outline would be found faulty because it has more in it than the specific purpose sets forth:

*Specific Purpose:* To inform the audience of the species of trout in the Sierra Nevada Mountains.

   I. My trip to the Sierra last summer
  II. How to fish for trout
 III. Rainbow trout
 IV. Brook trout
  V. Brown trout
 VI. Golden trout

The first two points, while they may be interesting, are pieces of major material that make the six points, when added, total to more than the specific purpose.

The body of the same speech might be so divided that it would total to less than the specific purpose.

    I. Rainbow trout
   II. Brook trout
  III. Brown trout

This outline does not include enough: lacking the item "Golden trout" it totals only to "*some* species of trout," not to "*the* species of trout."

The speaker may have reason for not discussing the omitted point. It could well be the lack of speaking time. But where time or other conditions force a speaker to exclude a point, this fact should be accounted for in the background material or by a narrowed subject sentence. Since golden trout, for instance, are found only above 9,000 feet, the above organization is acceptable for the

> *Specific Purpose:* To inform the audience of the species of trout found below 9,000 feet in the Sierra Nevada Mountains.

Unless a speaker uses carefully this system of testing by addition, he may also produce an outline which contains both too much and too little, in that it includes an extraneous item and omits one that is essential:

> *Specific Purpose:* To inform the audience of the species of trout in the Sierra Nevada Mountains.

    I. How to fish for trout
   II. Rainbow trout
  III. Brook trout
  IV. Brown trout

The examples given here are of main points as they relate to the specific purpose. The same principle is applicable at lower levels of subordination.

## Important Technical Principles

### EACH HEADING A STATEMENT

Each of the points in an outline, both main heads and sub-heads, should be a statement. Do not use a question as an outline heading. The major fault with questions in the outline is that there can be no clear relationship between a question and either a superior or a subordinate point. Because a question makes no definite statement, it cannot be proved and it cannot be used as supporting material to clarify or to prove. Moreover, if a heading is phrased as a question, none of the suggested methods of testing the outline can be applied. The injunction against questions *in the outline* does not mean that you should avoid rhetorical questions *in the delivery of your speech.* An outline, however, shows the logical structure of a speech. As such, it should answer questions, not ask them.

> *Wrong:* What are the two basic types of evidence?
> *Right:* There are two basic types of evidence.

### EACH HEADING A SINGLE IDEA

Each of the headings in an outline should contain a single idea. An outline is not an essay with numbered paragraphs. Moreover, the purpose of the outline is to show the logical relationships among the individual ideas. These relationships are not properly shown if more than one idea is put into a single heading.

*Wrong:*

> 1. A six-year traffic survey in Los Angeles demonstrates an interesting paradox. Though approximately the same number of persons daily come in and out of the downtown area, traffic has increased 20%.

*Wrong:*

> 1. A six-year traffic survey in Los Angeles demonstrates the interesting paradox that approxi-

mately the same number of persons daily come
in and out of the downtown area, but that traffic
has increased 20%.

*Right:*

1. A six-year traffic survey in Los Angeles demon-
strates an interesting paradox.

   a. Approximately the same number of people
daily come in and out of the downtown area.
   b. Traffic has increased 20%.

## No More Than One Symbol for Any One Heading

To label a single item in the outline as both I and A or both
A and 1 is illogical. It suggests that a subordinate point is its
own main head, which is, of course, impossible. When a double
symbol is used, it ordinarily means that the writer of the outline
has a series of subordinate points and senses that they need a
head, but has not devised it.

| *Wrong:* | *Right:* |
|---|---|
| I. A. . . . . . . | I. . . . . . |
|   B. . . . . . . |   A. . . . . |
| |   B. . . . |

| *Wrong:* | *Right:* |
|---|---|
| I. . . . . . | I. . . . . . |
|   A. 1. . . . |   A. . . . . |
|     2. . . . |     1. . . . |
|   B. . . . . |     2. . . . |
| |   B. . . . . |

## Headings Discrete

There should be no overlapping among the divisions of an
outline. Advocating the repeal of child-labor laws, one speaker
argued that other cities in the nation might derive the benefits
Philadelphia got from its work-school program initiated to combat the labor shortage of the Second World War. Here is a part
of the argument:

I. The wartime work-school program was of great value in Philadelphia.
   A. The program helped reduce the number of dropouts from school.
   B. The program taught initiative and responsibility.
   C. Young people gained a new sense of importance from contributing to the family's resources.
   D. Discipline problems at home and at school diminished.

Notice that subpoint B overlaps both C and D. These two points (C and D), instead of being co-ordinate with B, are really pieces of evidence to show that B is true. They are effects of B. They should be subpoints 1 and 2 subordinated *under* B.

## At Least Two Co-ordinate Headings at Each Level of Subordination

It is not logical to use one subhead under a superior head. If we break a piece of chalk, the smallest number of pieces we can have is two. The same concept applies broadly to the partitioning of ideas. The purpose of subordinate statements in an outline is to break down the idea contained in the main head, to show its parts, or to show how it was arrived at. When an outline contains a single subheading it is not usually a true logical division of the idea to which it is subordinated. Instead, it is most often a restatement of the same idea with greater specification of detail.

*Wrong:*
   A. The President threatened to veto the bill increasing social-security payments if the increase was too big.
      1. He said the increase must not be more than 7%.

*Right:*
   A. The President threatened to veto the bill increasing social-security payments if the increase was more than 7%.

The exclusion of one-point subordinations does not necessitate exclusion of evidence. You may want to furnish a single piece of evidence or supporting material, an example, or a statistic by adding the desired detail to the main idea and introducing it with a colon:

*Right:*

    A. Most cars on the freeways in Los Angeles carry only 1 person: the average is 1.4 persons per car.

*Right:*

    A. Americans are often chauvinistic: American tourists frequently belittle the customs of the countries they visit.

## Revising the Outline

The first outline of a speech is usually weak. Oftentimes it is little more than the scratch outline mentioned earlier. Usually, when you begin to think about a topic, you lack detailed information and often fail to see the ideas in clear perspective. Moreover, as you gather information and as your ideas develop, you see that relationships you first perceived do not exist. New ideas come into the picture and less adequate ones are discarded. As your knowledge and understanding develop, you see the need for revision of the outline, both for clarity and for forcefulness of presentation. A constant examination of the ideas and frequent revision of the outline will be necessary, even to the actual moment of speaking.

## SUMMARY

In outlining, keep the following points in mind:

1. A complete-idea, rhetorical outline is preferable.

2. Partition the main ideas into a series of distinct, co-ordinate headings.

3. If a heading is not an immediately self-evident and self-explanatory statement, develop it with a minimum of two subheads.

4. Use statements, not questions, to express ideas.

5. Use proper indentations and symbols to show co-ordination and subordination accurately. Use one symbol per idea, one idea per symbol.

6. Check the outline for logical consistency and formal correctness.

7. Check the informative outline for completeness by applying the test of addition.

8. Revise the outline as necessary for greater clarity and force.

## QUESTIONS

1. What is the purpose of an outline?

2. When is a complete-idea outline the best and when is a topic outline better?

3. Why is it paradoxical to call a brief a brief?

4. Give the general format of a speech showing what goes into the Introduction, the Body, and the Conclusion.

5. Explain subordination and co-ordination.

6. How should the speaker mark his outline to help him where he wants to deliver the evidence before stating the idea it supports?

7. What is the customary order of subordination in which the various symbols are used?

8. How many main headings should a speech have? Why?

9. How can the outline be tested by a system of adding ideas?

10. The text gives five technical principles for outline development. Explain the three you feel are most important.

11. How much should an outline be revised?

## EXERCISES

1. Using the following points, make an outline for the body of a speech
   showing subordination and co-ordination by the use of correct symbols and indentations. First find your main heads (there are two of
   them), then look for the subheads, then proceed to further levels of
   subordination.

   *Specific Purpose:* To inform the audience about the major activities
      open to students on a college campus

   Students attend classes
   Pamphlets
   There are extracurricular activities
   Plays
   Students plan and attend their own social events
   College football team
   College fencing team
   Volleyball
   They take tests
   Periodicals
   Students have a variety of cultural activities outside the classroom
   College track team
   Art exhibits
   Softball
   Dances
   College basketball team
   The primary activities on a college campus are curricular
   Books
   College wrestling team
   Golf club
   Parties
   College baseball team
   Students use the library as a source of information
   Clubs and fraternities have a league
   They write papers and deliver speeches
   Maps
   Touch football
   Concert series
   Tennis club
   They listen to lectures by the instructor
   Students attend athletic events as spectators and participants
   Swimming club
   Intercollegiate athletics
   Lecture series
   Minor sports

They engage in class discussions
Major sports
After-school sports are available to everyone
Intramural-athletics

**2.** State the specific purpose of one of the following speeches and then
outline the speech.

*Inaugural Address, Nelson A. Rockefeller,
Governor of New York**  ◈

As this sixth decade of our twentieth century nears its end, we
are nearing, too, what could be the fatal testing time for free men
—and freedom itself—everywhere.

Over the span of many a century, many a generation thinks its
own age is a moment of historic decision. We know it.

We know it because we have witnessed—for more than twenty-
five years now—the tragic ordeal of freedom. We have seen the
tyrant—first Fascist, then Communist—strike down free nations,
shackle free peoples, and dare free men everywhere to prove they
can survive.

We know this to be such a time of historic decision, because we
see the world divided, the weapons of war perfected to deadly extremes, and humanity seeming, at times, about to turn and prey
upon itself.

And we know something else: We know how and why this
world is divided and imperiled.

It is divided, essentially, between those who believe in the
brotherhood of men under the fatherhood of God—and those who
scorn this as a pious myth.

It is divided between those who believe in the dignity of free
men—and those who believe in the monstrous supremacy of the
totalitarian state.

It is divided between those whose most potent force is their
faith in individual freedom—and those whose faith is force itself.

It is divided between those who believe in the essential equality
of peoples of all nations and races and creeds—and those whose
only creed is their own ruthless race for power.

This division of the world—and this time of decision—leave no
corner of the earth, no fraction of humanity, untouched. From
this basic struggle, there can be no refuge, nor escape.

Our neighborhood is the world. History and technology, the

* Delivered January 1, 1959. *New York Times,* January 2,
1959. Reprinted by permission of the editors.

hope of free man everywhere and the menace to freedom everywhere: All things have conspired to make this so. The speed of the rocket and the force of an atom bomb, the strength of America and the strength of her enemies; such things mean that every state in our union, every community in our state, every citizen in each community—all face a common challenge and share a common cause.

The graveness of the challenge is matched by the greatness of our opportunity to serve that common cause.

Knowing this, we have no reason to fear—but every reason to strive.

For the spiritual resources of free men are unique, and the strength of free men is unsurpassed—if united in common purpose. Our history itself, as a people, is living and lasting testimony to this. As a nation, we were born of a free association of individuals—a concord of states—joining with one another in the modern world's most astonishing story of national adventure and creation, the stirring story of America.

In the same spirit and on a wider horizon, the twenty-one American republics of this Western Hemisphere, freely joined in common purpose and in friendship, have given practical demonstration of their dedication to peace and human dignity. Today throughout the world such free associations of free peoples, working together in their mutual interests, can achieve the universal aspiration of man for individual opportunity.

From the individual's faith in his own worth, to his voluntary role in his own free community, to his own community's service to his nation, and to his nation's dedication to the common cause of all free men—thus is the force of the faith of freedom steadily raised to a higher power.

And as we know the strength of this faith, we know, too, there is still further reason for confidence and courage in the material means and devices we can employ to serve this faith. For the first time in history the revolution of science and industry makes possible the realization of man's ageless dream of individual opportunity and well-being. The commonwealth of humanity at large can be served now as never before in the story of man. Disease can be conquered. The hungry can be fed. The homeless can find shelter. Such things can come to pass in a measure no earlier generation of man has dared imagine.

Through these means can we serve, as no other age has served, the true end of freedom: Not merely checking menace and peril to free peoples—but assuring to free men of all nations the chance to nourish their spirit, enrich their mind, each to live a life of promise true to his chosen destiny.

I speak to you today—obviously—as citizens of America and of the free world.

We can serve—and save—freedom elsewhere only as we practice it in our own lives.

We cannot speak of the equality of men and nations unless we hold high the banner of social equality in our own communities.

We cannot speak of a rule of law among nations of the world unless our own laws faithfully serve the needs, and guard the rights, of our own citizens.

We cannot be impressively concerned with the needs of impoverished peoples in distant lands, if our own citizens are left in want.

We cannot hope to spur economic progress and prosperity in the world unless such a state as New York can itself help to lead America herself toward new horizons of well-being and equal opportunity for all our citizens.

We cannot pretend to help inspire new young nations in the ways of freedom and its institutions—if our schools do not enable our own youth to be enlightened citizens.

We cannot hope to serve the cause of peace among nations—if classes or factions in our own society war among themselves.

Thus does our role in the world—and our duty to ourselves—coincide as if they were one. We are called upon to conduct ourselves like free men—with the will and the wisdom to make freedom work.

We do this not with rhetoric—but with action. We do this not simply by what we say—but by how we live.

We must speed our economic growth—for upon the vitality of our economy depend jobs and incomes for all. We must help industry prosper and expand. We must face realistically our transportation problems. We must wisely develop our natural resources. For only in all such ways can we guard our truly priceless resources: Our citizens and their well-being.

We must make more orderly, efficient and responsible our governmental processes. We must put the state's fiscal house in order. We must review—and revise—outmoded methods of the executive branch. We must erase all administrative abuses, all marks of waste and inefficiency, from our government. For only by such repairs and reforms can this Government by the people be, seriously and literally, government for the people.

We must, wherever appropriate and proper for the state, effectively serve the needs of popular welfare. We must improve and expand the security provided in our programs of social insurance and health insurance. We must encourage urgently needed investment in private housing. We must do more and better work in the fields of physical and vocational rehabilitation. We must improve all our programs for the aged: Health and recreation, housing and employment.

With our rising standard of living and increasing leisure time it is important that the state give increasing encouragement to the intellectual and cultural facilities for the people. For—in all these areas of human want and need—government must have a heart as well as a brain.

We must truly strive to perfect the rule of our laws. We must promptly strengthen our whole court structure by thoughtful and thorough reorganization. We must—through the efficient mobilization of all enforcement officers and agencies—not only declare, but aggressively wage, war upon organized crime. And in all our laws and their enforcement we must and shall never forget the crime that is committed by any assault upon civil rights: Here our vigor must match our vigilance. For it can be said of any state or nation: By their laws, you shall know them.

And we must work, perhaps hardest of all, on the field where the future can be won or lost: In our schoolrooms. We must attack the problems of juvenile delinquency. We must continue urgently needed state aid to our schools. We must plan—years into the future—expansion of our state institutions for higher education. For what we do not teach, we cannot save—and this is true of freedom itself.

In all such ways may we citizens of New York prove worthy of being citizens of the nation that is the best and strongest hope on earth for free men everywhere.

In such tasks, we can give little time or care to conventional labels or slogans. They have little meaning in terms of the realities of life today.

We shall be conservative—for we know the measureless value that is our heritage, to save and to cherish and to enrich.

We shall be liberal—for we are vastly more interested in the opportunities of tomorrow than the problems of yesterday.

We shall be progressive—for the opportunities and the challenges are of such size and scope that we can never halt and say: Our labor is done.

Above all, we know the world we live in—and the values for which we strive.

We shall never surrender to the belief that man is a soulless device made to serve a machine or a state. We know that the state —and machines—are properly conceived and designed to serve man.

We shall never yield our faith in the spiritual nature of man:

Not a common creature truly designed to serve his Maker and his own true God, his own full promise.

Let us unite in common cause—with hope and faith and love, with vision and courage. Together we can thus work toward the goal of freedom of opportunity for men everywhere in a world of peace.

I shall need your help and your trust.

I ask that help—and I pledge myself consistently to serve that trust.

### The United States in Asian Eyes*

Mr. Chairman, Mr. President, and gentlemen of The Economic Club: That was a very nice introduction. Nice introductions of course make you feel good inside. They have the disadvantage, however, that your audience expects you to live up to the billing, and that isn't always so easy.

Some of you men have been in Asia—a lot of you have, in fact. One morning in January I was having breakfast in our house, which is called a bungalow, and I read in the paper that a delegation of the Detroit Board of Commerce had just arrived in Karachi where we were at the time, although we lived in Lahore. So instead of going to the office, I hurried down to the Metropole Hotel and encountered Willis Hall and some of his friends and they insisted—I mean they *insisted*—that I have breakfast with them. So on that day I had two breakfasts.

As all of you know who have been there, Asia is fascinating. There is so much to tell that I am afraid I shall be tempted to digress from the topic for today which is "How We Look to the Asians." I hope that I don't succumb to the temptation.

Before I go on, I must say that Asians and Americans think differently, or at least we approach situations differently. I have in mind an American in Lahore who is a good friend of an educated and enlightened Pakistani. Most Pakistanis don't use a knife or fork; they eat with their fingers. The American protested to the Pakistani that eating with the fingers is not sanitary. The Pakistani replied, "It all depends on how you look at it. I know that my fingers have never been in anybody else's mouth, but I am not so sure about that fork of yours."

* An excerpt from a speech by Clement J. Freund, Dean of the College of Engineering, University of Detroit, and Consultant in Higher Technical Education to the Government of West Pakistan, delivered before the Economic Club of Detroit, April 4, 1960. *Vital Speeches of the Day*, July 15, 1960, pp. 590–592. Reprinted by permission of the editors.

◈  The Islamic religion specifies fasting during the month of Ramazan, a period of thirty days in the spring of the year. During this time the strict Muslim takes no food from sunrise to sunset, and drinks nothing, not even water. It is a rigorous discipline. I know a Muslim official in Karachi who hired a servant and paid him well to fast for him.

Instead of giving a running talk, perhaps I should just try to answer a number of questions which Americans ask over and over. For example: *Is There Any Main Idea or Purpose Which Animates Asians when They Think or Talk about the United States?*

I think there is. They want to be our equals. For centuries Asians have been looked down upon, often despised, as inferior races. They are getting mighty tired of it. This attitude is directed not only against the United States; not even principally against the United States. It is directed against all Western nations.

As you know, Asian countries are getting rid of foreign rulers in rapid succession. This is not so much because they think Westerners have been cruel, or unjust, or avaricious. I believe it is mainly because Westerners have been uppish and superior.

Fortunately, we Westerners are rapidly discarding the notion that the Asian is classified somewhere between ourselves and one of the higher animals. But some of us are still learning. Here are two Americans. They are big fellows, deep voiced, extroverts, obviously successful. They are wearing sun helmets, dark glasses, and all the other paraphernalia of the tourist. They have come upon a construction job where a thousand laborers are carrying dirt in baskets on their heads. One of them booms to the other, "Charley, have a look. Isn't this something? What couldn't you do in a couple of hours with a bulldozer?"

Now the Asian superintendents and engineers on this job understand English very well. They know all about bulldozers, but they just can't afford them.

The Asian contends that both he and we have the same human nature, the same dignity, and that we are entitled to the same respect. He feels that he is no less a man because a bulldozer costs so much.

I am firmly convinced that President Eisenhower's tour of Asia was so successful—and it was successful in spite of what Democrats may say—because he had the special knack of meeting with and talking to Asians as one man to another, as equals. He made them feel that he welcomed them to the Western brotherhood of nations. The dirtiest beggar in Karachi knew that the President would shake hands with him if he could get near him.

A by-product of the Asians' desire for equality is their desire for national independence. My good British friend, Bill Hawkins, said to his good Muslim friend, Zafar Rathor, "But British rule of Pakistan was more efficient than your own rule is now." Rathor's answer is one you have often heard: "This may be so, but we much rather govern ourselves badly than have foreigners govern us efficiently.'

Another question: *How Do Asians Size Us Up?*

One could spend a couple of hours on that one.

They take us very seriously; too seriously. Three Americans served as consultants to the Commission on National Education in Pakistan. The Commission was made up of a number of the leading men of the nation. Whenever any one of us spoke, all of them listened most respectfully, they hung on every word we had to say. It was embarrassing. None of us were *that* smart.

What Asians think of us depends, at least in those countries we visited, on the class of people you are talking about. In each of these nations there is a very small percentage—three to five per cent, perhaps—of educated and enlightened people who exert a considerable influence and pretty much dominate the nation. Ninety to ninety-five per cent of the people are illiterate, ignorant, and desperately poor. They exert no influence whatever unless a demagogue arouses them and then they can take the country over.

The educated and enlightened Asians are intensely interested in everything American, our cars, our radios, our television, our Coca-Cola, our motion pictures, our record players. Unfortunately, they know much more about these superficial aspects of American life than they know about our feelings about liberty, the dignity of the individual person, human rights, and belief in God. We have not publicized these values very well.

They admire our knack of organizing, our enthusiasm, our machines and factories, our newspapers and universities, especially our universities, and our representative form of government.

While they admire us, they are not exactly in love with us. Perhaps they are just a little afraid of us. If you get to talking confidentially with a lawyer or a chemist, he will remind you that we are the most powerful nation in the world. Then he says, "This makes us nervous. Historically, the powerful nations have always been conquerors; they have always overrun the weaker nations."

I explain that we have no such intentions. I point out that our country has never, or almost never, overrun and oppressed any other country. "Perhaps not," he replies, "but they all begin some time. And how do we know you won't begin? The stronger you are, the more severely you will be tempted."

So much for the upper classes. Now for the great majority of the population.

We have become friends of a clever woman, who is mother of a

very nice family, and is an important official, just under the director, in the Village Aid Department of the Pakistan Government. About ninety per cent of Pakistanis live in the rural vil-
lages. They are poor and uneducated. Village Aid is the branch of
the Government which is responsible for improving the lot of the
villagers. This woman knows her villagers. Besides, she has a fast
moving mind, a smart tongue in her head, and a doctor's degree
from Harvard. This is what she has to say: "Many of the villagers
are very suspicious of the United States. All around them they see
evidence of American aid, free seed, agricultural advisors, veteri-
narians, machinery, vehicles, powdered milk, medicines. The
Americans they say, obviously are not giving us all these things
just to be generous. When they set out to conquer the world, they
will expect or force us to serve in their armies."

Perhaps Americans in foreign service and consulting can do
something to correct these false notions. There are many American advisors in the Pakistan Village Aid.

In spite of some nervousness, I believe that the average Asian
thinks well of us. In the small towns of Ceylon, the little boys
wave to you, grin across the full width of their faces, and shout,
"hello; OK!" which is all the American they know.

In any case, the prestige of the United States in Asia is enormous.

A further question: *Do Americans Handle the Problem of
Communism Effectively?*

The educated Asians don't think so.

You have often heard it said that all we need to do in order to
win the Asian nations for the West is to fly over them and throw
out thousands of Sears catalogues. It is argued that they would be
so fascinated by our abundance of all kinds of goods available to
the common people that they would adopt our viewpoint.

I doubt if the argument holds. The trouble is that the average
Asian, the typical Asian, is no more interested in radios, or plumb-
ing, or nylon hosiery, or refrigerators than I am in solid gold
bathtubs. There is just one all absorbing topic the average Asian
cares about. All he cares about, or thinks about, or talks about is
food, enough food. The average Asian is always hungry.

Americans in Asia talk democracy, education, sanitation, liberty,
private enterprise, the good life. We talk these things remotely,
often through an interpreter. The Communist agent in Asia talks
just one thing: food. And he talks it in the Asian's language, to
the poor people.

Food is always a problem. I know a young stenographer, about
nineteen years old. He is a boy. Practically all the stenographers
are boys. He can't afford to go to college so he is studying at home.

I asked him if he is making progress. His answer was quite matter of fact. He simply said, "No, I'm not. The trouble is that my younger brothers and sisters cry too much on those days when we have no evening meal."

But I believe that we are holding our own against the Communists in Asia, even if the upper class people think we are not too smart with our propaganda. The reason I believe we are holding our own, is that the Communists *talk* food to the Asians, but we *give* them food.

Still another question: *Are the Asians Grateful for the Foreign Aid They Get from Us?*

I don't think so, for a number of reasons. First of all, the most of them can't appreciate the help they get. The typical Asian is simple and uninformed. He just doesn't understand. He is much like a six year old boy who does not appreciate the care and protection his parents give him. He takes them for granted. I suspect that there are many young people in Asia who think that American aid is part of the over-all scheme of things, like sunshine and fresh air. It never occurs to them that they might not always have American aid.

There is another reason why they are not grateful. They believe that we are incredibly and fabulously wealthy, and that what we give them is a trifling fraction of what we might give if we had a mind to.

To the typical Asian, an automobile is evidence of unspeakable riches. A new Ford car in Karachi—or a Plymouth, Mr. Chairman —costs more than the total lifetime earnings of most Pakistani citizens. These citizens look at American picture magazines or spend a few annas to attend an American movie. They see pictures of the late afternoon stream of cars out of downtown Detroit or Los Angeles. They draw only one conclusion.

A new Ford or Plymouth at the curbstone in Lahore attracts just the same kind of crowd as the yacht of the Queen of England would attract if it were tied up at the foot of Woodward Avenue.

Asians think that Americans are generous, but that we could be much more generous if we wanted to be.

Here is another question we often hear: *What Do Asians Think About Our American Habits and Ways of Living?*

The common Asians think we are materialistic, irreligious and immoral. The enlightened Asians think we may not be as materialistic, irreligious and immoral as we seem to be.

Asians judge us by their own standards. In Asia, at least in Muslim Asia, and probably in Hindu and Buddhist countries as well, religion is the paramount factor in the life of the citizen. He craves more food but in order that he may more effectively worship his God. He needs food to exist, but religion is the principal reason for existence. Everything else is secondary and incidental. I am speaking of the average Asian; there are many exceptions. Because many of us do not have this same attitude toward religion, they call us irreligious.

American motion pictures are shown all over Asia. The Asians see them and enjoy them. But they conclude that most of us are crooked politicians, gangsters, or degenerate, wealthy parasites.

I know a smart young man very well who is in the Pakistan Embassy in Paris. He told me that if he is to judge by motion pictures, Americans spend most of their time going into bars through swinging doors, touching somebody on the shoulder, and when he turns around, giving him a terrific wallop in the jaw.

Very many Muslim women are still veiled. All of them, all who are respectable that is, are shrouded from head to toe. American women are not. So the Asians say we are immoral.

An American and a resident of Hyderabad arrived at New York and put up at the Plaza Hotel. It was the Hyderabad man's first visit to the United States. The American was busy for an hour or two and suggested to the Asian that he take a walk down Fifth Avenue and have his first look at the United States. It was a very warm day.

When he returned, the American asked him what he thought about it all. The Asian replied, "Wonderful; beautiful; magnificent; remarkable in every way. But there is one thing that puzzles me. I have never in my life been in a city where there were so many prostitutes."

On the other hand, Asians have a high regard for American honesty and general integrity. In that special respect they believe we are just as good as they are, or better.

Mrs. Freund and I spent five or six days in the Oberoi Palace Hotel at Srinagar, in Kashmir. We ran short of rupees but the manager of the hotel told us not to worry. When it was time to pay the bill, he took our personal check on a Detroit bank without blinking an eye. He had never seen us and knew that he never would again. He had never even heard of us. Half a dozen Americans have told us of similar experiences of their own.

Well, there you are. I have not answered all the questions Americans ask about Asia but I have answered those they ask most frequently—or I have tried to answer them.

If you never have, you ought to take a trip to Asia if you can arrange it. You won't be quite as comfortable as in Europe, on the whole, but what you see will be more spectacular and dramatic. It appears to me at least, that Asia is now the center of the world stage.

I don't know much about international affairs, but if you live in Asia you get distinct impressions or feelings. I certainly have the feeling that the key to the future of the whole world is where India and China rub on each other down there, and it might be fun for you to go down and take a look if you can.

# ATTENTION AND INTEREST

I. The nature of attention
  A. Attention factors
    1. Intensity
    2. Change
    3. Unity
    4. Familiarity
    5. Novelty
    6. Repetition
  B. Principles in the use of attention factors
    1. Attention factors should appear throughout the speech
    2. Attention factors should be emphasized in the introduction
    3. Attention factors should be pertinent to the speech
    4. Attention factors should be appropriate to the interests of the audience
II. Determinants of interest
  A. Habits
  B. Set
  C. Values
  D. Suggestion
  E. Projection
III. Summary, questions, and exercises

# Chapter IX

## ATTENTION AND INTEREST

From a psychological standpoint, a book about speech is a study of perception. It examines the ways in which a speaker may encourage a listener to receive sensory impressions and then perceive their meanings. The speaker has an idea; he wants his listeners to understand it. He wants that idea to be reproduced in the listener's awareness in such a way that it will have essentially the same meaning and significance for the listener that it has for him.

The speech serves as a kind of map. It is a complex series of reference points made up of literally thousands of visual and auditory impressions which merge to form for the listener a single, over-all interpretation of the idea. The listener's perception of the speaker's idea is analogous to the traditional psychological concept of stimulus-response.

When a psychologist uses these terms, he is speaking of a single unit of energy directed at a single receptor to which the receptor will respond in some observable way. The speaking situation, however, is a complex of interacting stimulus-response relationships. The speaker initiates whole complexes of stimuli to which he asks the audience to attend and eventually respond. The listener's response is no less complex than the speaker's stimulus. From each momentary complex of stimuli, a listener abstracts and selects what he will respond to on the basis of his needs, attitudes, and expectancies. His responses take a multitude of forms ranging from overt action to contemplation. A new speaking situation is created every time there is a change in the complex of

stimuli presented by a speaker or a change in the interest of the
audience.

Two aspects of perception, then, are important to a speaker:
the stimuli which he conveys, and the response which the audience makes to them. The success of the speaker's communication
depends upon the extent to which he can command the attention
of the audience and control the audience's selection of the parts
of the speaker's message to which it will respond.

This chapter will consider these two aspects: the factors which
determine the attention value of the stimulus complex conveyed
by the speaker, and the role of the listener's interests in determining his response.


## The Nature of Attention

In every speaking situation, a listener has a multitude of
stimuli to which he might give attention. He is being con-
tinually bombarded by stimuli from the room, the seating, the
temperature, the outside noises, the people around him, and
his own objective and subjective concerns apart from the speaking situation. The speaker's problem is to cause the listener to
give attention to the particular group of stimuli he provides. The
speaker must make himself (and his message) the predominant element in this ocean of sensations. He must stand out as a striking
figure against a pale background. To do this he must make use
of factors in his speech which focus the attention of the audience
on him.

But attention span is quite short. No person can completely
concentrate on a single group of stimuli for more than a brief
time. Thereafter, his attention will wander and the speaker will
be pushed into the background by competing sensations whose
attention values had previously been ignored. For this reason,
the speaker must provide a continuing pattern of stimuli which
command the listener's attention.

In the moment of perception, the listener's interests leap out
to anticipate and mix with the speaker's presentation so that a
unification of stimulus and response occurs. For purposes of anal-

ysis, however, the speaker's presentation can be examined apart from the listener's interpretation. This presentation, the stimuli initiated by the speaker, can make use of certain intrinsic characteristics of stimulation which command attention apart from the listener's interests. Let us examine these attention factors now.

## ATTENTION FACTORS

There are six factors which will normally command attention regardless of the selectivity of the listener. These are: intensity, change, unity, familiarity, novelty, and repetition.

*Intensity.* Among a group of stimuli, listeners will tend to respond to those which are most intense. Thus, a loud noise, a bright light, or a strong smell will attract attention. To the speaker, this means that the stimuli he conveys must be the most intense in the room. He must be louder than the general babble around him. He must be more forceful in stating his case than his competitors.

Intensity here does not mean just loudness or gross physical gesture. It includes, also, the speaker's attitude toward the situation and his subject. If his attention seems to wander, if he looks out the window, if his arguments sound copied without interpretation from last month's *Reader's Digest,* if the total impression which the audience gets is that he doesn't really care, he can be said to lack intensity. If he wants an audience to pay attention to what he says, a speaker must show that the subject he discusses is of concern to him and that he has a commitment to his own convictions.

*Change.* If intensity were the only criterion, then the loudest, most positive, and most physically active speaker would get the most attention. You know that he does not. You know that unrelieved intensity in speakers frequently makes listeners tired of hearing them. The intensity of loudness, for instance, can be so constant that it becomes a general characteristic of the occasion. It has nothing about it which sets it apart from the background and it is, therefore, no longer useful in differentiating the speaker from competing stimuli. The audience's attention moves as yours does when you are studying in your room and someone begins to use the typewriter. It attracts your attention because it is different from the stimuli you have become used to. As you become habituated to the sound, however, it fades into the background and as you study you do not even hear the typewriter. This fading is an example of the way we attend to *changes* in the nature and intensity of stimuli more than we do to a continuous level of stimulation.

Not all stimulation which involves change will command attention. A repeated pattern of flashing lights, like a neon sign above a grocery store, fades into the background of attention after the viewer becomes habituated to the patterned change. A speaker with a sing-song pattern of speech changes his pitch and quality but, once the listener finds the pattern, the speaker's rhythmic patterned changes command as little attention as a monotone.

Speakers make use of change to build attention and thus give greater emphasis to ideas. If, at certain points in the speech, you seem more intent, argue more carefully, and heighten the motivational aspects (more about these in Chapter XI), your audience will give more attention to those points. You can thus direct the attention of the audience to your major ideas. But observe care not to emphasize minor points in this way, or the audience will pay more attention to them. You would be putting them in the foreground of your listeners' observation and relegating your major points to the background. Frequently a speaker is confused by the listener's insistence that he did not "hear" a point when the speaker is sure that he "said" it. Both listener and speaker are right. The speaker "said" what he thought he said, but not in a way that made the listener "hear" it. The listener did not perceive from the speaker's manner that the point was important, so he ignored it or forgot it.

***Unity.***     If speaking were like the visual perception of a bright light, which is a single stimulus, intensity and change could be regulated more conveniently. But speaking is not thus simple. It involves subtle abstractions of language and logic; it involves a visual image which is not a single strong light but many different stimuli which reach the eye from clothes, stance, facial expression, and movement. The vocal characteristics of pitch, force, time, and quality also provide multiple impressions. Over and above such external stimuli as the hard seats, the ventilation, the whispering in the row behind him, the listener receives millions of stimuli from the speaking situation. If he is to comprehend them, they must be organized. The speaker must, therefore, order his actions so that at any given moment the listener will receive all the discrete stimuli as if they were one.

Ideally, every movement and change in voice should support the speaker's idea. There must be a focusing of attention: the diverse stimulus components must be so related to one another that they may be taken as a whole. An analogous element in visual attention is sharpness of outline. The speaker must assure himself that all the stimuli at any given moment focus on a central idea.

It is with the purpose of helping speakers to achieve this focus that teachers caution against unnecessary physical movements, unusual patterns of speech, or irrelevant ideas. Unless all stimuli are linked together as a unified stimulus field, the listener will respond to distracting elements which stand out. These distracting sensations will produce injurious reactions like: "He kept fumbling with his keys." "She sounded as if she were 'preaching' to us." "What was all that talk about his uncle's farm for?" Unless there is unity, the listener may well fail to perceive the central purpose of the speech.

*Familiarity.* Things which are familiar to an audience will frequently command attention. When the ideas in a speech are unfamiliar to the listeners, their minds will tend to wander, to look for more understandable stimuli in which they are already interested. The speaker must, therefore, relate his subject to what is familiar to his audience. "You may not know, or care, what a differential is but if your car didn't have one you wouldn't be in class today," said one student speaker. "The Chinese food you get in a restaurant is not the same food the people in China eat," said another. In each case the speaker was trying to link his subject to what was familiar to his audience.

*Novelty.*    A habitual cigar smoker might give his attention to the sight of a man smoking a cigar. What kind of cigar is he smoking? How many does he smoke per day? Questions like these occur to the cigar smoker; the man who does not smoke cigars is likely to say, "Who cares?" But anyone will pay attention to a woman smoking a cigar. That sight is novel. It is so novel that it is almost humorous.

The out-of-the-ordinary will almost always attract attention. A student speaker brings a strange machine to class. The members of the audience look up. "I wonder what that is all about," they say to themselves.

While novelty will get immediate attention, it must be linked to the familiar if interest is to be sustained. Most listeners will cease paying attention to a thing after they become aware that it has little to do with their interests.

In Chapter XVI (Speaking to Entertain), the principles of humor will be discussed in greater detail. But it can be noted here that the attention-getting quality of humor is based on its novelty.

*Repetition.*    Since attention span is short and listeners are continually attracted by competing stimuli, it is quite common for main ideas to be forgotten, even those which have been force-fully stated. One method of reinforcing a listener's attention to an idea is repetition.

Judicious repetition of ideas and phrases will strengthen the speech. The speaker can make use of repetition through parallel sentence structure and phrasing. In one section of his Annual Message of January, 1936, President Franklin D. Roosevelt used fourteen consecutive rhetorical questions beginning with the word "shall." Ten of the fourteen questions begin with the words "shall we say." "That government of the people, by the people and for the people shall not perish from this earth," has a repetition of phrase pattern and words which holds attention. The speaker who weaves each new point into the pattern of his speech by associating it with the central thought uses repetition to reinforce his main idea.

If, however, repetition is used too much or wrongly, it is likely to become all the listener hears; it will draw attention away from important ideas and make the audience conscious only of the repetition. Unconscious periodic repetition of distracting mannerisms like "ah" and "uh" reinforce the unnecessary and force the main idea of the speech into the background.

## PRINCIPLES IN THE USE OF ATTENTION FACTORS

The factors of attention are valuable in selecting and developing the materials of a speech. These factors are not the only criteria for choosing material, for your first obligation is to select materials that support the central idea of your speech. (Chapter VI has discussed this matter.) But having determined what you want to say, you use the attention factors to help you in achieving your purpose. Look now at some of the principles which should control that use.

**Attention factors should appear throughout the speech.**    A speaker needs the attention of his audience through his entire speech. When and if attention lags, something important may be lost. Because the span of attention is quite limited, it must be constantly renewed by the speaker. Material should be selected, points should be organized, and delivery should be used to sustain the attention of an audience from beginning to end.

**Attention factors should be emphasized in the introduction.** The first and perhaps the most important point at which attention must be developed is in the introduction of the speech. When a speaker arises, he is, in a sense, a blur of movement, unfocused in the attention of his audience. As he goes to the speaking stand and arranges his notes, he becomes a human being; he has distinctive clothing; he has a distinctive face. Then he begins to talk. If the audience continues to see just a human being with dark hair, black shoes, blue suit, white shirt, and blue tie, the speaker will not hold attention. So it is that the introductory part of his speech must direct the attention of his hearers to his main idea. If the speaker fails to seize the attention of the audi-

ence at the beginning of his speech, it will be extremely difficult
to do so later on.

*Attention factors should be pertinent to the speech.*    It is easy
for a speaker to catch attention by using methods that are completely extraneous to the ideas in the speech. A young man began
a speech one day by holding out his hand at arm's length and
dropping a large number of glass marbles on the floor. The
marbles made a marvelous flash of color as they rattled and
rolled and danced around the room. The audience was immediately and completely attentive—to the marbles, not to the
speaker. To make it worse, as soon as they discovered the marbles
had nothing to do with the speech, their attention was lost. Such
*involuntary* attention is like the response to a sudden bright
light, or the firing of a shot. It will not last long and is of little
use to a speaker.

Listeners will also give a kind of *voluntary* attention which is
motivated by something extraneous to the speech itself. For example, a student may voluntarily set himself to hear a dull lecture because he wants to get a good grade in a class, or a workman will force himself to listen to instructions that he must have
in order to hold his job.

Outlandish attention techniques will send listeners away remembering the technique and not the idea. "Boy, was he loud!"
was a remark we once heard from a listener leaving a lecture hall.
"That was really a funny joke he told. I have to remember to tell
my wife when I get home," said one man after a political speech.
Such reactions as these indicate that what may be popularly regarded as a "good speech" may actually be a poor one because
the idea of the speaker is lost in the techniques of attention. The
speaker wants responses to his *ideas.* He must be sure, therefore,
that his attention techniques complement rather than over-
shadow the ideas.

*Attention factors should be appropriate to the interests of the
audience.*    The kind of attention a speaker gets when he
appeals to the habitual concerns of an audience is the most use-

ful. He must look for the best attention factors in a speech and not just the obvious ones. He looks for the factors which will be close to the experience of the audience, for the ones to which the audience can most easily respond.

## Determinants of Interest

To this point, our discussion has concerned itself with the speaker's active part in controlling the audience's perception of his ideas. Through the proper attention factors, he influences the selection and interpretation of the stimuli that compete for the attention of the audience. There are, however, other conditions in the audience itself which help to determine its response. These may be referred to as the determinants of interest.

There are five major conditions which will determine whether a member of an audience will select the stimuli a speaker intends him to select: habits, set, values, suggestion, and projection.

### HABITS

People perceive objects and ideas as they have been in the habit of perceiving them. When a sensitive critic looks at a poem, he sees form, idea, quality of language. A dullard sees in poetry only words, and perhaps dull words at that. The one responds to the beauty of the poem, the other to its dullness. The poem is different only in the habitual response of its two readers. Much of education is a process of developing new habits of looking at things. Students learn new habits of perceiving a picture, a microscopic organism, an event in history, a novel, a business organization.

A speaker may change some of his listener's habits but he cannot, with a speech, expect to construct new systems on the instant. Since audiences have certain habits of perception, a speaker must make some adaptation to those habits.

Politicians have learned to say "federal health insurance," instead of "socialized medicine." Psychologists, psychiatrists and social workers use the term "mental illness" in discussing what used to be called "insanity." Words like "health" and "insurance" evoke favorable habitual responses, while "socialism" and "insanity" tend to evoke habitual negative responses.

## Set

Habits in an audience are the personalized, internal dispositions of an individual listener. Its set is its generalized, external predisposition. Listeners tend to have certain predispositions about what should come from a speaking situation. Their level of interest is determined by their expectations, by their set. Therefore, a speaker must meet the anticipations of his audience or must change its set. If he does not, he will be misinterpreted and interest will lag.

How would you like to be introduced to an audience of a thousand people in a strange town this way: "And now I give you Miss Mary Watkins whom we all know as one of the most inspirational speakers of our times. We are all anxious to hear what Miss Watkins has to say to us for we know that our lives will be enriched by her message." If you wanted to fall through the floor at that moment no one could blame you. The chairman establishes a set in the audience which you know you cannot meet. Apropos, a word of warning to chairmen of meetings: give the audience a set which will help the speaker. Introduce the speaker and his topic and create a favorable impression for them both. But do not make the audience expect too much.

## Values

A listener's values will affect his response to a speaker's ideas. Value differences have been demonstrated by an experiment with children and coins. A group of children were shown various coins. A beam of light was then projected on a screen and the children were told to adjust the circle of light to the size of the coins. Invariably, the children from poorer families perceived the coins as larger than they actually were. The coins had a greater value for them than for the other children.

Some audiences see greater value in religious ideas than others.

Some audiences will give higher values to athletics, agriculture, politics, or books than others do. A skillful speaker understands the system of values which is operative in an audience and adapts his speaking to it. He may be able to change those values somewhat, but he must not ignore them lest his listeners reject him and lose interest in his ideas.

## SUGGESTION

Suggestion is an important part of the conditioning of an audience. It means simply that a listener is influenced by those around him. One form of political suggestion is known as the "bandwagon" technique. A candidate for office tries to create the impression that there is no doubt he will be elected. If this notion can be established, other politicians and some voters may support him because they want to be on the winning side. In one well-known experiment, an audience was told that a bottle contained a fluid with a strong odor. Each member of the audience was asked to hold up his hand when he could smell the odor. Then the bottle was opened. Actually, there was nothing in the bottle. The most suggestible members of the audience soon put up their hands and others followed. Some never did. One significance of the experiment is the fact that the people who raised their hands later were clustered in groups around the more suggestible whose hands had gone up first. There is an indication not only that some people are more suggestible than others, but that they help to influence those around them.

This fact is important to a speaker. When several individuals agree, they reinforce each other's convictions and modify, by suggestion, the ideas of other listeners in the group.

## PROJECTION

Perhaps the most frequently overlooked determinant of a listener's response is the phenomenon of projection. You are aware of the projective techniques used by psychologists. The Thematic Apperception Test presents a series of pictures which are deliberately vague. When a viewer is asked to tell a story based on a picture, he will project himself into the picture and express his underlying values and attitudes. An auditory form of projection technique is the "tautaphone," an instrument which produces meaningless sounds. When a listener is asked to interpret these, here too he projects his own ideas into the meaningless sounds.

If purposely vague pictures and sounds have meaning because a listener or viewer projects his own ideas into them, is it not also to be expected that listeners will do the same with a vague speech? Listeners not only *accept* or *reject* what a speaker says because of habits, set, values, and suggestions; they actually *change* his ideas to make them mean what the listener wants to hear. The more vague the speech, the more personal is the meaning the listener will get.

For a speaker, the implications of this phenomenon are clear. He must make sure that ideas and words are concrete. He must repeat his main ideas and use specific examples, for if the speaker is vague in word and idea, the listener will fill the gaps with what he wants or expects to hear. Experiments have been conducted with classes of college students who were read a meaningless speech like the one in Chapter XII, "Cooperation—An Opportunity and a Challenge." When asked to explain it, most of the students who thought they understood the speaker's point had heard ideas which were compatible with their own. An overly technical speech will also encourage projection. If a speaker's language is so technical as to be unclear, then a listener in his desire to find meaning, will project his own meaning, perhaps incorrect, into what the speaker says.

Projection can also work to a speaker's advantage. Realizing that a listener has certain interests in an idea, a speaker knows that he need not go into great detail. In argument, for example, some of the steps in the reasoning process are omitted. The audience will fill them in. It is a necessary condition of the speaking situation that no speaker can completely develop all his ideas. Listeners would become bored if they were subjected to every detail. A speaker, however, must know his listeners' interests and build a framework that will cause them to project those ideas which are compatible with the speaker's ideas.

## SUMMARY

In addressing an audience, a speaker initiates systems of stimuli which a listener accepts, rejects, or interprets in terms of his own interests. In order that the listener may perceive the speaker's ideas correctly, the speaker uses certain devices to focus the attention of his audience on the central idea of his speech. These devices are called attention factors:

1. Intensity
2. Change
3. Unity
4. Familiarity
5. Novelty
6. Repetition

To make his ideas effective, the speaker uses these attention factors throughout the speech, but he develops them with particular care in the introduction. He chooses attention factors that are appropriate to the ideas in his speech and pertinent to the interests of his audience.

Five conditions influence the level of interest which an audience will have in a speaker's ideas and help to determine whether listeners will select the stimuli the speaker intends them to select:

1. Habits
2. Set
3. Values
4. Suggestion
5. Projection

## QUESTIONS

1. How do both speaker and listener affect the way an act of communication takes place?

2. The chapter discusses six different attention factors. What three do you consider most important? Why?

3. How is a singsong pattern of speech like a monotone?

**4.** What principle of attention is in danger from unnecessary physical movement, unusual patterns of speech, or irrelevant ideas?

**5.** Why should attention factors be emphasized in the introduction?

**6.** How valuable to a speaker is involuntary attention in an audience?

**7.** How do listeners' habits affect interest?

**8.** What is set?

**9.** What kind of a speech will invite the greatest listener projection?

## EXERCISES

**1.** Report some experiences that show how people are suggestible.

**2.** Develop and bring to class the outlines of two or three different introductions to the same speech, emphasizing different attention factors in each.

**3.** Write a paper (no more than three double-spaced typewritten pages) in which you analyze a specific audience, explaining what values you believe would be most significant to them. Consult Chapter V in writing this paper.

**4.** Evaluate some speech delivered in class in terms of what the speaker did, or failed to do, to arouse your attention and sustain your interest.

# ARGUMENT: LOGICAL ELEMENTS

# Chapter **X**

# ARGUMENT:
# LOGICAL ELEMENTS

Consider two men, neighbors, living side by side for years in friendship and harmony. Assume that these two men hold opinions which make them almost as different as men can be. One drives a Chevrolet, the other prefers a Ford. One is a Dodger fan, the other supports the Braves. The one is a Republican, the other a Democrat. They belong to different churches. One owns his own small business, the other works for wages and, at the place where he is employed, is shop steward of the union to which he belongs.

In spite of their thoroughly differing views on these and many other subjects, two such persons might spend years in quite close contact as friends, neighbors, colleagues, or business associates without a word of controversy. The many differences between them will persist without being a source of controversy, however, only as long as neither of them is motivated to change an opinion of the other so that it agrees with his own. At whatever moment either of the two feels the necessity for concurrence between them, passive difference becomes active disagreement. In that moment, an occasion for persuasive speaking has been created.

Noise, wrangling and ill temper have come to be so closely associated with argument and disagreement that both are frequently identified with quarreling. Certainly the effort to resolve differences can be carried on in an atmosphere of harsh, angry words and raised voices, but these do not constitute either the disagreement or the argument. On the contrary, it will become clear in this chapter that *eliminating* disagreement is the occasion for persuasive speaking.

In persuasion, a speaker tries to bring about concurrence with his views by stating and defending the position he holds. The expression he uses to state his position is called a proposition. We have already discussed (Chapter III) the three kinds of propositions which may be advocated by a speaker: propositions of fact, value, and policy. Each of these says what the speaker believes to be the proper answer to the corresponding kind of question.

A proposition of *fact* (the alleged answer to some question of fact) expresses a speaker's belief that certain conditions exist and, at the same time, indicates what he intends to prove to his audience. For example:

> Southern whites are afraid that, given equal rights,
> Negroes might persecute white people.

A proposition of *value* (the alleged answer to some question of value) is a statement which indicates the value judgment a speaker has made about a subject. In persuasion, the speaker attempts to make his audience agree with his judgment. An example is found in a remark Nikita Khrushchev made to East Berliners:

> The friendship of our two peoples is one of the
> great achievements of our time.

A proposition of *policy* (the alleged answer to some question of policy) identifies the course of action which the speaker believes his audience ought to adopt. For instance:

> To fight Communism in Asia, the United States
> should encourage mutual agreements among Asian
> nations.

You can readily see that none of the above three propositions will be universally accepted at first utterance. Each of them requires to be justified, for merely expressing an attitude or a belief does not always make it acceptable to others. The process of defending a proposition, of getting it accepted by an audience, is called argumentation. In order to create belief in his proposal, a speaker advances *arguments* to support it. If the arguments are effective, the audience accepts the speaker's proposition. An argument may be defined as a statement or group of statements intended to support a proposition.

## Persuasion on Rational and Nonrational Grounds

When a controversy arises, each of the parties to it likes to think that the position he holds has a rational basis. People feel more secure if there are adequate *reasons* to justify what they believe and do. Adequate reasons as grounds for decisions and judgments are firmer than whim, emotion, and guess.

There are, of course, other than rational grounds for decisions about what to do and for judgments about what is good or bad and true or false. To think otherwise would be naive, for human beings have emotional responses that significantly influence them. But it would be a pity if there were no other grounds than emotion for decisions that must be made: emotion is influential, but reason should be satisfied.

An argument based on emotional appeal and without a clear rational basis can undoubtedly be effective in persuasion. It is quite conceivable also that appeals to reason alone may be persuasive. But when they are used together, appeals to reason and emotion satisfy both the rational and the nonrational elements that seem to form the basis for most of the beliefs that people formulate about the problems of day-to-day experience.

## Probability and Proof

Under ideal conditions, the arguments a speaker uses to persuade would constitute conclusive proof of his proposition. Actual conditions are such, however, that conclusive proof is a virtually unattainable goal. The subjects of persuasive speeches grow out of controversies that will have at least two sides: Is a

factual judgment true or false? Does a person or condition have
an alleged merit or lack it? Should a proposed policy be adopted
or rejected?

The evidence on both sides of any proposition is almost inevitably so limited and so divided that clear-cut decision is difficult.
Even if it were possible to know all the evidence and all the arguments for and against any proposition, decision would still be
difficult because most audiences are so heterogeneous that a
speaker can find in them no inclusive standard of values on
which to base his arguments. Consequently, proof in persuasion is
not the same as scientific demonstration. That is to say, proof
will not be absolute, for no matter how firmly a conviction may
be held, there is always the possibility that it may be wrong.

But on the other hand, it is not enough to prove only that a
proposition *can* be true. An audience may readily agree that a
candidate elected from one political party *might* be more beneficial to the country in the presidency than the candidate from
another. The demonstration of such a fact would not be sufficient grounds to vote for either candidate.

Because it is impossible to give absolute proof, and because it
is necessary to prove that a proposition is more than possibly
true, a speaker's efforts in persuasion are aimed at proving that
his proposition is *probably* true. An audience looks at the two
sides of a given proposition, recognizes that there is evidence and
argument on both sides, and then gives its assent to the side
which seems to have the weight of probability in its favor.

In demonstrating the probability of a proposition, "making a
case for it," there is a wide range in the strength the case may
have. The proposition can be made to seem only plausible; that
is, the audience can agree that there is some reason to believe it
might be true. A stronger case is one that shows the proposition
is likely to be true. The stronger the likelihood, the stronger the
case. Insofar as it is possible, an audience wants assurance that
its decisions are right. Listeners will accept a proposition when
the speaker has demonstrated its likelihood to a degree that satis-
fies them. That is, the proposition must not only be more likely
to be true than false but the likelihood must be strong enough to
satisfy the audience's desire for assurance. An audience is com-

pletely satisfied when a speaker's case is so strong that his proposition can be accepted as *true*. In these instances, the listener feels that the proposition is more than likely, has more than a good chance of being true. He is convinced; he believes; for him, the proposition is true. This same listener may change his mind later, or new evidence may prove him wrong, but at the moment his decision is reached, he is convinced that the speaker's proposition is true.

Arguments are evaluated from two points of view. First, the evidence presented must be examined to determine its adequacy; second, the process of reasoning by which conclusions are drawn from that evidence must be characterized as correct or incorrect. Sound arguments may be defined as those which combine sufficient, adequate evidence and correct reasoning procedures. The forms, uses, tests and sources of evidence have been discussed in Chapters VI and VII. It is our purpose in the present chapter to see how the rational part of argument operates in persuasive speaking.

## The Structure of Argument

Every argument used in persuasion performs an identifiable operation: it presents (or suggests) evidence and specifies the implications of that evidence. The common practice is to speak of the evidence as the "premises." The implications are stated in what is called the "conclusion."

Traditionally, arguments are considered to be of two types: inductive and deductive. For both kinds of arguments the claim is made that their premises provide evidence of the truth of the conclusion, that the conclusion follows from the premises. Only in the case of deductive argument, however, is the claim made that the premises provide *conclusive* evidence. In a properly formulated deductive argument, the conclusion follows *necessarily* from the premises. Inductive arguments are those whose premises offer *some* evidence of the truth of the conclusion. The degree to which the premises of an inductive argument support the conclusion will vary with the amount and quality of the evidence. In no case, however, will an inductive argument provide more than probable proof of the conclusion. Let's examine briefly the structure of these two kinds of argument.

## INDUCTION

By inductive argument we mean this: From the fact that something is true of certain examined members of a class, the conclusion is drawn that the same thing will be true of unexamined members of that class also. The conclusion can be applied to an unlimited number of the unexamined members of the class. Thus induction is often a reasoning process that moves from particulars (or the less general) to the universal (or the more general). Another induction may extend the conclusion to a limited number of unexamined members of the class, for example to the next one which appears. In this case, the induction moves from known particulars to a new unknown particular. The process of induction can be described as taking place in three steps:

1. *Isolated facts, conditions, or phenomena are experienced.* As an amateur entomologist, you collect various species of butterflies. The first butterfly you find proves to have a fine powder on its wings.

2. *Similarities appear among the specific instances which you examine.* Your second specimen is also seen to have a powdery substance on its wings. You observe that the same condition exists in all the butterflies that make up your collection.

3. *A conclusion is drawn.* You conclude that what has been true of all the butterflies you have found thus far will be true of butterflies in general, and that any butterfly you find in the future will have powder on its wings.

It is obvious that such a conclusion is no more than probable. Adding more and more evidence to support it does no more than increase the probability.

## DEDUCTION

We have said that a deductive argument is one whose premises are claimed to provide conclusive proof of the conclusion. This is not to say, however, that the conclusion of any deductive argument is necessarily true. It means merely that in a valid (that is, a properly constructed) deductive argument, the conclusion is necessarily implied by the premises. The premises of the argument may be true or untrue and the argument itself may be valid or invalid. Only when the premises are true and the argument is valid must the conclusion be true.

Deductive arguments take several forms. Among these, the one most commonly used to illustrate deduction is the categorical syllogism. You have surely seen the classic example that has been appearing in textbooks for perhaps twenty centuries:

> All men are mortal.
> Socrates is a man.
> Therefore, Socrates is mortal.

Let's illustrate the relationship between the premises and the conclusion of this syllogism. First, we draw a large circle to represent *all mortal beings.* The circle is intended to include not only men but all animals, birds, trees, insects, fish, and anything else that lives and is subject to death. Next, we represent *men* with a smaller circle inside the large one. The smaller circle has to be inside the larger because inductive experience has shown that men, as a class, do die and therefore are a part of the larger group. Finally, we come to the specific instance in the form of the individual, *Socrates,* whom we represent by a third circle. Since Socrates belongs to the class of men, this third circle must be inside the one representing men. Diagrammed, the syllogism looks like the structure on p. 172, overleaf.

Immediately, it becomes evident that Socrates could not be classified as a man without at the same time being included in the group of mortals. It is easy to see why deduction is such an effective form of argument.

The categorical syllogism is only one of several forms the syllogism may have and the syllogism is itself by no means the only form a deductive argument may take. Consequently our discussion of deductive argument is merely illustrative. It is certainly not intended to be exhaustive.

The point is worth repeating here that proofs in persuasion

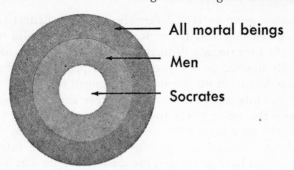

All mortal beings

Men

Socrates

FIGURE X–1. THE CATEGORICAL SYLLOGISM.

are not absolute. It is true that the conclusion of a valid deductive argument follows necessarily from the premises. But this says nothing about whether the conclusion is true. When speakers deliberate on policy decisions and on judgments of fact and value, the premises which provide evidence for their conclusions are only probable. The conclusions of a deductive argument can never be more probable than the premises. The implication of this fact is clear: The most a speaker can usually show is that a proposition of policy, value, or fact is "probably true" or "best."

## Persuasive Forms of Argument

More than 2000 years ago, Aristotle observed that when a speaker uses arguments to prove a proposition, he uses inductive and deductive reasoning in forms especially adapted to persuasion. Let's see how inductive and deductive arguments operate when they are used by a speaker to build persuasive proof.

### INDUCTION IN PERSUASION

In describing the structure of inductive arguments, we said that their conclusions can be extended to either a limited or unlimited number of unexamined members of a class. Each of these two possibilities serves as a basis for argument in persuasion. If the conclusion is unlimited in its extension, a generalization is

made about the whole class. When a speaker makes such a generalization and offers evidence to support it, he uses *argument by
example*. When the conclusion to an induction is limited in its
extension and is applied to some particular unexamined member
of the class, the speaker uses *argument by analogy*.

*Argument by example.*     The generalizations a speaker makes
in persuasion may be either true or false. For our purposes, it
must be assumed that the speaker himself believes them to be
true and that he would not otherwise bring them to bear in an
argument. Many of the generalizations that are useful to a
speaker are propositions which an audience already holds to be
true. Such propositions may vary widely, from the rashest kind of
generalization to highly credible beliefs carefully distilled from
intelligent interpretations of broad experience. In other instances,
when an audience cannot be expected to know, understand, or
readily accept propositions that are important in a speech, the
speaker must establish them inductively through argument by
example.

Suppose in arguing against socialized medicine you were to
contend that the quality of medical service under such a system
could always be expected to be poor. You might adduce a number of specific instances in which socialized medicine has afforded
medical care of poor quality. On the basis of these specific instances, you would conclude that what is true of the known examples cited would be true of all other unexamined instances of
socialized medicine, even those not yet in existence.

A large number of examples is not always necessary in effective
rhetorical induction. It is quite possible that a single case in
point might be sufficient to create belief in a proposition. In the
example just cited, although there are several countries where
socialized medicine has been adopted as a policy, instead of listing a number of instances wherein the government pays the cost
of medical care, you might develop an extended and detailed
description of its failure in one specific place. It is evident that
in drawing a universal conclusion from no more than one specific
instance there is grave danger of forming a hasty and untenable
generalization. If such an argument is to have any persuasive

force, it must be drawn from a carefully selected and well-developed example which an audience can easily accept as truly representative of the proposition it supports.

Since generalizations depend upon the evidence that supports them, the critical element in argument by example is the quality of the examples themselves. These examples are precisely the kind of supporting material described in Chapter VI (Supporting Material: Types and Use) and must meet the criteria described there. Let's list these criteria briefly again.

1. The examples must be representative.
2. Negative instances must be accounted for.
3. The examples must be sufficient in number.

*Argument by analogy.* Confusion sometimes arises over the term analogy because it is used in two ways: In the first sense, the word refers to the language device a speaker may use to illustrate or clarify an unfamiliar idea by comparing it to a similar idea with which his audience is familiar. For example, you might say that the gills of a fish serve much the same purpose as the lungs of an animal, or that a world federation of nations would be quite like the United States in its political structure. An illustrative analogy has great merit not only for clarifying an idea but also as a means of lending vividness to the idea. "We all know," says Emerson, "that as the human body can be nourished on any food, though it were boiled grass and the broth of shoes, so the human mind can be fed by any knowledge."

To the extent that clarity and interest are necessary in any speech, an illustrative analogy may be useful in persuasion. It will do nothing, however, to build proof. The speaker who wants to prove a proposition will build analogies in the second sense of the term. In this second sense, analogy is used to mean the reasoning process by which a speaker infers that what is true of one specific instance will also be true of a similar specific instance. No one has to learn to drive each of the makes of automobiles separately. Automobiles are enough alike in the way they operate for a driver to be able to move easily from one to another and drive it without learning how to operate each new one that comes along. Even if he learned to drive in a Chevrolet, and has driven only this one car, he knows by analogy that he will be able to drive a Ford should the occasion arise.

For a clearer understanding of how this kind of reasoning operates, let us examine *literal analogy* and *figurative analogy,* the two forms in which it appears in argument.

*Literal analogy.* A literal analogy draws a conclusion about two items, events, or conditions which belong to the same class. It is a prediction that because two things are alike in certain known respects they can be expected to be alike in other respects where the similarity is as yet unknown. Using this kind of reasoning, a speaker argues that because socialized medicine has operated successfully in Great Britain it would operate successfully in the United States, or that since two cities are nearly equal in population, have similar kinds and amounts of industry, and are alike in other important respects, they may be expected to equal each other in, say, wealth, or number of children of school age, or some other point of comparison.

Franklin Delano Roosevelt used this analogy in his "Arsenal of Democracy" speech, December 29, 1940:

Tonight, in the presence of a world crisis, my mind goes back eight years to a night in the midst of a domestic crisis. It was a time when . . . the whole banking system of our country had ceased to function. . . . I tried to convey to the great mass of American people what the banking crisis meant to them in their daily lives. Tonight I want to do the same thing, with the same people, in this new crisis which faces America. We met the issue of 1933 with courage and realism. We face this new crisis—this new threat to the security of the nation—with the same courage and realism.

Suppose you were trying to prove that part-time students, taking all their classes at night, ought to meet the same rigorous standards set for day students. You might say:

Look at it this way. A swing-shift worker can't be any less capable and efficient than a fellow on the day shift. The work he turns out has to be just as good. What if you had a part-time job on the swing shift at Norco Aircraft? You wouldn't last a week if you did poor work there. If you ever told your boss the work you turn out shouldn't have to pass inspection because you're there only part-time, how long do you think you'd last? Well, the same thing is true in school. The fact that you are a part-time student and take only late afternoon and evening classes doesn't mean you can get by with low quality work.

The chief benefit of drawing an inference by analogy is that it allows one to profit from experience; the chief danger lies in the fact that some important difference may have been overlooked in making the original comparison. The driver who has operated only late-model cars with automatic transmissions will not be able to drive a car with a standard shift solely on the basis of his earlier experience. The British system of socialized medicine can be expected to operate successfully in the United States only if the two countries are similar in respects that are important to government operation of a medical program. If, however, careful analogies are drawn, and if the phenomena compared are similar in important respects, arguments from analogy will have probative force helpful to a persuasive speaker.

*Figurative analogy.* A figurative analogy makes a comparison between objects that are not in the same class. A few years ago, colleges were debating the topic of a guaranteed annual wage. A speaker used the following analogy to defend his contention that labor was unwise in demanding a guaranteed income.

The labor movement has made tremendous strides in this country since the pioneering days of Samuel Gompers. At the same time, labor has made many enemies who distrust unions as the weapon of the laboring man's greed. Right now, when the unions themselves are shot through with corruption, it would be foolish for labor to demand a guaranteed annual wage. Do you remember the story of the dog with the bone? He saw his reflection in a pond. It looked to him as if the dog he saw had a bigger bone, so he dropped his bone to take the bigger one— and lost both. If the workingman insists upon reaching for the bigger bone of a guaranteed annual wage, he may lose many of the advances labor has made up to now.

Obviously, this analogy compares items that are not at all alike in any literal sense. The argument draws its force from the fact that it establishes an apparent or plausible ratio: the greed of the dog bears the same relationship to his loss of the bone that the laboring man's greed would bear to his loss of hard-won advances.

In the Cooper Institute address, Abraham Lincoln addressed a portion of his remarks to Southern politicians:

In [the] event [that a Republican President is elected], you say, you will destroy the Union; and then, you say, the great crime of having destroyed it will be upon us! That is cool. A highway-man holds a pistol to my ear, and mutters through his teeth, "Stand and deliver, or I shall kill you, and then you will be a murderer!"

In 1850, John C. Calhoun clashed in a debate with Henry Clay and Daniel Webster over the question of extending slavery into territory recently acquired from Mexico. The great call of Webster and Clay was for Union. Calhoun answered, "The cry of 'Union! Union! The glorious Union!' can no more prevent disunion than the cry of 'Health! Health! glorious Health!' on the part of a physician can save a patient lying dangerously ill."

Ordinarily, figurative analogies are more colorful than literal analogies but, at the same time, they lack the probative force of the carefully drawn literal analogy. Nonetheless, a good figurative analogy can make it possible for a speaker to defend a proposition successfully when otherwise he might fail. Indeed, a good analogy, either figurative or literal, may be worth ten thousand syllogisms, much as a picture is worth ten thousand words.

## DEDUCTION IN PERSUASION

When a speaker uses deductive inferences in persuasion, he may on occasion put his arguments into syllogistic form. Most often, he will not. Logically, a syllogism is an ordered structure of simple beauty, but stylistically, its formal and often stilted language leaves much to be desired. Speakers, then, almost always put their arguments into the ordinary language of conversational speech. Instead of using complete syllogisms, they use syllogisms in an elided or abbreviated form. That is, they omit whatever premises the audience can infer for itself, and give only those parts of the argument that are necessary. The name "enthymeme" is given to deductive arguments that appear in this shortened form. According to Aristotle, who gave enthymemes their name, deductive arguments are not only abbreviated in structure but, like inductive arguments, they are also probable rather than certain proofs.

The reason for stating deductive arguments as enthymemes is mainly one of style. The attention and interest of an audience are so important that a speaker must do everything he can to retain both. If he forces the audience to plod through every detailed step of his arguments, he tires them, he bores them, and often he gives the impression of talking down to them. Consequently, he says only what must be said to make the argument clear.

Wendell Willkie, in his "Loyal Opposition" speech, delivered after his defeat for the presidency by Franklin Delano Roosevelt, defended the right of the minority to debate issues in those dangerous times just prior to World War II. Note that the premise upon which the argument depends, the proposition that any totalitarian idea should be rejected, is not expressly stated. Instead, the speaker assumes that the audience will supply the missing proposition. Willkie said:

It has been suggested that in order to present a united front to a threatening world, the minority should now surrender its convictions and join the majority. This would mean that in the United States of America there would be only one dominant party—only one economic philosophy—only one political philosophy of life. This is a totalitarian idea—it is a slave idea—it must be rejected utterly.

Willkie's argument not only illustrates the tendency of a speaker, for the sake of style, to elide the deductive arguments he uses, but it also exemplifies the second characteristic of the enthymeme—the fact that the proof it elicits is only probable. It is in no sense an absolute truth that any totalitarian idea should be rejected. Mr. Willkie could safely assume, however, that his audiences would accept the proposition as being probably true. Consequently, the argument was effective.

When a speaker uses deductive reasoning in persuasion, his inferences take the form of *argument from sign* or *argument from cause.*

*Argument from sign.*     In using argument from sign, a speaker observes directly some fact or condition. Using this as evidence, he draws the conclusion that some other fact or condition, not immediately observable, is true. A good example of inference based on signs may be seen in the diagnosis a physician makes. When he examines a patient who has, let us say, pneumonia, the doctor cannot directly observe the disease. Instead, what he looks for are symptoms, a set of conditions which are directly observable. These symptoms are a set of signs from which he can infer the presence of the disease.

Argument from sign may be thought of as deductive. It is always based on a generalization either explicit or implied and can be put into syllogistic form. This generalization alleges a relationship between an observed sign and what it shows. It asserts that the observed phenomenon and the condition it signals always occur together, that the former does not occur without the latter. If the alleged relationship is accepted or believed by an audience, and if the condition taken as a sign is known or believed to exist, the conclusion follows without question.

The Londoner of Shakespeare's day knew that he could see a play whenever a flag was raised over the Globe Theater. The presence of the flag was taken as a sign that a play would be presented. The conclusion is drawn from two premises: "A flag on the theater always signals the production of a play," and "The flag is flying." If these two propositions are true, the conclusion necessarily follows that a play is to be produced.

A student speaker, defending the proposition that the United States should continue to support UNESCO, contended that

UNESCO has been instrumental in preserving art. In support of this contention, he offered these occurrences as signs that UNESCO has indeed labored to preserve works of art:

1. It advised the Austrian government on the restoration of a number of old paintings.
2. It helped Yugoslavia restore murals and frescos.
3. It advised Syria and Lebanon in their efforts to restore ancient monuments and archeological sites.
4. It helped Peru in the restoration of her historical monuments.

On December 8, 1941, the day after the Japanese attack on Pearl Harbor, Franklin Delano Roosevelt delivered the famous speech in which he asked the Congress to declare that a state of war existed between the United States and Japan. In that speech, the President said:

Yesterday, December 7, 1941—a date which will live in infamy—the United States of America was suddenly and deliberately attacked by naval and air forces of the Empire of Japan. . . .
Yesterday the Japanese Government also launched an attack against Malaya.
Last night Japanese forces attacked Hong Kong.
Last night Japanese forces attacked Guam.
Last night Japanese forces attacked the Philippine Islands.
Last night the Japanese attacked Wake Island.
This morning the Japanese attacked Midway Island.
Japan has, therefore, undertaken a surprise offensive extending throughout the Pacific area. The facts of yesterday speak for themselves.

The President was right. The signs of a Japanese surprise offensive were incontestable.

*Testing sign relationships.*    In argument, the sign relationship alleged by a speaker must be accepted by his audience. It is the crucial point in the argument. Consequently, before an argument from sign is used in persuasion, the reliability of the generalization upon which the argument depends must be examined in the light of three questions.

1. *Is there a reliable relationship between the observed fact and the conclusion drawn?* An accidental relationship is no sure basis for argument from sign. The conclusion you draw in such cases is likely to be a coincidence or just plain superstition.

A little boy, returning from an afternoon at the beach with his parents, sees another car on the street. He says, "Look, those people have been to the beach, too." He bases his inference on the fact that two long, pointed sticks protrude from the trunk of the other car. They look to him like poles for a pair of beach umbrellas. The basis for the inference is quite tenuous, because even if his supposition is correct, and the pointed sticks are a sign that there is a beach umbrella in the back of the car, their presence is by no means a certain sign that the people in the other car are returning from the beach.

There may be a splendid correlation between the number of smogless days in Los Angeles and the number of days of rain in Phoenix, Arizona, but a smogless day in Los Angeles is nonetheless a poor sign of rain in Phoenix. Perhaps you have heard it said that when more boys than girls are being born at any given time the fact is a sign of impending war. Such a condition is about as trustworthy a sign of coming war as left-handedness is of superior intelligence.

2. *Do changed circumstances of time or place alter the relationship between sign and conclusion?* The reliability with which one condition can be taken as the sign of another condition can be altered by time and place. In the first half of the nineteenth century, the fact that a Southern farmer was a man of means would be a very reliable sign that he was a slaveowner. Today, no amount of wealth would be a sign that such a man owned slaves.

3. *Is the conclusion supported by the concurrence of other signs?* A single sign may often be insufficient evidence of the condition it seems to point to. Additional corroborating signs are frequently needed to support the conclusion of an argument from sign. Circumstantial evidence in a criminal case is an example. To say that a man is guilty of burglary because he was in the vicinity at the time the crime was committed is a weak argument. To show, in addition, that he was seen leaving the

burglarized home and was arrested with stolen articles in his possession is to offer further and more substantial signs of his guilt.

In problems as complex as those that arise in human society, a single sign will seldom be a sure indication of a given fact or condition. Much more often than not, several are required to establish probability. Stock-market analysts make forecasts based on very tenuous data. What kinds of facts are such predictions based on? In July of one year, employment set a new record and unemployment dropped. For the second quarter of the year, the gross national product increased $5,000,000,000 over the first quarter. Personal income for the first seven months of the year is 1.06 times that for the same period in the year before. Now, do these facts *prove* that the over-all economy is in a healthy state? They may prove the proposition for some; for others not. At any rate, the conditions described are *signs* that indicate something about the condition of business. From them, one can draw inferences about the present and future states of the economy.

*Argument from cause.*     Every effect must have a cause, and no agent can properly be considered a cause unless it produces an effect. The two are inevitably associated. When an occurrence or condition is the direct result of an antecedent occurrence or condition, the relationship between them is that of cause and effect. The one that exists prior in time and operates to bring about the other is said to be the cause. The one that exists as a direct result of the first is said to be the effect. Inferences based on causal reasoning appear either as arguments *from cause to effect* or as arguments *from effect to cause*.

1. *Cause to effect.* In a recent classroom speech, the speaker proposed that the state government should operate clinics to dispense narcotics at low cost to addicts. His speech contained these examples of argument from cause to effect: Lack of availability, plus the greed of peddlers, causes the price of narcotics to be high. High prices cause narcotics addiction to be very expensive. The expense of being an addict forces addicts to turn to crime for money to support their habit. He argued further

that the clinics he proposed would reduce the cost of addiction, thus removing the cause of a large proportion of present-day crime, and would, at the same time, eliminate narcotics peddlers by removing their source of profit.

Do you remember Mark Antony's funeral oration over the body of Caesar? Shakespeare has Antony use this *cause-to-effect* argument.

> It is not meet you know how Caesar loved you.
> You are not wood, you are not stones, but men:
> And, being men, hearing the will of Caesar,
> It will inflame you, it will make you mad.

Arguments of this kind move forward in time. That is, in reasoning from cause to effect, a speaker infers from one event or condition that a second event or condition will follow, the first being the cause, the second its result. This kind of reasoning is used to support an appeal for or against an increase in taxes, the choice of a man for public office, a program of disarmament, or any specified course of action.

2. *Effect to cause.* The second kind of argument from causal relation moves backward in time from a given condition and attempts to establish a probable cause. This kind of reasoning determines why the Roman Empire fell, why there has been a war, what causes juvenile delinquency, what causes a high divorce rate, or the cause of any other of the host of society's problems. When someone is ill, he reasons from signs (the symptoms) *that* he is ill. In order to know *why* he is ill, he must look to the germ, or virus, or condition that *caused* the illness or discover the conditions that made him susceptible to it. Only an intelligent understanding of probable causes will permit more than temporary, symptomatic relief in any situation that demands improvement. Aspirin may stop a headache, but it will not stop the eyestrain that causes the headache. Not knowing that eyestrain is present may lead to effects even more serious than headaches.

In the British House of Commons, in 1780, Charles James Fox delivered a speech in which there appears the following clear example of argument from effect to cause.

It is this cursed American war that has led us, step by step, into all our present misfortunes and national disgraces. What was the cause of our wasting forty millions of money, and sixty thousand lives? The American War! What was it that produced the French rescript and the French War? The American War! What was it that produced the Spanish Manifesto and Spanish War? The American War! What was it that armed forty thousand men in Ireland with arguments carried on the points of forty thousand bayonets? The American War! For what are we about to incur an additional debt of twelve or fourteen millions? This accursed, cruel, diabolical American War!

Patrick Henry used reasoning of this same kind in his speech to the Virginia Convention of Delegates, March 23, 1775.

I ask . . . , sir, what means this martial array, if its purpose be not to force us to submission? Can gentlemen assign any other possible motive for it? Has Great Britain any enemy in this quarter of the world, to call for all this accumulation of navies and armies? No, sir, she has none. They are meant for us; they can be meant for no other.

*Testing causal relationships.*     Arguments from cause, like arguments from sign, should be thought of as deductive. They, too, depend upon a stated or implied generalization—in this case, that in all instances a given event or set of circumstances can be expected to bring about a second event or condition as a direct result. Here again, as in the case of inference from sign, it is essential to the argument that the audience accept the premise which states the causal relationship upon which the speaker's conclusion depends. If the causal relationship stated or implied by the speaker is accepted by the audience, and if conditions described by the speaker are known or believed to exist, arguments from cause will be accepted as conclusive proof. In order to avoid the many dangers inherent in causal arguments, test their rhetorical soundness before you use them in persuasion.

1. *There must really be a causal relationship.* We have said that a cause always precedes its effect. That is, it comes earlier

in time. This one characteristic is often an occasion of the fallacy called *post hoc, ergo propter hoc*—"after this, therefore on account of this." The fact that one event follows another does not mean that the second is the result of the first. Time sequence, then, does not constitute causal relationship. Superstitions are good examples of faulty causal reasoning of this sort. Either a causal faculty they do not possess is attributed to certain occurrences ("Oh, you broke a mirror. Seven years bad luck!") or, on the basis of coincidental time sequence, a causal connection that does not exist is alleged ("I sprained my ankle when I stepped off the curb because I walked under a ladder just before it happened.")

It is easy, but naive, to allege a causal relationship where none really exists; many factors can intervene to destroy a neat chain of causal reasoning. One is often tempted to assert the truth of a conclusion on the basis of an event that he would expect to cause a certain result. He fails to notice that other causal factors intervene. Having the engine in an automobile overhauled should result in improved performance and economy of the car. But if the driver tries to economize further by using paint thinner for fuel, he introduces another factor that will completely prevent the engine overhaul from having the desired effect. By the same token, a fisherman plagued by mosquitoes can expect little help from an insect repellant if he washes it off because he doesn't like the smell.

2. *Avoid oversimplification in determining cause and effect.* Rarely, if ever, are cause and effect found in simple one-to-one ratio. Most often, an effect comes about through the operation of a whole series of contributing causes. It is quite simple to say that a president *caused* a depression or a war. It is also quite foolish to make such an assertion. The tremendously complex nature of social ills makes oversimplification both a temptation and a danger. If, however, a speaker undertakes to show that a president's policies made a substantial contribution to certain unfortunate events, he is on safer and also more reasonable ground.

More often than not, a cause generates, or at least influences, multiple effects. Any course of action, when put into operation, has results; that is, it becomes a cause operating to bring about effects that may be good, bad, or indifferent. If a speaker argues that juvenile delinquency results from bad comic books (itself a thoughtless analysis) he may conclude that censorship of reading materials would cause a reduction of juvenile delinquency. But censorship involves side effects which may very well be worse than any good it accomplishes.

Determining cause and effect is usually a complicated and difficult process. Yet causality may be the most important concept in the whole of argumentation.

***Distinguishing between sign and cause.***     Arguments from sign and from cause are often difficult to distinguish. For one reason, English has a limited number of logical connectives such as "because," "since," "hence," and "therefore." These or similar words are used to indicate argument and conclusions to argument regardless of whether a speaker is basing his inferences on sign or on cause. Moreover, if argument from sign is to be effective, there must be some kind of causal relationship between two events when one is the sign of the other. Otherwise, signs are merely accidental.

An argument from sign is called a *ratio cognoscendi*—a way of knowing that a proposition is true. When you see a flock of geese pointing northward across the sky, you know that spring will soon be here. If a man buys a new car every year, wears expensive clothes, and lives in an exclusive section of town, you take these indications to mean he suffers no immediate lack of money. In each of these instances, the signs are interpreted to mean that the conclusion drawn from them *is* true. No attempt is made to say *why* it is true: why spring is coming, or why the man in question is wealthy.

Arguments from cause, on the other hand, lend credibility to propositions by offering reasons that will explain *why* they are true. This kind of inference is a *ratio essendi,* a way of accounting for the existence of something.

The major distinction, then, between arguments from sign and arguments from cause is in what they attempt to show. An argument from sign, making no use of causal relationships, attempts to show *that* a condition has existed, does exist, or will exist.

An argument from cause assumes the condition and offers to explain *why* it is so.

## SUMMARY

Controversies arise when one person is motivated to change an opinion of others so that it agrees with his own. In so doing, he uses arguments to justify belief in his point of view. The arguments he uses will be examples of either inductive or deductive inference. If the former, they will be said to offer *some* evidence of the truth of the conclusion. Inductive arguments help to establish the probability of the conclusion drawn. Deductive arguments, on the other hand, are said to provide conclusive proof. That is, if the argument is valid, the conclusion is necessarily implied in the premises.

Although the conclusion of a valid deductive inference follows necessarily from the premises, this consequence says nothing about whether the conclusion is true. Only when the premises are certainly true *and* the argument is valid is the conclusion certainly true. But when speakers deliberate on proposed policies, judgments of value, and allegedly factual conditions, the premises that provide evidence for their conclusions are only probable. Hence, the proofs in persuasion are only probable. The arguments a speaker offers, then, are used to give a rational basis to belief. They do not constitute absolute proof.

Inductive arguments in persuasion appear either as generalizations or as analogies. In making generalizations a speaker presents evidence in the form of examples to justify the belief that what is true of the instances cited will be true of all unexamined instances of the same phenomenon. An argument by analogy does not use its premises as evidence that exemplifies something about a whole class. Instead, it concludes that what is true of examined instances will be true of another *particular* instance of the same class of phenomena.

Deductive arguments appear in persuasion either as arguments from sign or arguments from cause. The first of these is called a *ratio cognoscendi,* a method of knowing *that* some statement is true. An argument from cause, *ratio essendi,* provides a reason for being, by offering to explain *why* a statement is true.


## QUESTIONS

1. What conditions set up an occasion for persuasive speaking?

2. What is a proposition?

3. What is an argument?

4. What is meant by: "a speaker's efforts in persuasion are aimed at proving that his position is probably true"?

5. What are the two points of view from which arguments are evaluated?

6. What are the steps in the process of induction?

7. Explain the categorical syllogism as a form of deductive argument.

8. What must a speaker do to establish a persuasive generalization from a limited number of examples?

9. Differentiate between analogy as argument and analogy as a language device.

10. Does the literal analogy have any advantage over the figurative analogy?

11. What is an enthymeme?

12. What is argument from sign?

13. Explain two of the tests of sign relationships.

14. Differentiate between argument from sign and argument from cause.


## EXERCISES

1. Write a short essay (no more than three double-spaced typewritten pages) in which you explain how the principle of probability is applied to some problem in your major field of study. You need not go

into extensive detail. Write the paper so that it reflects the general understanding of experts in the field. The following topics might suggest the kind of subject you should choose:

(a) Can history predict future events?
(b) What is the nature of probability theory in genetics?
(c) How much do intelligence tests and intelligence quotients tell an elementary-school teacher about her students?
(d) To what extent does chemistry provide absolute truths?
(e) What is the theory behind minority rights in a democracy?
(f) In what sense is human personality predictable?
(g) Is mathematics an absolute science?
(h) How do economists know when a country is in a depression?

2. Examine the texts of several speeches delivered in the last presidential campaign. (See the *New York Times, Vital Speeches of the Day,* or *Representative American Speeches* for texts of many of these.) Find the specific proposition the speaker is advocating and decide whether it is a proposition of fact, of value, or of policy.

3. In the editorials of such news magazines as *The Reporter* and *U.S. News & World Report* (or in newspaper editorials), find samples of arguments from example, from analogy, from sign, and from cause. For inductive arguments (example and analogy), evaluate the evidence presented; for deductive arguments (sign and cause), evaluate the generalization upon which the argument is based.

4. Collect examples of arguments you hear in conversation and evaluate them as in exercise 3. Here are some samples of what you might listen for:

"I didn't think you were at home. I didn't see your car in the driveway."

"I want to see *Psycho*. I sure liked *Vertigo* and *Rear Window*." [All three movies were directed by Alfred Hitchcock.]

"My eyes are bothering me. I must have been studying too much."

"Don't make so much noise; you'll wake your mother."

"All the best television viewing times are filled with westerns. Look at Saturday night's schedule."

Incidentally, can you tell what kind of argument is used in each of the examples given in this exercise? How would you counter these arguments if you disagreed?

# ARGUMENT: PSYCHOLOGICAL ELEMENTS

I. Motivation
   A. Motive appeals
      1. Self-preservation
      2. Happiness
      3. Ego enhancement
      4. Well-being of family and friends
      5. Financial well-being
      6. Preservation of the society
   B. Using motive appeals
      1. Make the motivation a product of the ideas of the speech and not vice versa
      2. Choose the motive which is best adapted to the audience
      3. Keep the motivation consistent throughout the speech
      4. Use multiple motivation where appropriate
      5. Let the materials of the speech develop the motivation
      6. Avoid the overuse of emotion
II. The *ethos* of the speaker
   A. Reputation as *ethos*
   B. *Ethos* in the speaking situation
      1. Integrity
      2. Intelligence
      3. Good will toward the audience
III. Summary, questions, and exercises

*Chapter* **XI**

# ARGUMENT:
# PSYCHOLOGICAL ELEMENTS

If listeners could be persuaded by logic alone, this world would probably be much better organized. It would probably also be much duller. The fact is, however, that people are *not* so persuaded, that the world *is* largely disorganized, and that it is surely *not* dull. In view of these conditions, a complete understanding of what happens in a persuasive-speaking situation will not be found in the study of logic. Speakers and audience act and react according to patterns of thought which are not always logical in any strict sense. Persuasion is to be understood psychologically. The necessary pyschological insights can be gained only if each speaking situation is viewed as a unique event in which the speaker and the audience co-operate at a particular moment in the act of persuasion.

In the preceding Chapter, we said that proofs in persuasion are only probable, and that it is the audience which determines what is probable and what is not. Even so, a listener's door to objective reality is no more open than is the speaker's. He knows the world only as he perceives it. And his perceptions of what is probable are colored by all his experiences: the set of values he gained from his parents, the impressions he received while he was growing to maturity, his reactions to contacts with other people in the streets, in schools, in the army, on athletic teams, or where have you. All these experiences influence perception and lead to conclusions about life which have not undergone the tests of rigorous logic but which, nonetheless, are fervently held convic tions.

The convictions a person has about men in general, about groups, about events, and about himself may be called assumptions. When anyone sits as a member of an audience, his own assumptions are rarely up for debate. Instead, they serve him as measures of the acceptability of a speaker's ideas and arguments. In order to persuade, therefore, a speaker must argue within the framework of the assumptions of his audience.

We are not saying that persuasion is nonlogical; it is logical, at least in part. To understand what happens in persuasion, it is necessary to know the logical structure of argument. Any audience a speaker addresses has learned, formally or informally, the accepted patterns of what is logical and what is not. The speaker must operate within these patterns in order to be persuasive. But the framework of audience assumptions within which the patterns operate differs from one speaking situation to another.

Since the early studies of public address in Greece, teachers of speech have recognized that audiences respond to three things: to logic, to emotion, and to the character of the speaker. This three-element response means that to gain approval for his proposition, a speaker supports it with arguments which are logically valid, which are consistent with the audience's assumptions, and which win a favorable reaction to himself as a person. The art of persuasion lies in a speaker's ability to select and conjoin these logical and psychological elements of proof in one persuasive effort. In this chapter, we will examine the psychological components of effective persuasion. We will look first at motivation: the process of inducing listeners to accept a proposition by using appeals which draw on the assumptions of those listeners. Then, we will examine what is called *ethos:* those aspects of the speaker's character which help to make his proposal acceptable.

## Motivation

No textbook can do more than draw an outline of the factors which influence an audience. This chapter is a start, a place from which you will be stimulated, we hope, to think seriously about how people react and for what reasons. After a speaker has made a careful analysis of his audience he must search for the motive appeals which will tap the feelings of his listeners.

## MOTIVE APPEALS

The motive appeals which become immediately identifiable are those which relate to a listener's self-preservation, his happiness, his ego, the well-being of those close to him, his own financial condition, and the well-being of the society to which he belongs.

*Self-preservation.* Perhaps the strongest motivation is that which appeals to a listener's desire for his own well-being. On this ground, he is encouraged to drive more safely, to have a cancer check-up, or to give up smoking. Self-preservation is not always the strongest possible motivation, but it is a human drive so powerful that it is a primary basis for many of the persuasive appeals we hear.

*Happiness.* When the basic drive of self-preservation has been satisfied in the individual, he will make his own happiness a basic objective. He will want to find the best place to take a vacation, the right kind of car for his enjoyment, the kind of job he will like best.

*Ego-enhancement.* Frequently, a listener will take action to enhance his ego even at the sacrifice of personal safety. Men may even give up their lives in personal sacrifice to achieve a desired goal. Others give up high-paying positions to work for the government or a charity for a dollar a year. In part, they do these things from a desire to help bring about some social good, but they also do it for ego satisfaction. Men want to see the organization to which they belong become recognized for its excellence. At least a part of their motivation is their self-satisfaction. In short, a man may feel that on a given occasion, ego-enhancement is more important than self-preservation or happiness.

***Well-being of family and friends.***        Closely related to the emotions of self-preservation and ego-expansion is the desire to provide a better life for family and friends. Even when a man knows
that what he does will not benefit him, he may do it for the good
of his family and friends. On these grounds he buys insurance
and fights a "war to end wars." A person is willing to sacrifice
now to prevent suffering among his descendants. This feeling is,
of course, closely related to self-preservation; it is often difficult
to separate the two motivations. Listeners want to preserve themselves and to preserve those whose loss would bring them pain.

***Financial well-being.***        Surely many would deny that the acquisition of physical goods is their primary motivation. To some
people, money means little but, on the other hand, many members of an audience will measure almost everything by its mone-
tary value. These two conditions are extremes but they serve to
illustrate the variety one can find in attitudes toward financial
security. It must be agreed, nonetheless, that financial well-being
is an important motivation to which substantially all Americans
react in differing degrees of intensity.

***Preservation of the society.***        Almost by nature men are conservative; they want to preserve what they know. Even the radical
has an association with other radicals so that, though he may
wish to topple the general society, he wishes to preserve and expand the society of radicals to which he adheres. Thus, when one
speaks of preserving the society, it means more than sustaining
city, ethnic group, state, or nation. The listener you are trying
to motivate may be a member of all of these but at the same
time may give active allegiance to some other group. He may be
more a Republican than a Chicagoan, more a laboring man than
an Italian. Many people give only passive allegiance to their
country. For such people, patriotism is not a great motivation.
With those who give active allegiance to a church, an appeal to
religion will probably tend to be more effective than it will be
with those whose membership in a church is passive. So, when
you make an appeal on the basis of the common good of the

group, you need to be sure to motivate in the name of the group which has the greatest allegiance of the audience.

## USING MOTIVE APPEALS

Six principles are helpful in selecting motive appeals. A speaker should:

1. Make the motivation a product of the ideas of the speech and not vice versa.
2. Choose the motive which is best adapted to the audience.
3. Keep the motivation consistent throughout the speech.
4. Use multiple motivation where it is appropriate.
5. Allow the materials of the speech to carry the emotion.
6. Avoid the overuse of emotion.

*Make the motivation a product of the ideas of the speech and not vice versa.*     Your first responsibility is to tell the truth as you see it, not merely to win a favorable audience response. In public life when a speaker bends with the wind of public passion, he is at best overambitious, at worst, a rabble rouser. He is like the man who says, "The mob is in the streets. I must follow them, for I am their leader." Such an attitude is unacceptable in a college speech class. The student who chooses one side of an issue because he knows that the class or the instructor agrees with it puts emotional reaction before truth and abandons his right to his own opinions.

*Choose the motive which is best adapted to the audience.* A representative of the police department speaking to a high-school audience on highway safety might use the motive of self-preservation. Frequently, however, adults have lectured teen-agers on such a subject only to discover that the motivation had no effect. Why? Because young people don't have the same fears of death which adults have. The solemn warnings of adults seem to teen-agers to be pretended fears intended to thwart youth's natural independence and interest in adventure. The motive of ego-enhancement might be more meaningful to an audience of young people. The speaker would better say, in essence:

No doubt about it, you are old enough to make your own decisions on what you should do. Adults have already put a lot of responsibilities on you and in return we should be willing to give you some deserved privileges. Everyone should be allowed to clown a little, but you can see that too much fooling around in cars can be dangerous. It's up to you to police yourselves. Tell the fellow who goes too far and endangers others that he is not the kind of person you want to associate with. It is the few of that kind who make it tough on the great majority of high-school drivers who are a real credit to themselves.

This argument seeks its motivation in what *will* move the audience. Too many speakers use the motivation they think *should* be effective. But if an audience is not religious or patriotic or acquisitive then it will not respond if you try to appeal to it via those motives. Build motivation on the emotions your listeners actually feel. You can do so only when you have made an accurate evaluation of what an audience thinks and feels about the subject of your speech. Here again the importance of audience analysis becomes clear.

**Keep the motivation consistent throughout the speech.**     It would be a confused use of motivation for a speaker to argue that tests of nuclear weapons must be ended because of bad genetic effects on our children, and then, in the conclusion, to omit this argument and say the tests must be ended for our own self-preservation. Such jumping from one appeal to another will destroy a speech. A program which offers self-preservation here, ego-expansion there, financial gain at another time is likely to lose the audience. It evokes no consistent response and so cannot bring to a climax the reactions of the audience. Diffusing emotional appeal builds a shotgun motivation that may wound opposition but never kill it.

A comparison with logical argument may be helpful here. Although emotion is regarded as a nonlogical appeal, it is not lacking in rationale. Just as a listener's thoughts must be led step by step through a logical process based upon a single purpose which can be recognized by the audience, so the motivation must move step by step through a consistent pattern of appeal. The necessity for consistency in motivation does not mean, however, that only one motivation may be used.

*Use multiple motivation where appropriate.* You may wish to tell a group at a service club that support for the Children's Camping Fund will benefit the community and at the same time increase the stature of the club and its members. Thus, you use both social and personal motivations to win their support.

Multiple motivation is useful in meeting the problem of the possible differences within audiences. In one audience there may be those with emotional concern for the community. Others in the audience may be impervious to such an appeal but susceptible to the motivation of ego-enhancement. One appeal reaches one listener and a second reaches another and so both are persuaded.

Remembering that motivation must be consistent throughout the speech, be sure when you use two or more motivations that they are compatible. It is compatible to support a camping fund by offering the good of the community and the listener's ego-enhancement as motivations because the listener fulfills his ego-needs by doing what is "right" for the community. But suppose a speaker were to urge the retention of capital punishment on the grounds that it protects the listeners against murderers and also saves them tax money by eliminating the cost of keeping convicted murderers in prison. These motivations are not compatible despite the fact that on the surface they might seem to be. For the second motivation runs counter to a strong societal belief that saving money is no justification for putting a man to death (if it were, who might not justifiably be executed?). Thus the speaker who uses this double motivation counters his own appeals. In essence, he expects the listener to respond to an appeal to self-preservation and also to a second appeal which, if accepted, would endanger the listener's self. Emotional responses must be motivated in the audience without establishing grounds for arousing those same emotions *against* the proposition.

When multiple motivation is used be sure that the con-

sistency among the appeals is clear. Allow them to develop together so that they become, in a sense, parts of one motivation.
Do not jump from one to another.

*Let the materials of the speech develop the motivation.*     A
speaker cannot gracefully say to an audience, "And I tell you
this for your own self-preservation." Effective emotion is developed through the concrete details of the speech. Persuasive
speaking is not made up of some magic combination of emotional words. Such misconceptions are perpetuated by those
lovers of language who ignore the fact that behind words must
lie ideas. If you wanted to appeal to a man via the emotion involved in an auto accident, which would you do:

1. Discuss the emotion of those who give speeches about auto
   accidents?
2. Discuss the emotion of those who view auto accidents?
3. Discuss the emotion of those who are in auto accidents?
4. Show a picture of an auto accident?
5. Show a picture of an auto accident in which someone dear
   to the viewer was injured?

Obviously, this list moves from the less to the more personal. At
the same time it moves from what is less concrete to what is more
concrete. The more personal and the more concrete the idea, the
more impact it will have on a listener. He has neither the duty
nor the capacity to feel emotion through the abstractions of a
speaker. You must look over your materials and select those examples, statistics, and comparisons and contrasts which will call
forth the emotional reaction desired.

*Avoid the overuse of emotion.*     Overworked emotional motivation can hurt the speaker in the long run, as many rabble
rousers have learned to their own discomfort. Excessive emphasis on emotional appeal may get temporary results with an over-
anxious audience, but in time, when the listeners have a chance
to think through the ideas, they will reject them. Listeners who
know they have been duped will not often again listen to that

speaker who duped them, and they may even turn on him in hostility. No one likes to know that he has been fooled.

Think of your own fraternity or club. It probably has at least one member who sees every minor problem as a major crisis, who is always giving explosive speeches on every subject that comes up. In time, the members let him speak but ignore what he says. They may even be quite cruel in telling him that he is a loud-mouth or a troublemaker. It doesn't really matter which they do; the person is no longer effective and, like the boy who cried "Wolf," gets no attention when he does point out a real problem. No matter how well he has mastered the techniques of speech, he has lost his persuasive ability.

The speaker should be sure his motivation is justified by his subject.

## The Ethos of the Speaker

Most of the elements of speaking that we have examined thus far—subjects, analysis, argument, supporting detail, and motiva-tion—are sharply focused in the mind of a listener by the ques-tion, "What kind of person is the speaker?" Audiences are con-tinually being asked to believe what a speaker says despite the fact that in a strictly logical sense he offers proof of only limited scope. However regrettable it may be that evidence and argument develop proof that is no more than probable, the fact cannot be avoided. It must be recognized, therefore, that much of the per-suasion which a speaker effects is the result of his own influence *as a person*. This personal influence of a speaker, insofar as it serves as an element of his proof in persuasion, is called *ethos*.

The concept of *ethos* or, as it is often called, "ethical proof," is not to be confused with *ethics*. A speaker may be quite un-ethical and still have commanding *ethos*. The most outrageous liar, for example, can deceive a listener and foist off on him thoroughly untrue ideas if the listener accepts the speaker as a person worthy of trust. The very name "confidence man" suggests the importance of winning the trust of others, even for a swin-dler. Indeed, one of the great foibles of human nature is the casualness with which people bestow their trust, the tendency for one person easily and willingly to put his faith in another. But until he wins this trust from his audience, a speaker will fail to be persuasive.

*Ethos,* then, may be defined as that part of a speaker's persuasiveness which results from the audience's favorable impression of him as a spokesman for truth. Whether he actually is speaking the truth is another matter.

## Reputation as Ethos

There are two aspects to a speaker's *ethos.* The first of these, which can be called reputation, includes all that an audience knows about the speaker apart from the speaking situation. A person who is known to be illogical, loose with facts, given to emotional outbursts and personal grudges, has an obstacle to overcome when he gives a speech. Another, whose previous actions have been pleasing to an audience, will be a more acceptable speaker. Former President Eisenhower is a good example. Despite the fact that in many ways he is not a good public speaker, what he says is often persuasive because of the favorable picture most Americans have of him as a man. Every speaker should try to gain and maintain the respect of others. But how to do so cannot be taught in a speech class.

## Ethos in the Speaking Situation

The second aspect of a speaker's *ethos* consists of traits of character which he reveals to his audience through the way he handles the actual speaking situation. It is generally agreed that if a speaker is to be persuasive he must demonstrate to his listeners by his words and by his conduct that he is a man of integrity, and intelligence, and that he bears good will toward his audience.

*Integrity.*     What a speaker is can frequently be seen through what he says. But he cannot just tell people of his honesty and moral soundness. He must show the external evidence of good character as a sign of integrity within. And the first requirement for showing integrity is that the speaker find it within himself. A speaker must know which of his actions and attitudes lend themselves to the demonstration of his own excellence and the high virtue of his purpose in speaking. True, a speaker cannot practice "techniques of integrity," but he can be aware of his own strengths of character and so organize and deliver his speech that these strengths are recognizable to his audience.

What are some of the evidences of integrity that audiences look for in a speaker? For one, they are likely to accept a person who is temperate in claiming virtue for his own position and in attacking the lack of virtue in those who oppose him. Listeners react favorably to a speaker who is sincere even to the point of admitting weaknesses in his position or in his knowledge. An audience will tend to give a favorable response to a speaker who displays tact in dealing with problems that are associated with tensions. All of these qualities—temperance, sincerity, and tact—should be demonstrated in a way that will represent the speaker to the particular audience he addresses as a person of moral character and high purpose.

*Intelligence.* The speaker must show his audience that he has intellectual tools fitted to the problem on which he speaks—both general intellectual capacity and knowledge of his subject. These constitute intelligence. In some cases, this intelligence is established before the speech. Listeners go to hear an "authority" speak or they listen because the speaker is known as an "intelligent man." When you listen to one of your professors in class his intelligence is established by his position, by what other students have said about him, and by many other factors.

But *ethos* in respect to intelligence must also be built during the speech. How does the listener recognize the character of the speaker's intelligence from signs he gives them in the speech? A speech should reveal that the speaker has knowledge and insights that listeners do not have. If the signs of the speaker's intelligence are not obvious, the listeners may sit quietly but pay little attention to what he says. Your classmates have little reason to believe that you are an authority on any subject. Consequently, you will need to indicate the background, reading, and thinking which qualify you to talk. You must cite facts. If

you just recite opinions your listeners won't pay attention to
what you say.

To enhance your *ethos,* your speech should reveal your knowledge of the subject under discussion, evidence a rigorous logical
development, and display what we frequently call "common
sense."

**Good will toward the audience.**    An effective public speaker
indicates to his audience that he advocates a proposal for their
good as well as for his own. Without overdoing direct praise,
he shows that he regards them as intelligent and good people. In
short, the speaker will show his audience that he wants them to
be there, that he regards them as worthy of what he has to say,
and that he wants the best for them.


# SUMMARY

Persuasion is a product of a combination of proofs. In addition
to logical proof (argument) there are psychological proofs which
help to persuade. These take the form of motive appeals and the
*ethos* of the speaker. Motive appeals provide a basis for the audience's emotional acceptance of a proposition. The speaker
adopts these appeals from the emotions which the listener already has. The six basic motive appeals defined in this chapter
represent the major emotional feelings which audiences have:
self-preservation, happiness, ego-enhancement, well-being of family and friends, financial well-being, and preservation of the
society.

In using these motive appeals, a speaker should follow these
principles: The motivation should be a product of the speech
and adapted to the audience. The motivation should be consistent throughout the speech, even when motivation is multiple.
The motives used should be compatible with one another to insure consistency of effect. The materials of the speech should
carry the emotion and the speaker should avoid overusing emotion.

A speaker creates a favorable *ethos* for himself by the clues he gives to his own good character. Reputation with an audience is important in persuasion but is not a problem for study in a speech class. *Ethos* is most concerned with the ways in which the speaker gives clues to his character during the speech itself. He gives these clues in order to show that he has integrity, intelligence, and good will toward his listeners.

## QUESTIONS

**1.** Which motive appeals do you suppose will most often be effective with college students? Why?

**2.** Should the speaker find a good motivation and then select a subject to fit it?

**3.** What is wrong with using a large number of different motive appeals in a speech?

**4.** How can multiple motivation be effective?

**5.** How obvious should you be in identifying for your audience the motivation you use?

**6.** Give an example of overused emotion.

**7.** What is *ethos*?

**8.** How does *ethos* differ from ethics?

**9.** How do the two aspects of *ethos* differ?

**10.** What are the three evidences which a speaker must give of good ethos?

## EXERCISES

**1.** Consider some prominent public speaker you have heard recently. What did you know about his reputation before you heard the speech which affected your reception of his ideas? What did he do in the speech to confirm or deny your opinion of him? Write a short paper explaining your reactions.

2. Which do you consider most important to a speaker's effectiveness: motivation or *ethos?* Why?

3. Examine one of the two following speeches. What motive appeals does the speaker use? How well do you think he adapted his appeals to his audience?

4. Examine one of the two following speeches. How well does the speaker use the motive appeals according to the principles discussed in the section on using motive appeals? The two speeches were made during the 1958 Congressional campaign by Vice President Richard M. Nixon and former President Harry S. Truman. Remember as you read the speeches that both were delivered to partisan audiences. Mr. Nixon spoke at a dinner in support of Governor Harold V. Handley, senatorial candidate from Indiana, on September 29, 1958. Mr. Truman spoke at a Democratic fund-raising dinner in Washington, D.C., on February 22, 1958.

### Mr. Nixon's Speech*

I am delighted that again as in 1956 I am making my first speech of this campaign in my mother's home state of Indiana. It would be natural for me to say this in view of the fact that 1956 proved to be a winning campaign. But this year in particular I am glad to be with you because if there is one thing you can be sure of it is that Indiana's Republicans are full of fight.

As a matter of fact, you like to fight so much that you have a few good fights among yourselves. But you can always be counted upon to get together against your Democratic opponents in a final campaign. And one thing is certain—you don't put your tail between your legs and run because things look bad.

This is the kind of spirit we need in this year 1958. Because we would just be kidding ourselves if we did not recognize right now that we Republicans have the fight of our lives on our hands this November. The Democrats are talking seriously of gaining as many as 60 seats in the House and as many as 12 seats in the Senate.

Some of my Republican friends have even urged me to do as little as possible in this campaign so as to avoid being associated with a losing cause. I appreciate their advice. But I want to tell

* Reprinted with the kind permission of Mr. Nixon, from the exact text as released publicly; the speech as delivered may have differed slightly. Mr. Nixon commented, in a letter that accompanied the text: ". . . I generally add or subtract as I go along, in actual delivery."

you and the whole country here and now that I don't intend to take that advice.

Why? Because I can think of nothing more contemptible than running from a fight when things are tough. Because the stakes are too high for anything less than an all-out effort this year. Because I believe there has never been a year when Republicans had less reason to lose and Democrats less reason to win than this year, 1958.

I have heard as you have the cry-baby, defeatist talk of some of our faint-hearted Republicans. "What can we talk about?" "The Democrats have all the issues." "This just isn't a Republican year."

My answer to that kind of talk is a word my Ohio father used to use—poppycock. If we Republicans lose this campaign it will be our fault and not our opponents'. We will lose if we continue to back-pedal and to allow ourselves to be a punching bag for the cheap, below-the-belt cracks of Harry Truman and his ilk. We aren't going to win by giving the voters a diet of dishwater and milk toast. But we can win if we start slugging with the truth about our own record and the truth about the frightening alternative offered by our opponents.

We've been taking it on the chin for months with the same worn-out old charges. "The Republican foreign policy is a war policy." "The Republicans are for the rich and against the poor." "The Republican Administration is corrupt and dishonest." It's time we started fighting back with one simple dramatic statement of the truth.

The six years of the Republican Administration of Dwight Eisenhower have been the best six years in the history of this country. I can hear our critics starting to bleat already—For whom? For big business? For the rich? My answer is—the best six years for the great majority of the American people.

I suggest we test the accuracy of this statement by applying the standards by which we judge any administration. What do people want and expect from the federal government? Above all, they want a government that can defend the nation and keep the peace. How does this Administration measure up on that score?

We have heard a lot of criticism of our foreign policy over the last six years. We have been too tough on the Communists and too soft. We have put too much emphasis on defense and too little. We spend too much for foreign aid and too little. We were wrong in Suez, wrong in Lebanon, wrong in the Formosa area.

But the major test of the success of a foreign policy is—does it keep peace with honor? And all the criticism in the world cannot obscure this solid fact: This Administration got the United States

out of one war, it has avoided other wars, and it has kept the peace
without surrender of principle or territory.

The Administration's policy of strength, firmness and fairness
in which we constantly wage peace is the only policy which will
work in dealing with the Communists, and I believe this policy
deserves and has the support of a great majority of Americans—
both Democrats and Republicans.

There is no doubt that next to the peace issue, the so-called
pocketbook issue is the one uppermost in the minds of the people.

At this point I want to tackle head-on the malicious and false
charges of Harry Truman and other Democratic orators that this
Administration's policies have been good for big business and the
rich, but bad for the 65 million American wage earners.

We can say without fear of contradiction that America's wage
earners have more jobs at higher wages, with better working conditions than in any year of the New Deal or the Fair Deal. And
what is most important, during the Eisenhower Administration,
America's workers have had prosperity with peace, while during
the twenty years of the New Deal and Fair Deal the only prosperous years were during wartime or as a result of war.

On the pocketbook issue, therefore, I say that the Republican
record and Republican policies deserve the support of a majority
of our people regardless of their party affiliations.

With this kind of a record, why is it then that the Republican
Party seems to be in trouble in this election. It is said that some
want to cut the budget and some add to it—some favor foreign
aid—some are against it. Some Republicans are modern and some
are old-fashioned.

Let us recognize that there are differences among Republicans
just as there should and will be in any party which is one of a
two-party system. But when you consider our differences, remember that they are small compared to the differences which divide
the Democrats. And also, and far more important, our differences
are infinitesimal when you consider the gulf between the principles in which most Republicans believe and those held by the
radical ADA wing which dominates the Democratic National
Committee today.

Here we come to the key issue of this campaign. We say elect
more Republicans and assure continuation of the policies of our
Republican President and his Administration. They say elect
more Democrats so that those policies can be changed.

What changes will they make? To answer this question we must
find the answer to another one. If more Democrats are elected,
what kind of Democrats will they be? To which Democratic Party
will they belong?

They will not come from the conservative Southern wing of the
Party. Newly elected Democrats will come from the radical ADA
wing which controls the Party in the Northern and Western states.
Because these are the states in which the key contests for control
of the House and the Senate are being fought out.

What will electing more Democrats of the ADA radical type
mean? Let me answer that question by asking what you want
from government. Do you want to cut government spending?

Here is what you would get if more Democrats are elected this
year. The budget for this year is 5 billion dollars larger than
it would have been because of bills voted by the Democratic-
controlled Congress over the amounts requested by the President.
In addition the President vetoed bills which would have added
another one and one-half billion dollars to our deficit.

And Democrats in the last Congress introduced bills which
would cost $206.5 billion over the next five years in addition to
the amounts planned by the Administration. One Senator alone,
Proxmire of Wisconsin, introduced five bills in the last Congress
which would cost by his own estimate $35 billion over a five-
year period.

You can see what you would get if more Senators of that
philosophy are elected this November. You will be in for a wild
spending binge by radical Democrats, drunk with visions of votes
and not pink but dead elephants.

What would this mean? This means that when you vote for
more Democrats in the House and Senate you are voting to raise
your taxes, cheapen your money, and to stifle the new investment
and enterprise which means more jobs and more progress for the
American people.

Do you want to control labor racketeering? You can kiss good-
bye any chance for effective labor legislation if you increase the
number of those Democratic Congressmen and Senators who will
owe their election to contributions and support of the very labor
politicians they are supposed to control. Because remember, labor
politicians don't give support unless they get 100 per cent domination of the man they help to elect.

Do you want to resist the trend to big government? By electing
more of the radical ADA-type of Democrats to the House and
Senate, you can be sure that a flood of bills will be introduced
with the object of moving toward the nationalization of health,
housing, power, farming and other American institutions. Because these radical ADA-type Democrats honestly and sincerely
believe that government enterprise is superior to private enterprise in providing for the needs of the people.

What does all this add up to? America has had its greatest

◈  progress in history in the last six years because we have had an
Administration in Washington that has recognized that there is
only one sure way to progress—one sure way to get the schools,
the highways, the hospitals, the security that we all want. That
way is through government policy which encourages and un-
leashes the creative energies of 170 million individual Americans
and which further recognizes that government action in any area
is justified only when individuals will not or cannot do what
needs to be done for themselves.

Our progress can continue if we continue that policy. But if
we go back to the bankrupt ideas of the New and Fair Deals
which failed to produce prosperity and peace in 20 years, you
will stop America's progress in its tracks.

The issue very simply stated is this—guarantee progress for
America by electing more Republicans. Stop progress by electing
more Democrats. This issue is bigger than any division in the
Republican Party. It is bigger than any differences between Republicans and Democrats. It is as big as America itself.

I have traveled to 55 countries in the last six years as a representative of the President and of the American people. I have
seen many kinds of government policies in operation in that
period. And every time I return to the United States I realize
how fortunate we are to live in this country. We can lose what
we have if we don't fight for it—work for it—and vote for it.

That is why I ask you to join me tonight and to go forth and
tell this story so that we can win a victory not just for the Republican Party, but for America.

◈              *Mr. Truman's Speech**

Thank you very, very much.

Mr. Chairman of the National Democratic Committee, Mr.
Chairman of the Dinner Committee, my able and distinguished
Governor from Missouri, who knows me better than most anybody here except my own family, I am highly appreciative of what
you had to say about me. I am overwhelmed by what the leader
of the majority in the Senate and the greatest Speaker the country
ever had in this world had to say about me.

And to you, my fellow Democrats, I am deeply grateful for the
great demonstration  and for what the Democratic party has done
for me. I've been able to fill, due to your support, the greatest
office in the history of the world. I won't say that I filled it, but
I had the office and did the best I could with it, thanks to you.
Now I'm trying to show you that I am grateful for that privilege.

* *New York Times,* February 23, 1958.

When our National Democratic Committee Chairman first told me that you intended to call this meeting the Truman Dinner, instead of the Jefferson-Jackson Dinner, I thought it probably was a great mistake. I very much feared that there wouldn't be a handful or more than a half dozen people here to listen to what I had to say, and that I'd have to spend my time talking altogether over the radio and be much more careful with my language than I have to do when I'm talking to an audience I can see.

I am overwhelmed with the turnout. It means, my friends, that we're on our way to restore the country to the people once more for their welfare and benefit, instead of turning it over to the people who don't need to have it turned over to them.

I am very happy that the committee decided on the twenty-second day of February for the purpose of holding this dinner, the birthday of the first President of the United States. Now our first President was a very able and considerate man.

He commanded the troops in the field as a citizen soldier in the Revolutionary War for independence for the British colonies; he presided at the Constitutional Convention in 1787, and he made that Constitution work after it was put into effect—the greatest, greatest document of government, in my opinion, that's ever been written.

He was roundly abused by the press of that day because he was a President of the whole country. The special privilege coteries of the modern day try to make him their patron saint, along with Alexander Hamilton. But if you read your history, there never was a man in the Presidency who was more roundly abused and he was publicly called everything under the sun. So I know he must have done a good job; whenever the press quits abusing me I know I'm in the wrong pew.

I don't mind it because when they throw bricks at me—I'm a pretty good shot myself and I usually throw 'em back at 'em.

You'll find, if you read history of the situation, that George Washington was really a Jeffersonian, no matter what they say about him in the history books. You see, the historians were the columnists of those days, and you have to read them with care.

It is now a little more than five years since the country has had a Democratic President. Five years is really a long time in these days when history moves at such a rapid pace. There have been a lot of changes in the last five years, but very few of them were of the kind promised us by the Republican ballyhoo artists in 1952.

In fact, most of the changes made were for the benefit of the people who needed no special benefits. I believe the people of the nation realize this. I think they're fed up with the Republican hucksters and their campaign oratory.

Until the Democrats have once more made the people prosperous, as we did in 1933 to 1953, I do not believe those people will be gullible enough again to fall for the Republican Administration—if they do, they'll get what they deserve, and I hope they do.

You know, people are all alike. We all have the same complex emotions because we are just humans. As we become prosperous and happy, we begin to think that—well, I did it myself, now I'll get along without any help and I'll do as I please and I'll go where I please and it doesn't make any difference who's President of the United States, or who's in control of the Congress of the United States, I can get along, 'cause I did it myself.

You have a shining example now of what happens to you when you pull things like that.

People in this country are emotional and sentimental. They like a hero and often fall for all sorts of soap and toothpaste advertising about him. I believe that the Americans are disillusioned and disturbed and that they have learned their lesson—at least I hope they have. The Democrats will win sweeping victories in 1958 and in 1960.

But I want to warn you Democrats. Profit by an example that was carried out in 1948 when there was a certain fellow from New York thought he had the thing in the bag and didn't have to work; he didn't care whether he was nice to people or not, and he got licked. And that's what'll happen to us if we don't keep working.

Now, I don't put very much confidence or reliance in public opinion polls, as you all know. Except the polls of an actual election. I usually believe that, and sometimes that has to be recounted.

I saw a poll the other day, by a pollster, that finally caught up with what the voters have been doing on Election Day. It showed that the voters are now 55 per cent for the Democrats and 45 per cent for the Republicans. If the pollsters are still making the same mistake they made in 1948 of underestimating the Democratic vote, that would give us a most handsome margin of victory.

You won't get that victory, though, if you don't work for it. Let me tell you that, and I'm speaking from experience. That's exactly what the voters gave us every time they had a chance last fall.

In the election in Wisconsin of Bill Proxmire.

On the landslide in New Jersey for Bob Meyner.

We showed them exactly how the people are feeling, and there were all sorts of apologies for why that took place—it wasn't any —the fault of the Republican Administration, it was just because people didn't understand what the issues were—but you know what the reason was? 'Cause people did understand the issues, and they voted that way.

The Democratic tide was strong enough in 1953—in 1954 to elect most of the nation's Governors. In 1954 and 1956 to bring in and keep a Democratic Congress. That Democratic tide has been rising ever since. The election of that Congress in 1956 is a historical event worthy of notice.

In 1848—a hundred years before that—there was an election of a professional military man. The 1848 election and this one in 1956 are the only ones in the history of the country that the President has failed to carry the House of Representatives with him.

Now this 1956 election means that the people are tired of being bamboozled by the Republicans. They are tired of getting liberal pep talks and reactionary policies. They are tired of getting words when they ask for deeds. They are tired of being deceived about conditions at home and abroad.

The people want the truth. They want action at the top—for the good of the nation and for the welfare and benefit of the ordinary citizen.

The present great Republican illusion is coming to an end. All Republican illusions have usually ended in disaster. I'll cite you just three—1873, after a long Republican control of the Government, one of the most tremendous panics this country ever had. 1893—After a Republican President had served four years, another great blow-up.

And most of you—I won't say all of you because there are a lot of nice-looking young people here—know all about 1929, and my good friend the Speaker has just told you what happened then. Those great panics followed Republican control of the White House.

The last five years have been a curious interlude in the history of the United States. During this period the international problems have continued to grow in danger and in difficulty. During this period the needs of the American people have been increased.

With a population growth of nearly three millions a year, with the mushrooming of the suburbs around the great cities, with the increase in the number of our older citizens, with the advance of science and the increased scope of industrial productivity and the greatest farm production in the history of the world, we have new and difficult problems and new and greater opportunities.

But the present Government of the United States is not aware of these things. And I'm talking about the Executive branch of the Government, not the Legislative branch. It has not advanced with the times. It has squandered our goodwill with our friends abroad.

It has failed to understand our problems at home and abroad.

Instead of staying ahead of the Russians as a world power, it's followed a strange policy of cutting down our scientific and military strength. Instead of making an expanding economy the goal of its domestic policy, it has concentrated on high profits for the already bloated bond-holders and higher interest rates for the money lenders, all at the expense of the home-buyers and the small business man.

Now if the Republicans don't like these statements, they can make the most of them. But there's not a single statement that I'm making or going to make to you that can't be proved by the facts as they exist.

Now this policy, or lack of policy, has helped the Soviets and has hurt the free world. The Soviets have always hoped that we would have another 1929. Unfortunately the Republicans, like the old French Bourbons, never do learn anything and they never forget anything, and they never forget to do everything they can for a special privileged class. We can see the results all around us.

There are four or five million men and women looking out for work, and millions more are only on part-time—and that number is growing, I am sorry to say. This is according to the Secretary of Commerce, who, I'd say, is not on our side, and not likely to exaggerate that condition, I'd say.

Meanwhile, the farmers are told to get off the land and join the ranks of the unemployed. That's a wonderful thing to do. Let the Government pay you for no production. Fire your farm help and add 'em to the relief rolls. That's a good way to help things. Bankruptcies have never been higher than this since the last Republican depression.

Now I met the referee in bankruptcy on the street in Kansas City one time—they got a lot of places for rent down there, little businesses that were going up the creek—and he was saying what a great Administration this was. Now, of course, he was a Republican. What a great Administration this was and how nice it was for everything to get along.

I said, "Yes, the only business I know that's on the increase is the one that you represent. Just look at those stores up the line."

He turned around and ran off. He wouldn't argue with me. He couldn't.

While men and factories are idle, school programs are neglected, colleges are short of funds, hospitals are overcrowded, while half the people of the country cannot afford to pay the doctor and hospital bills; highways need rebuilding and slum clearance is lagging.

Our great New Deal and Fair Deal programs of security—for the aged, for the unemployed, for broken families—have been al-

lowed to stagnate until the level of benefits in this rich land of
ours is a national scandal.

And in spite of the Republican recession, the Republicans
manage to keep prices going upward. You know that's really some
feat. They have price inflation and a recession at the same time.
Beat it if you can.

This Administration had a hard time getting the satellite off the
ground, but it was no trick at all to shoot the cost of living into
outer space.

It doesn't make any difference what you call it. When a condition arises which causes you to lose your job, you can call it a
recession or a deflation or a panic or whatever else you want to
name it. When you don't have anything to wear, anything to eat
in the house and you have some small mouths crying for a place
to sleep and a place to eat, it doesn't make any difference what
you call it.

I only know when the word recession has been used, usually by
a general in the field that loses a battle, he's receding to another
position so he can go ahead and do something else. But these fellows don't recede to any position. They just recede and keep receding and that's all there is to it.

I think maybe when all this thing is counted up and gone over,
the people of the United States are going to waken to the fact that
those of us who believe in the welfare of the people are the ones
that ought to be in complete control of the Government.

Now I wonder what the Republican program is today?

Have they had any new ideas regarding overcrowded schools
and underpaid teachers? Not a single idea: only the Republican
attitude of do nothing.

Aid to hospitals? Cut it back, cut it out—don't make any difference, both are good. Either is good from the Republican idea.

Slum clearance? Abandon it.

Police and public assistance, particularly public assistance?
Turn it back to the states, or repeal it, or better yet, just forget it.

Stop stream pollution? Don't do it. Let 'em drink dirty water. It
don't make any difference. The Republicans buy a bottle of water anyhow, and they don't need clean rivers.

R. E. A. co-ops? Turn 'em over to the private power companies and strangle them to death. Dig up old man Insull and put
him back to work. You know I went through all that period as a
member of an investigating committee that found out what the
utilities were doing to the country, and these birds are trying to
bring that thing back again, and almost did with Dixon-Yates.

What are we going to do with G. I. loans? Best thing they think
they can do is to jack up the interest rates.

What about the aged and the increased number of old people in the country? Oh, just forget about it. They'll find somebody to take care of 'em. We don't have to do anything about it.

And the unemployed? They have a right to suffer, so one of the great Republican spokesmen says.

If they ever overlooked anybody in dishing out punishment, I don't know who it is. In fact, if you're not on this list in any other way, you haven't been forgotten—you're going to get a 5-cent postage stamp.

You know, that 5-cent postage stamp goes on that part of the mail that pays its own way. The objective in that is because it's a very painless way to subsidize the slick magazines with their whisky ads and cigarette ads—it's carrying them through the mail at a loss. That's what that 5-cent stamp is for.

Now you know I am inclined to think that this Republican Administration hasn't even helped the big business in the manner in which they thought they ought to be helped, in spite of everything. In spite of trying so hard, big business is not satisfied. Big business has had only one tax cut in all these Republican years, and it got more than double the tax cut in high interest rates. Quite a lot of help, maybe. I don't know why.

But I was up in New York not long ago, and down in that business section called Wall Street, and you never heard as much weeping and wailing and gnashing of teeth in your life about what a terrible Administration we had. They bought it and paid for it and put it in, but they're not satisfied with it.

Republican orators, campaign orators, say that while the Democrats are betting on a depression, the Republicans are betting on prosperity.

Now I'd like to ask 'em just one question: What are the five or six million unemployed betting on? Even more important, what are they betting with?

Are they betting their meager unemployment compensation payments—which the Republicans used to condemn as socialism?

What about the unemployed who don't even have unemployment compensation? I'd like for the Republicans to tell me what they're going to bet with.

The effort to label everyone who mentions the present serious economic situation as a prophet of gloom and doom who is betting on a depression is simply another version of the old Republican cover-up everything you don't like with a smear program on the other fellow. [*sic*] Why they're even blaming me for their not being able to put sputnik in the air because I did something back twenty years ago.

Whenever they do that I just laugh and make no comment, and

then they have to go after something else because everybody ◈
knows it's not so.

One of the worst results of this period of economic misrule is its
effect on the international situation. The present Administration
has acted like an overbearing banker with a glass eye, not like a
loyal and faithful friend to the other nations, and the crisis of
confidence in our leadership has sapped the strength and determination of the great alliance.

We have friends all over the world. All the free world in Europe and in Asia and all the South American countries were our
friends. There's hardly a single one of them that doesn't do just
what Wall Street's doing to this Administration—cuss them out
every time they get a chance.

Our Democratic approach to this fundamental question is in
contrast to the Administration's narrow-minded attitude. We believe that an economy of abundance can help to solve our international as well as our domestic problems. We know that a growing and expanding economy means that all the funds necessary
can be made available for defense, for health, for education, for
economic foreign aid.

The productivity of the American economy is so immense that
the United States need not be afraid of adopting a sizable additional national security program when they are needed to support
the security and liberty of the free world.

To those who ask what will happen to the United States economy as a result of a substantial increase in our defense effort, the
answer is clear.

On Oct. 20, 1957, the Democratic Advisory Council stated in
part, and I'm going to quote it. This is a quotation from the Advisory Council's bulletin:

"The dominant feature of our economy since 1933 is that great
new resources—factories, supplies of materials and production
and distribution channels—have come into being.

"This increase in national product, brought by these new resources and a forward-looking national economic policy, put it
well within our capacity to strengthen our national security and
to meet both our international responsibilities and the needs of
our own rapidly growing population.

"To say that greater expenditures wisely made weaken our economic structure is quite untrue. To base our foreign and defense
policies on such fears and ignorance invites the fate which usually
overtakes the timid and the weak." That's the end of the quotation.

Now my friends, the Republicans have always been timid and
weak. The Republicans have but one strong President that I ever

◇ read about, and his name was Abraham Lincoln, who unfortunately was assassinated.

They had one who was great for publicity in connection with those things which afterwards were put into effect by Woodrow Wilson and Franklin Roosevelt. That man was Teddy Roosevelt, whom the Republican hierarchy threw out of the party in 1912. And I remember that campaign as well as if it were yesterday, and it's a darn good thing they threw him out because that elected Woodrow Wilson—it was a fine thing.

The most terrifying result of this five-year period of Republican complacency, however, is that the Soviet Union has been determinedly driving ahead with all the fierce energy that a dictatorship can command while we've slipped backward in relative strength.

We've been slashing our conventional armed forces year by year. We've failed to bring our weapons up to date. And we've failed to go full speed ahead in the development of new weapons and missiles.

The Democrats have been pointing out this dangerous lag ever since 1953. Up to this point, the answer to any criticism of our military policy has always been: But we have a general in the White House and when it comes to national defense a general must be right. Sputniks woke 'em up.

Now what should the Democratic party do to prevent the present state of affairs. I'm going to give you five points on which the Democratic party can save the country, and they will:

First, the Democratic party is and must remain the party of the people. Our primary concern is with the vast majority who make the backbone of this nation—the working men and women, the farmers, the people on salary, the people of moderate income.

We are also concerned with the welfare of the well-to-do. And I've noticed that in the long run they, too, seem to fare better under the Democrats than under the Republicans. You understand, when everybody's at work and got a job, everybody's prosperous. But in the sort of trickle-down theory of the Republicans, it happens just like it's happening now under this Administration.

The Democratic principle No. 2—that the Democratic party must stand firmly and forthrightly for the full enjoyment and production of the civil rights and liberties of every citizen in the land, regardless of race, creed or color. I think that firm and far-sighted leadership might accomplish this without calling out the regular army for help.

Indeed I know that patience and persistent action, coupled with firmness, can work wonders in the field of civil rights. But unless a President works at it day and night, and shows the people where he stands, you can expect demagogues to move in at every chance.

But [be] that as it may, [in] the Democratic party there can be no compromise which will deny to any of our people the enjoyment of their basic rights,

*At this point the broadcast part of Mr. Truman's speech ended. The following is the prepared text of the remainder of his address.*

Democratic principle Number Three: The Democratic party must believe in, and work for, a constant economic growth and a rising standard of living. Progress is an article of faith with us. We believe that our economy can continue to grow steadily year after year, producing more and more goods and services for more and more people—and that there is no inevitable law of nature that requires periodic downturns where everyone is "put through the wringer."

Moreover, we believe the Government has a considerable measure of responsibility for creating conditions in which steady economic growth will take place. The Democratic party must be prepared to fulfill that responsibility completely and should constantly develop plans and programs to that end.

Democratic principle Number Four: In foreign policy, the Democratic party must stand firmly for cooperation and concerted action with other free nations. The business of working with allies from many lands, allies who have varied interests and diverse points of view, is always difficult and complex—and is frequently exasperating. But in the world of today there is no acceptable alternative.

The contest between our free way of life and the totalitarian system of the Communist bloc is a grave challenge to the continued existence of the United States as a sovereign nation and to our continued existence as free men. This is a contest we cannot afford to lose. And in the long run, it is likely to be determined by the economic strength and industrial power of the contending forces arrayed on either side.

Today, the free nations together have a preponderance of economic strength, but the United States cannot go it alone. It requires the cooperation of the whole free world to maintain our economic and military superiority. Russia and her satellites are gaining rapidly in strength. The free nations have an extremely tough struggle even if we stick together. If we fall apart, we can only expect the worst.

International cooperation must be not only the watchword of our foreign policy, it must also be the central theme of our whole national life—shaping our course in everything we do, domestic as well as foreign.

Democratic principle Number Five: The Democratic party must support an adequate national defense, whatever the cost. There are some basic facts everyone ought to understand in order to see this problem in the proper perspective. For one thing, there is the fact that our struggle with communism is a life-and-death struggle. We hope and pray that this struggle can be settled by peaceful means, but we know the Russians will settle it by conquest—if they can.

We are dealing here with the question of our survival. Modern weapons are so terrible we cannot assure our survival with certainty no matter what we do. But the best chance of survival is the maintenance, with our allies, of the strongest possible defense system. This is very, very expensive in terms of money. When we come to decide whether or not we are willing to pay the price, the question is not "what is it convenient for us to pay?" Rather, the question is "what is it worth to survive?"

The answer of the Democratic party must be clear and unequivocal: We are prepared to devote to our survival all our wealth and resources that are needed and can be effectively used for that purpose.

Remember the last sentence in the Declaration of Independence:

"And for the support of this declaration, with a firm reliance on Divine Providence, we mutually pledge to each other our lives, our fortunes and our sacred honor."

Remember this too, my friends—mere survival is not our only concern. How we survive is far more important—whether we survive as free men and a nation unafraid—or as a cowering, frightened people in retreat. We must do what is necessary to survive as a free people, no matter what the cost.

Indeed, I do not see how any sane man, whatever his politics, who has the courage to face the facts, and the sense to understand them, could arrive at any other answer. But apparently some people—people in high places—have arrived at a different answer and are now basing our national policy upon it. Or perhaps it would be more accurate to say that they really have not arrived at any answer and that we have no national policy on this vital question—except to follow the line of least resistance. Again, it may be that they have not arrived at the right answer because they have not even asked themselves the right question.

I hope, my friends, that as we get on about our business of winning the elections in 1958 and then the Presidential election in 1960, we will hold fast to these fundamental principles. Some of the principles may seem popular; some may not. But because they are right, we must stick to them, remembering that, in the long run, good government is good politics, and the best government is the best politics. If we don't do what we know is right, we don't deserve to win. Let's go ahead on that basis, and we will come out all right.

These principles will dispel the fears of the American people and justify the hopes they have placed in us. With these principles, we can win resounding majorities in Congress in 1958 and the Presidency in 1960. With these principles, this great Republic will regain the confidence of the world in our ability to lead the way to peace, freedom and security.

# LANGUAGE AND ORAL STYLE

I. How language works
  A. Symbolism
  B. Meaning
    1. Denotation and connotation
    2. Emotional coloring
II. Style
  A. Written and spoken style
  B. Characteristics of a good oral style
    1. Propriety
      a. Shoptalk
      b. Slang
      c. Taboos
      d. Formal English
      e. Informal English
    2. Precision
      a. Accuracy
        (1) Avoid exaggeration
        (2) Avoid ambiguity
      b. Concreteness and specificity
        (1) Avoid meaningless qualifiers
        (2) Avoid abstract terms
        (3) Avoid general terms
    3. Simplicity
    4. Directness
    5. Originality
  C. Making style vivid
    1. Figures of speech
    2. Parallel structure
    3. Rhetorical questions
III. Improving language and style
IV. Summary, questions, and exercises

*Chapter* **XII**

# LANGUAGE AND ORAL STYLE

The outline of a speech has on occasion been likened to the skeleton of a human body. The comparison is useful insofar as it suggests the relationship of parts to whole in functional order. Moreover, if outline is to speech as skeleton is to body, it is clear that a speech is not wholly represented by its outline. In much the same sense that the human skeleton requires ligaments, muscles, and nerves to function, a speech becomes a complete and living thing only when the sinews and flesh of language are added.

At least one further comparison can be made. The muscles of the human body are either weak or strong, flabby or firm. Language, too, is either weak and flabby or firm and strong. In this chapter, we will consider how language is used to give movement and strength to a speech by adding to the skeleton of the outline the firm, strong muscles of effective oral style.

## How Language Works

When a speaker addresses an audience, the ideas he wants his listeners to understand and accept cannot be transplanted directly from his mind to theirs. Ideas are not a material currency which can be circulated from hand to hand. Instead, the speaker must use some medium of transmission.

### SYMBOLISM

Language may be defined as anything written or spoken which is used to communicate meaning. None of these visible or audible signals *is* the thought it communicates. Instead, it is used to "stand for" the thought. Hence, the use of language as a means of communication is an enormous feat of symbol-making. To cite a fairly simple instance, the word *and* is widely symbolized by the mark "&" (and has been ever since 63 B.C.). The mark itself is called an ampersand, and this is a further verbal symbolization. So you see that a man can not only devise things which stand for other things, but he can also devise words that are names for these new things.

Words may be represented by graphic signs in writing or by combinations of sounds in speaking. Whether the set of graphic signs looks like

> W. Va.     or     West Virginia,

it is represented by roughly the same combination of sounds when put into speech. We say "roughly" because the sound signs, too, may undergo some variation, depending on the accent and dialect of the speaker. But despite differences in spelling (British *kerb* vs. American *curb*) or in spoken renderings (*tomayto* vs. *tomahto*), verbal symbols are created to describe or refer to the things they name.

Not all language is verbal. Certain kinds of communication dispense with words: a skull and crossbones on the label wrapped around a bottle will tell you something important about the contents as quickly as the verbal symbol *Poison*. The cross and the Star of David are almost universally known symbols, but neither of them is verbal language. Shaking a clenched fist communicates something quite clearly to a large part of the world's population, but it is not a word. Verbal language, however, is the primary means by which human beings have recorded and transmitted the accumulated experience and wisdom of the past. And, for the most part, speakers depend on verbal symbols to communicate ideas. A speaker uses words, spoken aloud, to tell his listeners what is in his mind. Since the speaker's words are not his ideas, but only stand for them, an enormous part of the effectiveness of any speaker's communication depends upon his ability to use words well. The problem in using words is to choose the right words to give the right meaning.

## MEANING

Because word-symbols stand for things and ideas, there is a tendency to think that words are the basic units of meaning. But words in themselves have only potential meaning; that is, a particular word has specific meaning only when it is used in a context. The answer to the apparently simple question, "What does *slip* (or *hand,* or *sack,* or *pool*) mean?" cannot be given unless one also knows the sentence in which the word is being used. The dictionary, despite popular misconceptions to the contrary, does not govern the English language. It is not the function of a dictionary to *define* any given word, but merely to *record* the many known definitions or meanings that the word has acquired in various contexts at various times. Words, then, have many potential meanings and their actual meaning becomes clear only in a specific context.

Because words change meaning as the contexts in which they appear change, it is clear that no word must necessarily have any single, unalterable meaning. The meanings assigned to words, then, are quite arbitrary and in no sense inherent in the words themselves. *Katz, chat, gato* and *cat* are all different "words," and yet they have the same meaning for one who understands German, French, Spanish, and English. Other words, spelled alike and pronounced alike, have quite different meanings: *bear,* the animal; *bear,* to carry. Still others, spelled differently but frequently pronounced the same, have different meanings: *bear, bare; pear, pare, pair.* It is clear, then, that meaning is not inherent in words.

Nevertheless, words assume with usage fairly widely understood and accepted meanings. Unless they did so, they would communicate little. Consequently, a speaker should use words within the general framework of meaning they have acquired. Theoretically, one may define a word to mean anything he chooses and then use it in this sense. If this use of the word is rejected, however, his communication suffers. A clear example of this fact may be seen in the following occurrence:

In this book, the word *proposition* is used to mean a statement which expresses a judgment concerning fact, value, or policy.

This is an ordinary use of the term in rhetoric. In logic, however, the word has quite a different meaning. To avoid possible
confusion, we thought we might use the word *conclusion* instead
of *proposition*. After all, a speaker's proposition is the conclusion to his line of argument and it is the conclusion at which he
wants his listeners to arrive. The word conclusion was aban-
doned, however, after one of us tried to define it in class one
day. A student objected to the definition quite vigorously, saying,
"You can't use the word conclusion that way. It really means
something else." This student must have felt as Alice did when
Humpty Dumpty said.

> "There's glory for you!"
> "I don't know what you mean by 'glory,' " Alice said.
> Humpty Dumpty smiled contemptuously. "Of course you
> don't—till I tell you. I mean 'there's a nice knock-down argu-
> ment for you!' "
> "But 'glory' doesn't mean 'a nice knock-down argument,' "
> Alice objected.
> "When *I* use a word," Humpty Dumpty said, in rather a scorn-
> ful tone, "it means just what I choose it to mean—neither more
> nor less."
> "The question is," said Alice, "whether you *can* make words
> mean so many different things."

There is no doubt that one can make words mean different
things. Somewhere between the rigid confusion that tries to make
words always mean the same thing and the arbitrary nonsense of
Humpty Dumpty there is an extensive continuum along which
words can be used in a variety of meanings determined by their
specific context. The context in which a word appears will give
it two kinds of meaning-content—*denotation* and *connotation*.

**Denotation and connotation.**     The hard-core meaning of any
word is called its *denotation*. This meaning is ordinarily what is
given in a dictionary definition. It is the direct, explicit meaning
of the term. The word *brother,* for example, means "male sibling," a boy or man who is blood relative of another by virtue of
having the same parents. This is the denotation of the word. It is

that part of the word's meaning which makes reference to a recognizable object in the tangible world. But like almost all the words a speaker uses, it has another kind of meaning. When an only child in modern times says, "He has been a brother to me," or asks, "Am I my brother's keeper?" something far more than the idea of "male sibling" is communicated. The example makes it clear that when word-symbols are used, they not only label things and ideas *objectively* but they also convey *subjective, emotional* attitudes. These secondary, emotional overtones that make up part of the meaning of a word are its *connotations*.

Connotations are complicating factors in the relationship between words and meanings. The connotations a word acquires are in some cases far removed from its original significance. There is an almost limitless number of examples. Words like *communist* and *propaganda* show how connotative meanings can all but obliterate the original denotation. The presence of connotative meanings in words gives them emotional coloration that has important implications for a speaker.

***Emotional coloring.*** Language serves not only to transmit fact and opinion to an audience but also to communicate a speaker's attitudes as well. In some instances, it is important that facts be reported with as little emotional coloration as possible. Informative speaking, for instance, is intended to communicate an idea in such a way that it will be *understood* and *remembered*. The speaker has no concern for his audience's attitude toward what he has to say. Consequently, his language should be as objective as possible. To the extent that his language is interesting and clear, it will serve him well.

At other times, understanding and retention are only part of a speaker's goal. In persuasive speaking particularly, language has the additional function of creating attitude. On these occasions, a speaker deliberately chooses emotive or attitudinal language—language that will influence the emotional reactions of his audience regarding the ideas he discusses. But the power of language to evoke emotional response can be used for good or ill. For this reason, the conditions under which a speaker may properly use emotive language must be outlined.

The greatest sin against language is committed when words are used to lie or to deceive. And they have great power to do this, for language encapsulates a whole complex of attitudes and reactions into a single word. When that word is honorific, it is called a euphemism; when the word is pejorative, its use is said to be name-calling. Both euphemism and name-calling have bad reputations and, for the most part, rightly so. They are two widely used substitutes for adequate evidence and sound argument. And herein lies the danger of emotive language. When attitudes and feelings are severed from evidence and reasoning, language is improperly used. A speaker should not pass over a disastrous blunder as "an indiscretion" nor castigate as "a dangerous subversive" a person whose reasoned views are slightly more liberal or conservative than his own.

The names that people apply to things often tell more about the people than about the things. Professor Felix Cohen, the noted philosopher of law, once remarked that if he were to be called an unbeliever, an infidel, and a Gentile, he would know that the people using these terms would be, respectively, a Christian, a Mohammedan, and a Mormon. When a speaker argues against the extension of social security to include hospitalization and health benefits by referring to such a proposal as "socialized medicine," we know more about his attitude than about the proposal.

But there is a proper use for emotive language. Once a speaker is convinced that he has a clear and correct understanding of the subject he discusses, then his language becomes a tool for communicating that understanding to others. Since the speaker's attitudes are a part of the truth as he sees it, he cannot properly be denied the use of whatever language will accurately and efficiently communicate his attitudes, as parts of his thinking, to others. Neither moral laxity nor intellectual fuzziness is involved when a speaker takes advantage of the emotive connotations of words to supplement the logical elements of his proof.

To put the whole matter briefly, attitudinal and connotative language is frequently a necessary and desirable tool of effective public speaking. It helps to communicate ideas and attitudes clearly, vividly, and interestingly. And this is precisely what a speaker tries to do. But if the speaker employs it to create bias; or if his language gives emotional coloration to a subject requiring objective treatment; or if attitudinal language is substituted for evidence and sound argument, then language creates distortion and is improperly used.

# Style

Any number of speakers may talk on the same subject. They may use the same sources of material, indeed the same materials. Further, they may organize their materials and ideas in the same manner. Yet when these speakers deliver their talks, no two speeches will be alike in every detail. Ignoring differences in voice, in physical appearance, and in such visual aspects of delivery as posture, stance, and gesture, there will still be one noticeable and substantial difference among the several speeches. This difference will be in the use of language. No two speakers will choose the same words to express what may be essentially the same idea. That variety in language which distinguishes one expression of an idea from another may be called style.

Style is defined in a variety of ways. Put simply, it is the choice of words a person makes to communicate what is in his mind. To use language well is to clothe the speech in suitable garments. Good oral style is that use of language which meets the intellectual and emotional demands of speaker, speech, audience, and occasion. In the following portion of this chapter, it will be our purpose to identify, as clearly as we can in a brief treatment, those elements of style which make for an effective use of language in speaking. As a first step toward understanding the style of oral communication, let's see how it differs from written discourse.

## WRITTEN STYLE AND SPOKEN STYLE

In writing, the expression of ideas is directed toward the eye. Some importance is ordinarily attached to the ability of a reader to comprehend a passage of writing quickly and easily. In general, however, there is relatively little demand on him to grasp an idea instantly when it is presented in written form. Under ordinary circumstances, a reader may examine a page at leisure. Whenever he wishes, he may pause to reflect on what he has read, to think about the ideas, and to absorb them at any rate he finds comfortable. When he finds a word whose meaning is less than clear, he can take the time to look it up in a dictionary. He can reread a passage any number of times his understanding requires and his interest allows. In short, the goal of a writer is to make his ideas ultimately intelligible to a reader.

For a listening audience, on the other hand, there is no such opportunity for leisurely consideration of the ideas presented to it. A listener cannot go back to rehear. If he pauses to reflect, he breaks the tightly woven chain of the speaker's organization, loses connection with the speaker's development, and is left behind. Often, he is completely lost as a listener. Consequently, whereas a writer must be ultimately intelligible to his readers, a speaker must be instantly intelligible to his listeners.

## CHARACTERISTICS OF GOOD ORAL STYLE

In the use of language, as in all other aspects of speaking, clarity and interest are indispensable qualities. That is to say, the task of language in a speech is to make ideas instantly, clearly, and accurately intelligible, and to do so in a manner that engages the continuing attention of the audience. The language usage that best attains this end constitutes good oral style. It will display these characteristics: propriety, precision, simplicity, directness, and originality.

*Propriety.* Style is appropriate to the extent that the speaker's language is adapted to his audience and to the occasion of his speech. As a matter of fact, in daily life one constantly adjusts his speech practices to different audiences without ever thinking of the process. During the course of a day, a man will talk to his children, his wife, his colleagues, his boss, his neighbors, casual acquaintances, total strangers, old friends: no two listeners are exactly alike. In each of these situations the process of audience analysis automatically and unconsciously precedes the speaker's selection of vocabulary, sentence structure, and figure of speech. A political orator speaking to members of his own party will use one kind of language and even certain terms which he will take pains to avoid when addressing an audience which also includes people of another political persuasion. For a man to address his wife in the same way he addresses the salesman who tries to sell him an insurance policy would be clearly unthinkable. A man who is signalling an S.O.S. doesn't use scientific or technical terminology, nor does he use the language of the *Congressional Record* when making love.

The choice of language, then, is habitually determined by the audience and the occasion. One of the hallmarks of an ineffective speaker is his inability to adapt his language to these two elements of the speaking situation. Linguistically ill-equipped, he is as handicapped as an automobile that can travel in one gear only.

*Shoptalk.* The phenomenon of "shoptalk" illustrates language propriety. Many occupations and activities have what amounts to a private system of language signals, a jargon incomprehensible to all but those in the activity. To describe familiar parts of a car, for example, the automobile industry uses a strange language known as "Detroitese." Brakes are called "anchors" or "binders." When a car is said to have a "furnace" and an "organ," it has a heater and a radio. The chrome strips around the headlights and door frames are known as "bezels," and the expression "loaded with scorch" means that the car has a high performance potential. The automobile stylists have other terms in their own special areas of the industry: "googoo" (overdone), "gorky" (clumsy), "gorped-up" (excessively ornamented), and "ipsipipsi" (just right).

Shoptalk sometimes provides a speaker with useful verbal shortcuts which accomplish the end of immediately identifying him with his audience. Used thus, it may gain him a vital psychological advantage. The limitations of such language usage are apparent. The jargon of the trade is useful only for talking to the trade.

*Slang.* Other language forms have even more limited useful-

ness than shoptalk. These forms should be considered totally inappropriate. Among them is slang. There is nothing wrong with
the motive that generates slang. It grows out of the attempt
to find fresh, colorful, sharp, or humorous expression of an idea.
Usually, however, slang is shortlived. If it does last, either it becomes a part of standard speech and is no longer slang, or it becomes the hackneyed, impoverished language of the speaker who
is illiterate or too lazy to find language that says what he really
means. A speaker may justify using slang on the ground that it
adds vividness to his expression, but he runs the danger that it
will add a jarring note to what he says.

*Taboos.* Even more to be avoided than slang is language that
violates the taboos of the speaker's audience.* These are many.
Among them are profanity, vulgarity, and obscenity. Language
of this sort may communicate very effectively—profanity, for
example, is notoriously expressive!—but it is not socially acceptable.

Linguistic taboos are more often applied to what are considered improper word forms or improper occasions than they are
to subject matter. Certain tribes avoid naming their gods for fear
of offending them. But they will use circumlocution to talk about
the gods. Among American audiences, it is considered improper,
except in serious speech to use various terms of religion: God,
hell, damn, and the like. Two terms with the same denotation
will often flourish side by side because one of them has connotations that make it taboo and improper in public discourse. Examples are certain words that refer to the functions of excretion
and reproduction. Whatever the taboos of his audience are, a
speaker who violates them exposes himself to reproof and a consequent loss of effectiveness.

*Formal English.* At another extreme from shoptalk, slang, and
linguistic taboos is a language style which a subject, audience,
and occasion sometimes require a speaker to use. It is called
*formal* English. This term is used to denote the variety of language used for communicating with people who demand precise
expression either because they are exacting in their language us-

* See Leonard Bloomfield, *Language* (New York: Holt,
1948), p. 155.

age or because the matter communicated is highly important. The language used in a Supreme Court proceeding, for example, must be formal in tone and precise in meaning—informality or flippancy would be highly inappropriate, imprecision a source of confusion. The English of a United Nations debate or report needs to be formal because only formal English approaches having the same meaning to all the people who use English for communication—a few being the Australians, Canadians, Ceylonese, Ghanaians, Indians, Irish, Jamaicans, Maltese, Pakistanis, and delegates from various parts of the United States. Moreover, formal English is better suited than colloquial English for accurate translation into French, Russian, Chinese, and the other languages used at the United Nations. Although relatively few situations call for a strictly formal usage, it is to the student's advantage to know how to operate at this level, for certainly in college he will be expected to write (and even to deliver orally) academic reports, reference papers, and, at the graduate level, seminar papers and theses. All of these are customarily expressed in formal English.

*Informal English.* All the styles of language we have been examining are, then, of limited usefulness for public speaking: Shoptalk is for specialists only, slang is normally inappropriate, linguistic taboos must not be violated, and formal English is used in the kind of speaking that is rarely heard in the course of ordinary life. What style of English, then, is widely and generally appropriate?

Stephen Leacock described it in his remark about the use of "English" for literature and "American" for speaking. The distinction he expressed is a linguistic fact: Written language tends to be formal English, whereas conversation is conducted in "American" or informal English. Informal English admits many words and sentence constructions that formal English excludes, words and forms customarily found in the casual speaking of educated people. Since such people are at ease in this language, a speaker may well use it in addressing them. Compilers of dictionaries label some of its words "colloquial," as indeed they are. But "colloquial" need not suggest inferiority or incorrectness; it is merely a descriptive label. Colloquial language is not necessarily incorrect and may be highly appropriate.

Informal English includes that large body of words and expressions employed by educated people in carrying on the public and private business of the contemporary world. This language is found in communications aimed at general listeners and readers: speeches, magazine articles, newspaper columns, and the like. This is the language that will be appropriate in the majority of speeches you will be called upon to make while in college and after graduation.

**Precision.**     For all his bumbling speech, Polonius knew well the functions of language. It was clear to him that Hamlet was reading *more* than "Words, words, words." Polonius understood that words have meaning, or, as he put it, "matter." You may smile at his clumsiness, but you should admire the old man's efforts to be clear and precise in what he said.

To be precise in language is to choose the right words for expressing an idea. The right words are those that say clearly what a speaker has in mind. They put his ideas sharply into focus and minimize the chance of confusion on the part of a listener.

We have said that good oral style is designed to make a speaker's ideas instantly intelligible. But a speaker will say clearly only what he has clearly in mind. Consequently, the first requirement for clear language is a clear idea. Assuming, though, that a speaker knows what he wants to say, his problem is to say it well.

There are two major characteristics language must have to be precise (and thus clear). The first of these is accuracy; the second is concreteness.

*Accuracy.* The two most important obstacles to accuracy in speaking are exaggeration and ambiguity.

Avoid exaggeration. Hyperbole is the name given to the kind of exaggeration that is used for dramatic effect. This sort of exaggeration is an acceptable figure of speech and is not likely to cause confusion or lack of clarity. When you say, "My car is as old as the hills," no one will take the statement literally. Such deliberate and intentional inaccuracies in language add vividness to expression. But this use of hyperbole is noticeably different from what happens when a woman says, *"Everyone* just *raved* about my new dress!"* It may very well be true that one or two of her friends made some polite remark about the dress but her statement is literally meant and is expected to be literally taken. This sort of exaggeration introduces unnecessary and thoughtless imprecision into what should be an accurate statement of fact.

The advertising vocabulary contains the most obvious offenses in using the kind of exaggeration that robs a statement of accuracy. "Big" isn't *big* enough, so advertisers use, in progression, "gigantic," "colossal," and, not even ultimately, "supercolossal." This kind of thinking leads toothpaste manufacturers to identify as their "large" size the smallest tube of toothpaste available through retail channels. But when the supersuperlatives have been exhausted, what next?

To exaggerate for emphasis has been called an American trait. It is more nearly universal. But exaggeration fails in its effect when it is used unceasingly, as the habit of using too much spice makes normally seasoned food seem flat.

Avoid ambiguity. Ambiguity is found in contexts, not in words. A statement is ambiguous when either of two meanings is possible and the context does not make clear which is intended. Grammatical ambiguity (often called *amphiboly* or *amphibology*) results from an uncertain grammatical construction. Newspapers offer frequent examples of amphiboly. More amusing than confusing, it is, nonetheless, an example of inaccuracy in the use of language:

"Throw the horse over the fence some hay."
"I like teaching more than my wife."
"Her hair was pulled back in a bun while at her throat which complemented her navy-blue tailored dress was a multistrand of beads."
"The restaurant is famous for its *foie gras* made from goose livers and its fine chef."
News notes about members of a woman's club: "We are sorry to report that our Past President, Mrs. Gertrude Sturtevant, is at home recuperating from an operation."
A headline: "Drowning dampens spirits at beach party."

Story on a society page: "A few youths swam in the chill night
air."

A second kind of ambiguity grows out of the fact that a word
may have a number of potential meanings and the context fails
to make clear which of these is intended. The lawyer who phoned
his wife to say he would be late for dinner because he was delayed
by a bar meeting was guilty of (deliberate?) ambiguity.

*Concreteness and specificity.* The greatest enemy of precision
in language, other than a lack of accuracy, is vagueness. It resides
in the words, not in their contexts. Once the actual meaning of a
word is determined within a context, ambiguity is removed and
the meaning is usually precise. A vague word, on the other hand,
is one whose meaning is so broad that no matter what its context,
left unaided, it will tend to be imprecise. We will mention three
classes of words that lead to vagueness: meaningless qualifiers,
abstract terms, and general terms. The implication is, of course,
that you avoid using them whenever possible.

Avoid meaningless qualifiers. Many words give the impression
of qualifying or quantifying when really they don't. What does
it mean, for example, to say that a man is "fat," "thin," "tall,"
"short," "middle-aged," or "bald?" The terms are so relative that
they mean virtually nothing except with reference to some scale
or some exact criterion. The images listeners get from such terms
as these will vary widely and also, no doubt, differ widely from
what the speaker intends to convey. How many is "some," "few,"
"several"? How much is "lots," or "very"? Whenever you can
(and this will be nearly always), give precise information.

Avoid abstract terms. An abstract term is one that names a
quality apart from any material instance of it. By their very
nature, abstract terms must be vague because they refer to no
tangible object. Abstract terms, like other vague words, lack precision because they can mean so many things. A speaker can
hardly avoid talking about such abstractions as *justice, honesty,
democracy, virtue,* and the like, but to do so without definition
or without clear examples that convey a precise image is to be
vague.

Abstract terms are tempting for several reasons. Most obvious of these is the fact that it is easier to use an abstract term than it is to force oneself to make clear distinctions among a number of borderline cases all of which are comfortably covered by the abstract term. A speaker can condemn "gambling" but avoid mentioning or thinking about church bingo parties. He can deprecate "obscene" books and let his hearers think of *Lady Chatterley's Lover* or something else. He can denounce "undemocratic nations" and let his hearers put the government of Trancisalpuria into that category if they wish. He can deplore "corruption" in "unions"; he need not then stigmatize Local 4321 of International XYZ.

Another reason abstract terms are tempting is that they make it possible to avoid definite commitments. When governments "rattle sabers," they do not make blunt threats but rather veil the threatened consequences in vague language. No government would say, "Stop putting missile bases in the countries around our border or we'll knock your head off." Instead, the language of diplomacy leaves enough room for doubt so that maneuvering is possible and backtracking causes no loss of face. "Inconsistent with national safety," "will strongly oppose any attempt," "lead to serious consequences." Analyses of conditions and forecasts of trends made by some stock-market analysts are splendid examples of precisely this sort of vagueness.

Avoid general terms. The use of general terms is a third cause of vagueness in expression. A comedian, whose name we have forgotten, makes fun of the practice of using what he calls the "vague specific." Good examples of the "vague specific" are found in several of the phrases student speakers seem to like to use: "authorities agree . . ."; "in my research I found that . . ."; "in an article I read . . ." Other examples of general terms: "A large midwestern city," "noted chemist (physicist, theologian, or whatever)," "government sources," "statistics show . . ."

The solution to problems of vagueness in language is, of course, to make the language as precise as possible. The way to do this is to use concrete rather than abstract terms, to use specific rather than general terms, to formulate meaningful definitions, to give clear examples.

Developing a sensitivity to language will make a speaker aware of the subtle shadings in idea and emotional coloration that may be achieved in his use of words. Moreover, it will make him intensely aware of the linguistic practices that exist in his own speaking. He will begin to strive for the word or phrase that carries the exact shade of meaning that he intends, and will not be content with one that is only a near approximation.

***Simplicity.***      A naive but common assumption is that "big" words are somehow better, because more impressive, than their ordinary and familiar counterparts. Acting on this assumption, speakers often sound pompous when they mean to be dignified. There is nothing more damaging to one's purpose than feeble elegance. Henry David Thoreau, whose own style is marked by economy and simplicity, commented that long words had a paralysis in their tails. (Thoreau said that he went for walks along the river, not on riparian excursions.) Far from being an elevated variety of English, self-conscious formality is pretentious and unnatural.

Former Representative Maury Maverick coined the term "gobbledygook" as a label for writing or speaking that is pompous, wordy, involved, and full of long, Latinized terms. Gobbledygook is almost totally destructive of clarity. What did the college administrator mean who listed these aims for education?

. . . the development of intellectual consistency, the creation of aesthetic awareness, the liberation of the personality, the awakening of non-verbal and non-rational sensibilities to amplify adult experience, and the structure of an insight into the eternality of human aspiration and frustration.

Multisyllable words from Latin and Greek roots may seem impressive to the one who uses them, but for English-speaking listeners one- and two-syllable words of Anglo-Saxon origin are better. As we recall, it was Thomas Aquinas who said that simplicity is the essence of beauty. Impressiveness in style is a part of its beauty, but pomposity is too easily mistaken for impressiveness. A young woman comparing the relative merits of two spools of thread said she found it "monetarily advantageous to purchase the larger spool." Her listeners might have been less amused to hear that it was "cheaper in the long run to buy the larger spool."

Lack of simplicity often robs style of propriety and precision. First, propriety suffers when language is too technical. The doctor who warns a patient of "an incipient carcinomatous condition in the duodenum immediately inferior to the pylorus" would be much clearer (to the layman) if he spoke of "the first stages of cancer at the upper end of the small intestine." Second, an attempt to use "impressive" language can often lead to embarrassing mistakes in accuracy. In Sheridan's play, *The Rivals,* the now famous Mrs. Malaprop made this kind of mistake:

> Observe me, Sir Anthony.—I would by no means wish a daughter of mine to be a progeny of learning; I don't think so much learning becomes a young woman; for instance, I would never let her meddle with Greek, or Hebrew, or Algebra, or Simony, or Fluxions, or Paradoxes, or such inflammatory branches of learning—neither would it be necessary for her to handle any of your mathematical, astronomical, diabolical instruments:—But, Sir Anthony, I would send her, at nine years old, to a boarding-school, in order to learn a little ingenuity and artifice. Then, sir, she should have a supercilious knowledge in accounts;—and as she grew up, I would have her instructed in geometry, that she might know something of the contagious countries;—but above all, Sir Anthony, she should be a mistress of orthodoxy, that she might not mis-spell, and mis-pronounce words so shamefully as girls usually do; and likewise that she might reprehend the true meaning of what she is saying. This, Sir Anthony, is what I would have a woman know;—and I don't think there is a superstitious article in it.

To achieve simplicity, use not only short, forceful words, but also as few words as possible to accomplish your purpose. Notice we say *to accomplish your purpose,* and not just to be understood, because your purpose includes being understood in a certain way.

***Directness.*** The style of public address is much more direct and personal than written style. A speaker uses first and second person pronouns "I," "you," "we," to a much greater extent than a writer. On July 26, 1952, Adlai E. Stevenson accepted the Democratic party's nomination to run for the Presidency. In the following excerpt from his acceptance speech, observe not only the directness and personalness of his style, but the simplicity as well.

Mr. President, Ladies and Gentlemen of the Convention, my Fellow Citizens:

I accept your nomination—and your program.

I should have preferred to hear those words uttered by a stronger, a wiser, a better man than myself. But after listening to the President's speech I even feel better about myself.

None of you, my friends, can wholly appreciate what is in my heart. I can only hope that you understand my words. They will be few.

***Originality.***     Change of pace is as important in speaking as it is in pitching a ball game. Nothing destroys interest or dulls attention as effectively as monotony. You remember that in Chapter IX (Attention and Interest) we identified change as being one of the characteristics of a stimulus that make it attract attention. Originality in style is a form of skillful change, one that helps to avoid monotony in language. Instead of using trite expressions, try to bring freshness and vigor to your speaking through saying what you have to say without the use of clichés, hackneyed phrases, and figures of speech that are tired from overuse.

William H. Whyte, Jr., constructed a composite business speech built out of some sixty badly overused expressions and constructions. It is an example of what Whyte says can be called *reverse* gobbledygook which "lends a powerful straight-from-the-shoulder effect to ambiguity and equivocation." Look at the style of that speech.

### Co-operation—An Opportunity and a Challenge*

#### An Address

It is a pleasure and a privilege to be here with you today. These great annual meetings are always an inspiration to me, and doubly so today. After that glowing introduction by our

---

* William H. Whyte, Jr., "The Language of Business," *Fortune*, November 1950, p. 114. Courtesy of *Fortune* Magazine.

toastmaster, I must confess, however, that I'd like to turn the tables and tell a little story on Chuck. When I say it's about the nineteenth hole and a certain gentleman whose baritone was cracked, those of you who were at the Atlanta conference last year will know what I mean. But I won't tell it. Chuck Forbes is too good a friend of mine and, seriously, I know full well we all realize what a tower of strength his yeoman service has been to the association in these trying times.

Yes, gentlemen, trying times. So you'll pardon me if I cast aside the glib reverberation of glittering generalities and the soothing syrup of sugar-coated platitudes and put it to you the only way I can: straight English.

We're losing the battle!

From every corner the people are being weaned from the doctrines of the Founding Fathers. They are being detoured from the high-speed highways of progress by the utopian highway-men.

Now, the man in the street is a pretty savvy fellow. Don't sell him short. Joe Doakes may be fooled for a while, but in the end he wants no part of the mumbo jumbo the global saboteurs are trying to sell him. After all, he is an American.

But he has to be told.

And we're not telling him!

Now let me say that I do not wish to turn the clock back. None of us do. All forward-looking businessmen see themselves as partners in a team in which the worker is a full-fledged member. I regard our employees as our greatest business asset, and I am sure, mindful as I am of the towering potentials of purposeful energy in this group of clear-sighted leaders, that in the final analysis, it is the rock foundation of your policies, too.

But the team can't put the ball across for a first down just by wishing it. The guards and the tackles can't do their job if the quarterback doesn't let them in on the play. And we, the quarterbacks, are muffing the ball.

How are we to go over for a touchdown? My friends, this is the $64 question. I don't know the answers. I am just a plain-spoken businessman. I am not a soothsayer. I have no secret crystal ball. But I do know one thing: before we round the curve into the homestretch, we have a job to do. It will not be easy. I offer no panaceas or nostrums. Instead I would like to suggest that the real key to our problem lies in the application of the three E's.

What are the three E's?

ENTERPRISE! ENDEAVOR! EFFORT!

Each and every one of us must appoint himself a salesman—yes, a missionary, if you will—and get out and do some real grass roots selling. And when we hit the dirt, let's not forget the customers—the greatest asset any business has.

Now, much has been done already. But let's not fool ourselves: the surface, as our chairman has so wisely said, has hardly been scratched. The program is still in its infancy. So let me give it to you straight from the shoulder. The full implementation, gentlemen, depends on *us*.

So let's get on the beam! In cracker-barrel fashion, let's get down to earth. In good plain talk the man in the street can understand, let's remind Joe Doakes that the best helping hand he will ever find is the one at the end of his own shirt sleeve.

We have the know-how.

With sights set high, let's go over the top!

## MAKING STYLE VIVID

The most important function of style in language is to give vividness to the ideas the language conveys. Language brings clarity and interest to a speech only if the speaker's style makes his ideas not only instantly intelligible but also vividly perceptible. Language which has the good qualities already discussed in this chapter will do much to make a speaker's expression vivid. We now turn our attention to a number of special devices which a speaker may use to reinforce the effectiveness of the language he uses.

*Figures of speech.*    Figurative language uses words to convey meanings beyond their literal meaning. It makes some change in the meaning or use of a word and thereby adds color and vividness to expression. The language of everyday conversation is abundantly sprinkled with figures of speech.

Of the many forms that figurative language takes, the most common are *metaphor* and *simile*. Both of these figures are formed by comparing one object with another. A simile makes a comparison between two things and ordinarily indicates the comparison with such a word as *like* or *as*. When a sports broadcaster told how spectators left a stadium in a dust storm, he said the event "looked like a mob scene being sandblasted off a billboard." This kind of comparison of the two events constitutes a simile.

If the things compared are closely alike, a simile is not vivid. If the broadcaster had compared the dust-driven spectators to people running indoors from a rain, he would have had a dull simile.

Adlai E. Stevenson said, "The world at our mid-century is, as someone has said, like a drum—strike it anywhere and it resounds everywhere."* Robert G. Ingersoll said of a speech by William McKinley that "he handled his facts as skillfully as Caesar marshaled his hosts on the field of war." Senator J. W. Fulbright said America was shocked to discover that "the newly emerging nations of Asia and Africa were awake and struggling like new children to grow up."† Senator Fullbright also said on the same occasion, "We are treating our relationship to the world of the twentieth century like a quack doctor who prescribes aspirin for tuberculosis."‡

A metaphor, like a simile, is based on comparison. But whereas in a simile the comparison is explicit, a metaphor is an implied comparison. The difference between the two figures is that while simile says one thing is *like* another, the metaphor says one thing *is* another. In October, 1896, Robert G. Ingersoll used this metaphor in a speech: "I know that labor is the Atlas on whose shoulders rests the great superstructure of civilization and the great dome of science adorned with all there is of art." Henry Clay said that the Union formed by the Constitution was "a marriage that no human authority can dissolve or divorce the parties from."

Similes and metaphors, used intelligently, can add greatly to

---

* Adlai E. Stevenson, *Call to Greatness* (New York: Harper and Brothers Publishers, 1954), p. 4.
† *Vital Speeches of the Day*, 26:24 (October 1, 1960), p. 74.
‡ *Ibid.*

the vividness of a speech. They will detract from it, however, when they are abused. Trite similes and far-fetched metaphors are fatal to effective expression.

Trite expressions in the speech of others are much more noticeable than are those one uses himself. Examples of tired speech abound. Here are a few instances of the sort of similes and metaphors that fail to interest because they have been used too much.

> Mad as a wet hen
> Nervous as a cat
> Slow as molasses in January
> White as a sheet
> To stick like a leech
> To be a bookworm
> Good as gold
> Fat as a pig

Avoid these and any other comparisons that have become hackneyed. Language is like a flashlight battery. It illuminates better when it is fresh.

*Overstatement, understatement,* and *irony* (identified as forms of humor in Chapter XVI) are used also as figures of speech to heighten the vividness of an idea without seeking to arouse laughter. Overstatement has already been referred to in this chapter under the name of hyperbole.* It consists in using a stronger word than is necessary to convey an idea. The result of this usage is to exaggerate, but for vividness, not deception. Observe the several examples of overstatement in the following excerpts from a single paragraph in a lecture by Adlai Stevenson.†

I am not a historian, but I doubt if anyone will dispute the *incomparably* dramatic qualities of the twentieth century. . . . In fifty years, distance has been *obliterated* by a technological revolution that has brought *all mankind* cheek to jowl, and that has released the creative and obliterative power of the atom. . . . National independence and democracy have scored *spectacular* victories and suffered *shocking* defeats. . . . Two new *colossi,* the

---

\* See also page 232.
† *Op. cit.,* p. 6. Our italics.

United States and the Soviet Union, have *suddenly* emerged. Ideas, on which the West has had an export *monopoly* for centuries, are now also flowing out of the East and colliding *everywhere* with our Western ideas.

Understatement* is the opposite of exaggeration. It deliberately says less than what might be said and thus calls attention to an idea. To say of a man one considers thoroughly dishonest "He is not the most scrupulous person I know," is to understate the case.

Irony† uses language to say one thing but to imply quite another. It is often found in the same context with either exaggeration or understatement. Note the combination of irony, understatement, and overstatement in the following passage. The speaker, Robert G. Ingersoll, is arguing *in favor of* the demonetization of silver.

In 1816 Great Britain demonetized silver, and that wretched old government has had nothing but gold from that day to this as a standard. And to show you the frightful results of that demonetization, that government does not now own above one-third of the globe, and all the winds are busy floating her flags.

There is no question that figures of speech add vividness to the expression of a speaker's ideas. But a word of caution. Figures can be used to excess. When they are, style becomes not vivid, but "purple." It becomes flamboyant, flowery, and weak. Here is an example of what can happen in a press release from the office of a Congressman:

If we throw stones of criticism we will break the glass houses and the idols with feet of clay will be toppled from their pedestals of self-exaltation by the angry winds created by the righteous indignation of Americans sacrificed on the cross of gold by selfish, greedy men and their stooges in high places.

***Parallel structure.*** Another method of making ideas vivid is to repeat phrases of identical or similar construction. The effect

* See Chapter XVI, p. 315.
† See Chapter XVI, p. 316.

of the repetition is to draw the attention of the audience to the speaker's ideas. A well-known example appears in Lincoln's Gettysburg Address. "Government of the people, by the people, for the people." In his first inaugural address, President Franklin Delano Roosevelt used this parallel structure.

> Our greatest primary task is to put people to work. . . .
> The task can be helped by definite efforts to raise the values of agricultural products and with this the power to purchase the output of our cities.
> It can be helped by preventing realistically the tragedy of the growing loss, through foreclosure, of our small homes and our farms.
> It can be helped by insistence that the Federal, State and local governments act forthwith on the demand that their cost be drastically reduced.
> It can be helped by the unifying of relief activities which today are often scattered, uneconomical and unequal. It can be helped by national planning for a supervision of all forms of transportation and of communications and other utilities which have a definite public character.

And in his second inaugural address, President Roosevelt said:

> I see millions of families trying to live on incomes so meager that the pall of family disaster hangs over them day by day.
> I see millions whose daily lives in city and on farm continue under conditions labeled indecent by a so-called polite society half a century ago.
> I see millions denied education, recreation and the opportunity to better their lot and the lot of their children.
> I see millions lacking the means to buy the products of farm and factory and by their poverty denying work and productiveness to many other millions.
> I see one-third of a nation ill-housed, ill-clad, ill-nourished.

*Rhetorical questions.*    A question is "rhetorical" when a speaker expects no direct answer to it from his audience. He knows the answer; he uses the question not to elicit an overt response but to add vividness to the expression of his ideas. A direct question, even one that requires no answer from a listener, engages his immediate, personal attention to a degree that statement often will not.

Rhetorical questions may be the speaker's method of forcing his listeners to formulate explicit (but silent) answers to his questions. In his famous "Compromise Speech," delivered to the Senate in February, 1850, Henry Clay used rhetorical questions in this fashion. In the paragraph quoted below, Clay refers to the first of eight resolutions he had proposed as a compromise between North and South over the question of slavery.

The first resolution, Mr. President, as you are aware, relates to California, and it declares that California, with suitable limits, ought to be admitted as a member of this Union, without the imposition of any restriction either to interdict or introduce slavery within her limits. Well now, is there any concession in this resolution by either party to the other? I know that gentlemen who come from slaveholding States say the North gets all that it desires; but by whom does it get it? Does it get it by any action of Congress? If slavery be interdicted within the limits of California, has it been done by Congress—by this government? No, sir. That interdiction is imposed by California herself. And has it not been the doctrine of all parties that when a State is about to be admitted into the Union, the State has a right to decide for itself whether it will or will not have slavery within its limits?

A rhetorical question may be used to summarize a point developed by a line of argument: "What better way, then, is there to destroy peace than by preparing for war?" The answers a speaker wants to these kinds of questions are obvious. They do not have to be put into words, though they may be answered by the speaker himself.

President Franklin Delano Roosevelt used rhetorical questions very effectively. In a campaign speech, delivered in Chicago, October 14, 1936, the President said,

To [the business men of America] I say:
Do you have a deposit in the bank? It is safer today than it has ever been in our history. It is guaranteed. Last October first marked the end of the first full year in 55 years without a single

failure of a national bank in the United States. Isn't that on the credit side of the government's account with you?

Are you an investor? Your stocks and bonds are up to a five and six year high level.

Are you a merchant? Your markets have the precious life-blood of purchasing power. Your customers on the farms have better incomes and smaller debts. Your customers in the cities have more jobs, surer jobs, better jobs. Didn't your government have something to do with this?

Are you in industry? Industrial earnings, industrial profits are the highest in four, six, or even seven years! Bankruptcies are at a new low. Your government takes some credit for that.

Are you in railroads? Freight loadings are steadily going up and so are passenger receipts because, for one reason, your government made the railroads cut rates and make money.

Are you a middleman in the great stream of farm products? The meat and grain that move through your yards and elevators have a steadier supply, a steadier demand and steadier prices than you have known for years.

In his annual Message to Congress, January 3, 1936, this same master of style put rhetorical questions into combination with the device of parallel structure to achieve a striking effect:

Shall we say that values are restored and that the Congress will, therefore, repeal the laws under which we have been bringing them back? Shall we say that because national income has grown with rising prosperity, we shall repeal existing taxes and thereby put off the day of approaching a balanced budget and of starting to reduce the national debt?

Shall we abandon the reasonable support and regulation of banking? Shall we restore the dollar to its former gold content?

Shall we say to the farmer—"The prices for your product are in part restored, now go and hoe your own row"? Shall we say to the home owners—"We have reduced your rates of interest—we have no further concern with how you keep your home or what you pay for your money, that is your affair"?

Shall we say to the several millions of unemployed citizens who face the very problem of existence—yes, of getting enough to eat—"We will withdraw from giving you work, we will turn you back to the charity of your communities and to those men of selfish power who tell you that perhaps they will employ you if the government leaves them strictly alone"?

Shall we say to the needy unemployed—"Your problem is a local one, except that perhaps the Federal Government, as an act of mere generosity, will be willing to pay to your city or to your county a few grudging dollars to help maintain your soup kitchens"?

Shall we say to the children who have worked all day—"Child labor is a local issue and so are your starvation wages; something to be solved or left unsolved by the jurisdictions of forty-eight states"?

Shall we say to the laborer—"Your right to organize, your relations with your employer have nothing to do with the public interest; if your employer will not meet with you to discuss your problems and his, that is none of our affair"?

Shall we say to the unemployed and the aged—"Social security lies not within the province of the Federal Government, you must seek relief elsewhere"? Shall we say to the men and women who live in conditions of squalor in country and in city—"The health and the happiness of you and your children are no concern of ours"?

Shall we expose our population once more by the repeal of laws to protect them against the loss of their honest investments and against the manipulations of dishonest speculators?

Shall we abandon the splendid efforts of the Federal Government to raise the health standards of the nation and to give youth a decent opportunity through such means as the Civilian Conservation Corps?

## Improving Language and Style

Facility in language and felicity in style are the goals a speaker seeks in his use of words. Neither of these is innate, and neither of them is easy to achieve. Your style will be what it becomes over the years, and it will be what you make it. We offer here a few suggestions to guide you in doing what every speaker must do—

build his own style through the experience of years. But start now!

*Become aware of your own use of language.* Listen to yourself. Record your speeches whenever you can. Instead of forgetting about a speech once you have delivered it, use it for practice material. Your primary concern in preparing a speech is with the ideas it conveys, and with the organization and materials that will make the ideas interesting and clear. In delivering the speech, with the ideas firmly at hand, and with notes to refresh your memory, you are free to give consideration to the language you use. This is the essence of extemporaneous speaking.

*Be curious about words.* As you read and listen, never let an unknown word pass you by. Make it identify itself. Examine its etymology and its usage. Find out what it means and then add it to your vocabulary. A good dictionary is one of the most valuable reference books you can own. But to keep a word in your vocabulary, you have to use it. If you do not, you will soon lose the word.

*Study the language of others.* Listening carefully to the speeches you hear in class is one good way of making a start toward being habitually aware of the language others use. An even better procedure is to read printed texts of speeches, to study them thoughtfully, to examine their structure and their materials and to analyze the speaker's use of language.

*Practice writing and speaking.* No matter how much you may learn about language or about style, your own use of words will improve little without practice. The speaking you do in class is, of course, only a beginning. The most significant progress comes through experience. Through practice in both writing and speaking you can work toward developing an artistic use of language that functions with the ease of habit.

## SUMMARY

The ideas a speaker communicates are not a material substance that can be passed from hand to hand like money; nor can they be poured into a listener's head like water from a cup. Instead, ideas are "stirred up" in an audience by the symbols the speaker uses to *stand for* the ideas. Almost all the word-symbols a speaker uses can convey many different ideas; that is, each one has many potential meanings. A word has actual meaning only when it appears in a context.

In a given context, a word has both denotative and connotative meaning: it has not only a literal significance but it carries emotional overtones as well.

Style in language is the way words are put together to express thought. Oral style differs from that of written discourse mainly in that the language of a speaker must make his ideas instantly, clearly, and accurately intelligible to his listeners.

Good oral style has these distinguishable characteristics: propriety, precision, simplicity, directness, originality. Language is appropriate when it is properly suited to the audience and the occasion of a speech. Informal English, as it is normally used by educated people in the majority of their writing and speaking, is the most widely appropriate. To be precise, language should be both accurate and concrete. Exaggeration, ambiguity and vagueness are the natural enemies of precision in language.

Simplicity in style is best achieved by avoiding flowery, impressive-sounding language in favor of short, forceful words of Anglo-Saxon origin. Simplicity also demands brevity, using as few words as possible to say accurately what is meant.

In their everyday communication, audiences use a liberal sprinkling of personal pronouns, contractions, and direct quotations. Their ears are attuned, therefore, to the relaxed idiom of informal conversation. A speaker lends directness to his style by using this same kind of informality and personalness in his language.

Clichés, trite expressions, and hackneyed, overused phrases rob a speaker's style of originality. Originality in style is best achieved by avoiding tired words and phrases in favor of language with freshness and variety.

The most successful style is that which makes a speaker's ideas come alive for his audience. We have mentioned only three of the several devices a speaker may use to give his style the vividness effective speaking requires: figurative language, parallel structure, and rhetorical questions. There are many others you should know and use.

To improve the style of your speeches, do these four things:

> Become aware of your own use of words.
> Be curious about words.
> Study the language of others.
> Practice writing and speaking.

A critical and responsible speaker understands that words may be weapons, not to be used without full knowledge of the consequences of their being uttered. He understands clearly the linguistic implements at his disposal. He neither uses them unscrupulously to make his points easily nor is he himself mastered by them. He is always in full and firm control.

## QUESTIONS

1. Define language.

2. What kind of language is the primary means of human communication?

3. What must you know to know the meaning of a word?

4. What is denotation? Connotation?

5. Under what conditions can a speaker be criticized for improper use of attitudinal and connotative language?

6. What is style?

7. What are some of the differences between written and oral style?

8. What usefulness is there in shoptalk?

9. When is exaggeration used improperly?

10. What three classes of words lead to vagueness? Give examples.

11. What is a malapropism? Give examples.

12. What is parallel structure? Give examples.

13. What is a rhetorical question? How is it used?

14. What should the speaker do to improve his style?

## EXERCISES

1. Construct a sample vocabulary of the jargon used in at least one occupation. Translate each word or phrase into language appropriate
   for a general audience.

2. Select an essay written in "formal" English style and convert one or
   more paragraphs into acceptable, colloquial, oral style.

3. Find the mistakes in Mrs. Malaprop's comment (p. 237) and suggest
   a more accurate word for each.

4. Note examples of vague terms used in classroom speeches (meaningless modifiers, abstract words, general words) and show how they may
   be made more precise through illustration and definition.

5. Write down trite expressions in one round of classroom speeches and
   suggest a phrase that expresses each idea more vividly.

6. This chapter considers only a few of the many widely used figures of
   speech. Make a list of several figures not mentioned and find examples of each in printed texts of speeches. For example: metonymy,
   synecdoche, personification, apostrophe.

7. Record a brief extemporaneous speech. Transcribe it and then polish
   the style.

# DELIVERY: PSYCHOLOGICAL ELEMENTS

I. Communication and expression
  A. Expressive elements of speech
  B. Communicative elements of speech
II. Factors affecting adjustment to a speaking situation
  A. Culture
  B. Past experience
  C. Conditioning
  D. The person spoken to
III. The conflict of expressive and communicative elements
IV. Some practical suggestions
  A. Don't blame yourself
  B. Adopt a conversational attitude
  C. Realize the importance of experience
  D. Prepare thoroughly
  E. Practice consciously the positive aspects of the speech role
V. Summary and questions

*Chapter* **XIII**

# DELIVERY: PSYCHOLOGICAL ELEMENTS

Speaking demands the immediate physical presence of the person communicating in a way that writing, painting, sculpture, and other forms of communication do not. His presence affects the audience. The importance of solid content in a speech is not diminished, therefore, by saying that good communication demands good delivery. For a listener, delivery is not only the vehicle for communication but also an important measure of the sincerity of a speaker and the significance of his ideas. Recall some of the times you have given your attention to a poised, self-confident speaker and withheld it from a halting and unsure one.

Such experiences are unfortunately frequent. Many worthwhile ideas are lost because of the inability of a speaker to give them the vitality they need. And many worthless trinkets have been accepted as sound ideas because they were delivered with enthusiasm and directness. Because delivery is so important to effective speaking, every student of speech needs to examine its principles. Competence in delivery will not by itself bring success, but success will be elusive if this competence is lacking.

Skillful delivery implies an understanding of some of its psychological, vocal, and visual elements. The next three chapters will examine these in that order. The present chapter will consider the relationship between a speaker's attitudes toward the total speaking situation and his effectiveness. Chapter XIV will discuss the vocal elements of delivery: how the voice is produced and how it can be used to make ideas forceful and clear. Chapter

XV will consider the visual elements in delivery: how the posture and movement of the body can help communication and how visual aids can be used for greater clarity.

## Communication and Expression

Speech is a human behavior, one of the behaviors by which people attempt to satisfy needs, to bring their environments and themselves into equilibrium. The environment of the speaker includes his audience, and his social needs include the need to minimize an entirely natural anxiety which speakers feel about the reactions of their listeners. We will try to examine the personal needs of speakers with this social need in mind. In this respect we can note that in the act of speaking the speaker is engaged in satisfying two different needs: his expressive needs and his communicative needs.

### EXPRESSIVE ELEMENTS OF SPEECH

Some speaking serves to meet the needs of the speaker's expression alone. That is, in such speaking the speaker is not concerned about what kind of a reaction he will get from others: he wants to get something out, to fulfill his need for expression. Everyone has had the experience of talking to himself, has had thoughts which he must get out if he is to maintain satisfying emotional equilibrium. He makes sure he is alone and then "tells off" the wise guy in the political-science class, saying the things that social training would not allow anyone to say to the wise guy's face: how obnoxious he is, how he disrupts the class with useless questions, how he insults people with whom he disagrees. The speaker, having vented his spleen through expressive speech, achieves a personal satisfaction. The next time he meets his obnoxious acquaintance face to face, he can smile and say, "Good morning."

Although such speech is used only to express feelings without trying to influence the attitudes and conduct of others, it is not always addressed to oneself. The principle of catharsis has long been recognized as a valuable psychological experience both by religious leaders and by psychotherapists. It is an essential part of everyone's life. A person often tells his feelings to a friend not because he feels that the friend can do something about them but because he has the need to express his feelings to someone— to get them out.

Feelings that invite catharsis evidently arise from problems that reside in the speaker rather than in his listener—audience, psychologist, confessor, or friend. Other feelings that reside in the speaker are his anxiety over being ridiculous, his embarrassment, his worries about his clothes or his haircut or his facial contours. To get this kind of expressive feeling out of himself is an imperative need for any speaker, for all speakers—because all speakers have these feelings in some measure.

## COMMUNICATIVE ELEMENTS OF SPEECH

In this book we are less interested in expressive elements of speech than in the kind of speaking which communicates to someone else. This sort of speaking is a means of gaining a response from a listener. It is a social act; both speaker and listeners are involved in the act because the speaker desires a response and looks for it in the listener. Expressive speech, in contrast, is not social: at the moment of expressive speech, if he lets himself utter it, a response is of no concern to the speaker.

## Factors Affecting Adjustment to a Speaking Situation

When a man goes into a service station to buy an automobile tire, what happens between him and the proprietor is called a transaction. The act that brings them together bears upon a variety of attitudes and needs on the part of each of them and each is changed by the experience. So it is with speaking. The total speaking situation—an interaction of speaker, speech, audience, and occasion—is a transaction in much the same sense that what happens between a merchant and a customer is a transaction. Speakers not only change the audience but it also changes them. The relationship between speaker and audience is more than one in which the speaker initiates a stimulus and the listener gives a response. As soon as a speaker begins to initiate stimuli, the listener begins to respond; this response in turn stimulates the speaker, frequently before he has finished speaking. A dynamic circular relationship of stimulus-response is set up. There are so many factors in the total speech situation that any attempt to decipher individual patterns of stimulus and response would be quite useless. There are, however, several general social factors which affect the speaker's attitude toward the act of speech and his perceptions of audience reactions.

## CULTURE

A speaker's ability to cope with a listener's reactions are determined in part by the culture from which he comes. Some cultural and subcultural groups put great stress on the ability to communicate and thus make success or failure in speaking a great source of reward or punishment. This condition automatically increases the emotional pressure on speakers. Some will respond favorably to the influence while others will want to escape from the threat of punishment for failure. They will seek to avoid the speaking situation or search for easy ways to satisfy its requirements.

## PAST EXPERIENCE

Past experience has an extremely important influence on a speaker's attitudes. It is for this reason that satisfactory experiences in communication should be provided for students in the elementary schools. The importance of success is a good reason for eliminating school exercises in speech which involve memorization and elaborate vocal and physical ritual through which a speaker must pass in order to win the approval of his teacher. Much of the nervousness of adult speakers today may well have been caused by the socially unsuccessful experiences they had as children when they were asked to "recite." The adult who is nervous today recalls only that the earlier situation was painful and that it involved speech. He forgets that it was completely different from the kind of adult experience in which he is now asked to participate.

## CONDITIONING

If past experience were merely a matter of recalling specific bad experiences and hoping to avoid them, the problem of anxiety would not be so great, for anxiety is oriented to the future. Conditioning extends the anxiety, for people have a tendency to repeat their first response to a given stimulus whenever that same stimulus is repeated. Furthermore, if the stimulus is repeated frequently enough the response becomes the automatic consequent of the stimulation. Thus if a speaker has had anxiety feelings about one speaking situation, apprehension will tend to be aroused by the situation each time he faces it. Unless some favorable experience takes place he will become more and more conditioned to have unfavorable feelings. As a result, the prospect of speaking in public will become a signal for anxiety to appear. One important contribution of your speech course is to teach you how to make speaking situations favorable experiences and become conditioned to meet speaking situations without the strong negative feelings that beset many speakers.

## THE PERSON SPOKEN TO

A further social influence which affects adjustment to the speaking situation is the amount of anxiety aroused in the speaker by the person spoken to. Many teachers who are very nervous before an audience of adults have no difficulty whatsoever when speaking before their classes. They have learned to expect favorable responses from children but not from adults. Sometimes being in a class poses a problem because the student speaker knows he will be graded by his instructor. The classmates, when the instructor is absent, do not constitute a threat and, therefore, are not the source of concern that they are when they are in the classroom situation.

Culture, past experience, conditioning, and the person being spoken to are by no means the only elements which affect the attitude a speaker will have toward a speaking situation. Many other social influences affect him. We have discussed these four to point up the fact that although each experience is different the social elements in a situation cause a person to generalize about his experiences, frequently to his own disadvantage. They teach him to expect success or failure and thus establish attitudes toward the speaking situation before it is ever confronted.

## The Conflict of Expressive and Communicative Elements

For a speaker, one of the most annoying reactions to a speaking situation is fear. The outward signs of a speaker's fear and anxiety are called "stage fright." In its milder form it is known as "nervousness." It may involve stumbling over words, vocalizing pauses (the injection of "uh" and "er" without regard to meaning), trembling hands and knees, or the inability to look directly at members of the audience. The type and extent of the symptoms differ from person to person. Regardless of the form the symptoms take, the fear reaction can be said to result from the fact that expressive elements in the speaking situation are interfering with the communicative purpose of the speech.

Speech may be thought of as a continuum with totally expressive verbalization at one end and totally communicative elements at the other. Speech can range, then, from the pathological condition of complete expressiveness to the machinelike exclusion of all but the communicative elements. But virtually all speeches will fall into the great middle group in which expressive and communicative elements mix and influence the speaking situation.

Obviously, a person who cares only about fulfilling his expressive (noncommunicative) needs in public speaking has a problem which a speech class cannot hope to cure. It is highly doubtful that such a person would remain long in a speech class. The notion that such a person might exist, however, helps to show what is behind fear reactions. Each fear reaction indicates a tendency for a speaker to concern himself with his personal ego needs rather than with the effectiveness of his talk. He worries not about how well his listeners understand his ideas, nor how persuasive his arguments are, nor how much the audience enjoys his humor. Instead, he frets about how they evaluate him, how he looks, and whether they are laughing at him rather than with him. A speaker should not come before an audience feeling he is to be judged on such personal grounds. He comes to share an idea with them. We might say that a speaker's anxiety and fear are proportional to the extent to which he questions his personal acceptability rather than the acceptability of the idea he espouses.

Needless, to say, no speaker can entirely divorce his person from his attempt to persuade. Nor should he try. No one has ever been a speaking machine. A speaker's personal involvement with his ideas is essential to the kind of enthusiasm which helps build satisfactory audience response. For this reason, even the most experienced speakers are anxious about the speaking situation. A competent speaker expects such anxiety, uses it by designing his speech so as to clear away as much anxiety as he can, and lives with the remnant of anxiety that no speaker can eliminate.

## Some Practical Suggestions

Understanding why fear and anxiety are present in a speaking situation will help you to develop proper attitudes toward speaking in public. Here are some practical suggestions to help you put this knowledge to work.

### DON'T BLAME YOURSELF

Speakers who find themselves subject to some of the physical reactions of fear and anxiety will frequently enlarge the problem by becoming angry with themselves. But stage-fright reactions cannot really be voluntarily controlled. If the speaker understands how powerless he is, he may be able to cease blaming himself and thus reduce the psychic feedback. He cannot will away the anxiety, no matter how much pressure he puts on himself. A speaker who learns to live with his anxiety has gone a long way toward relieving himself of fear.

## ADOPT A CONVERSATIONAL ATTITUDE

One of the most helpful attitudes to develop is the idea that public speaking is an expanded and formalized version of conversation. People speaking to a group of friends in informal surroundings have little difficulty in saying what they want to say. The person who thinks of public speaking as something enormously greater and more formal than private conversation burdens himself with pressures which are not a part of the informal situation. The more one can think of public speaking as conversation, the easier public speaking will be. The same direct, friendly, enthusiastic kind of communication which is so enjoyable in a friendly get-together is what makes public speaking effective.

## REALIZE THE IMPORTANCE OF EXPERIENCE

Just as unhappy experiences can condition a person to fear public speaking, so also can favorable experiences condition him to enjoy it. To attain this goal, a speaker must banish from his ideas about speaking as much of the mystery as possible: He must know what good speech is and he must study the methods of organizing speeches, supporting them, and delivering them. When he sees that making a good speech has no requirements which he cannot master, and that an effective speaker is an intelligent craftsman rather than a miracle worker, he can begin to have the kind of experiences which build confidence. Each favorable experience will reinforce the others.

## PREPARE THOROUGHLY

It seems obvious that anxiety will attack the speaker who isn't sure of what he wants his speech to do or whether his speech will do it. In the presence of these uncertainties, he is insecure about how his audience will react. Careful preparation is the only realistic solution to this problem. A speaker must study his subject well. He must be sure to understand the limited topic on which he will speak and he should also build a broad circle of information around it.

There are certain laxities that effective speaking does not allow: "I'm not too sure about this but I think you understand what I mean." "I think it is pronounced . . . " "I understand that Professor Kernaghan has a different view on this but I couldn't find his book in our library." "I had to work late last night so I didn't have a chance to check all the facts." These and similar statements merely say that the speaker is not expert on the subject. Listeners ask, "Why should I listen to him?" A speaker's confidence grows out of knowing that he is well prepared and out of seeing that his audience realizes he is qualified to speak on his subject.

## PRACTICE CONSCIOUSLY THE POSITIVE ASPECTS OF THE SPEECH ROLE

There is much value in deliberately adopting the pose of good adjustment to the speaking situation. Psychologists tolerate the view that the acceptance of a role makes a person do things which are compatible with it. A speaker may feel more composure because he adopts the body set and delivery of one who is composed. Actors have long recognized that audiences tend to do and feel what they see being done and felt. When they see someone in pain on the stage they "feel" pain. When the actor is happy they "feel" happy. This reaction is called *empathy*. Empathy is useful to a public speaker. If listeners perceive an alert speaker, they will tend to be alert. The speaker, seeing a favorable audience response, tends to become more confident.

Here are a few specific actions you can practice to help give you the appearance of emotional control.

*Walk briskly to the platform.* Walk directly and resolutely to the rostrum and put down your notes. Don't slouch or shuffle along the way. Don't glance nervously at the audience or fumble with your papers or clothing.

*Look directly at the audience.* When you reach the rostrum and have assembled your notes before you, look directly at the audience for a brief time before beginning your speech. Think of this as a moment when you "meet" the audience and make your first friendly contact with them. During the speech, concentrate on looking directly at the members of the audience. The speaker who seems unable to look directly at his listeners gives a sure sign of anxiety. Eye contact is perhaps the most important factor in good delivery. It will be discussed in more detail among the visual elements of delivery in Chapter XV.

*Use a good attention factor in your introduction.* Your introduction may set the tone for the reactions you will get to the rest of the speech. For this reason, you will want to get off to a good start. Make sure to plan an opening which will arouse the interest of the audience; then deliver it as you planned it. Don't let any anxiety you feel make you rush into the main body of the speech and so slide over the interest-gaining use of the attention factor. Attention factors have been discussed in Chapter IX, and further discussion appears in Chapter XVII under the heading "Gaining Attention."

*Control the rate of delivery.* When nervous fear strikes a speaker, his first reaction is to get his unpleasant experience over with as soon as possible. This reaction is understandable because the human organism always tries to avoid unpleasant stimuli. Your effectiveness can be hurt by the perfectly normal desire to escape an unpleasant situation. To avoid this reaction, measure the rate of your delivery. Talk more slowly than you might be inclined to, especially at the beginning of the speech.

*Keep your nervousness to yourself.* No matter what happens, don't tell your audience that you are nervous. Far too many speakers do this, as a defense. They try to break the ice by saying something like, "Well, I hope you're more relaxed about this speech than I am." Or when they fumble with words or have muscle spasms they look self-conscious or apologize or giggle. You might be able to gain sympathy this way, but you won't win respect.

If a speaker tells his listeners about his troubles, they will give him sympathy but they will withhold from him the very important thing he seeks—support for his ideas. Audiences can feel sympathy for a speaker in distress, but they will not follow one who finds it necessary to lean on his listeners.

If a speaker is obviously nervous, his listeners know it without having to be told. When a speaker has difficulty, empathy makes the audience suffer with him. Furthermore, there is some reason to believe that feeling sympathetic makes an audience uncomfortable. This discomfort can very easily turn to annoyance directed at the person who makes the request for sympathy. If the speaker fights out his problem his audience will react favorably to his perseverance. Many will admire him for doing what they feel they cannot.

## SUMMARY

Speech is used, often at one and the same time, to communicate an idea to someone, to elicit a response, and to fulfill personal needs without concern for a response.

Many factors influence the way each speaker adjusts to a speaking situation but all cases of poor adjustment come about because expressive elements break through into the social or communicative purpose of the speech. For this reason a speaker must do all he can to concentrate on the social purpose of his speaking and not on his personal needs.

Speech classes are not designed to resolve feelings of insecurity. If those feelings are relatively insignificant, a course in speech may be the means whereby they can be resolved. The practical suggestions offered in this chapter make no pretense toward performing psychotherapy. They are designed to help speakers learn how to control the disruptive interference of their personal needs so that the speaking they do will fulfill its primarily social aim. Students do learn to speak well in spite of the perfectly normal anxieties that assail all speakers.

## QUESTIONS

**1.** Differentiate between a speaker's expressive and communicative needs.

**2.** In what way can a speaking situation be characterized as a transaction?

**3.** Do you agree with what the text says about elementary-school recitations?

**4.** What is conditioning? How is it significant to a speaker?

**5.** What false emphasis is at the basis of fear reactions in a speaker?

**6.** The text mentions some practical suggestions which will help alleviate nervousness. Which two do you consider most important?

# DELIVERY: VOCAL ELEMENTS

   I. Voice production
      A. Respiration
      B. Phonation
      C. Resonation
      D. Articulation and pronunciation
        1. Pronunciation
        2. The speech alphabet
        3. Articulation
  II. Elements of voice
      A. Pitch
      B. Force
      C. Time
      D. Quality
 III. Using the voice to communicate meaning
      A. Emphasize the important words
      B. Make clear distinctions among the ideas
      C. Make words sound like what they mean
      D. Speak in a conversational manner
  IV. Summary, questions, and a list of special readings in voice

*Chapter* **XIV**


# DELIVERY: VOCAL ELEMENTS


One important means of making and keeping contact with the world is the sense of hearing. Through it come a large proportion of the stimuli that influence thought and action. These stimuli come to the ear in the form of sound. As far as the ear is concerned, sound is made up of four elements: pitch, force, time, and quality. It is these elements that the ear hears and transmits to the brain, where they are interpreted and given meaning. The ear is capable of distinguishing a wide range of variation in the pitch, force, time, and quality of the sounds that come to it.

The ear hears voice, as it hears any sound, in terms of these same four elements. Consequently, pitch, force, time, and quality are basic considerations for the speaker who wants to use his voice effectively. In order to explain clearly the function of each of these elements in good speech, we must examine the process through which speech is brought about.


## Voice Production

For the production of sound, two conditions are necessary. First, there must be an elastic system, that is, a body capable of vibration, and, second, there must be a force outside the elastic body to set it into motion. When these conditions occur, the oscillation of the vibrating body causes disturbances which are transmitted through some medium to the ear. In the voice, the part that vibrates (the elastic system) is the vocal folds. The force that sets the vibrators into motion is the breath stream controlled and supplied under pressure by the muscles of the breathing mechanism. The transmitting medium is ordinarily the atmosphere. The sound produced by a speaker is resonated in the chambers of his throat, mouth, and nose and is thus given the quality characteristic of that particular speaker's voice. Finally, this vocal sound is modified by the articulators into the various sounds of speech. Thus, four steps are involved in producing any given speech sound. These are respiration (breathing), phonation (vocal-fold vibration), resonation, and articulation.

## Respiration

There are many misconceptions about breathing in speech. The best way to avoid these false impressions is to understand how respiration helps to produce vocal sounds.

In breathing, both the air and the lungs are inert. They do not take an active part in respiration. It is muscles that do the work. Air moves into and out of the lungs, not through any power of its own, and not because the lungs pull or push the air, but because the muscles of the body serve to bring about changes in air pressure within the lungs.

Because the ribs are curved, and because they are fastened to the framework of the body, when they are raised through muscular action they tend to move outward from the center line. Put your hands in the center of your chest and press your elbows to your side. Now raise your elbows without moving your hands. Notice that as your elbows rise, they move away from your body and the distance between them increases. The ribs act in somewhat the same way. They are raised by muscles between the ribs and by other muscles fastened to the ribs from other parts of the skeleton. The rising action tends to increase the lateral dimensions of the rib cage. (See Figure XIV–1.)

The vertical dimension of the thorax (rib cage) is also increased in breathing. Separating the lungs from the abdominal cavity is the diaphragm, a somewhat convex or dome-shaped partition of muscle and tendinous fiber. When the muscular portion of the diaphragm is tensed, the convex shape of the diaphragm is, to a degree, flattened. This action increases the vertical dimen-

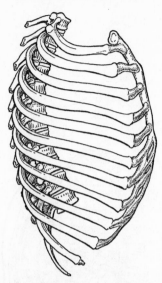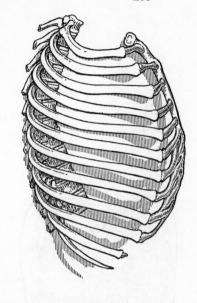

FIGURE XIV–1. SIDE VIEWS OF THE RIB CAGE. *Left:* POSITION
OF THE RIBS AFTER EXHALATION AND BEFORE INHALATION BE-
GINS. *Right:* POSITION OF THE RIBS AFTER INHALATION AND BE-
FORE EXHALATION BEGINS. OBSERVE THE INCREASE IN THE
VOLUME OF THE CHEST CAVITY.

sion of the thorax, enlarging the space within. (See Figure
XIV–2.)

Because the lungs within the thorax are elastic and open to
the atmosphere, as the space that confines them is enlarged, they
enlarge to keep the space filled. The pressure of air outside the
body forces air to enter the lungs.

Inhalation is always an active process. That is, muscular activity is always required to bring air into the lungs whether it
will be used for speaking or not. Exhalation, on the other hand,
is not so active a process in quiet breathing. When one is not
"out of breath," or when the breath stream is not used to vibrate the vocal folds, the muscles ordinarily used in exhalation
can remain passive. The weight of the body itself (the force of
gravity acting on the walls of the chest and on the abdomen)

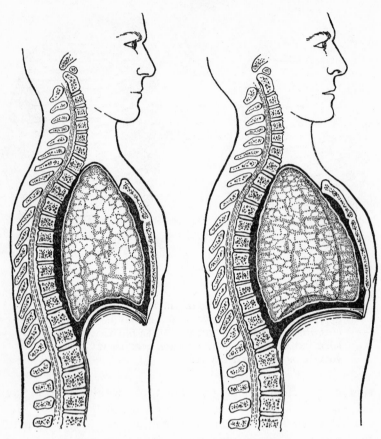

FIGURE XIV–2. SECTIONS OF THE THORAX (*left*) BEFORE IN-
HALATION AND (*right*) AFTER INHALATION. OBSERVE THE
FLATTENING OF THE DIAPHRAGM AND THE EXPANSION OF THE
THORACIC CAVITY WHICH THE LUNGS OCCUPY.

tends to make the thorax contract and creates enough pressure on the lungs to force the air out.

Speaking requires greater muscular activity than does quiet respiration. Otherwise, the breath stream will not be under enough pressure to vibrate the vocal folds strongly enough to produce a sound of desirable quality and sufficient strength. The additional pressure needed for good speech comes from muscles that surround the abdominal area of the torso. By contracting, these muscles force the viscera upward to press against the bottom of the diaphragm. As the diaphragm rises, it decreases the space within the rib cage. Other muscles pull the ribs down. These actions compress the air inside the lungs and expel it under pressure past the vocal folds, causing them to vibrate.

The muscles of respiration are quite strong and when they are used vigorously they can make the voice quite loud. Under ordinary conditions, however, sheer loudness of voice is not nearly so important as the control exercised over it. Co-ordination of muscular activity rather than simple muscle power achieves the necessary control.

As a final point in our very brief sketch of the breathing process, let us say one more word about the diaphragm. For many years the prescription has been constantly repeated that for proper use of voice one must "breathe from the diaphragm." To avoid unnecessary confusions and errors, this injunction must be clearly understood. There is little doubt that the diaphragm is one of the chief muscles used in inhalation. But other muscles must be used actively and directly to expel air from the lungs. The injunction to "breathe from the diaphragm" has little meaning, therefore, except as a psychological aid to voice production. The diaphragm is active primarily in inhalation. Physically, the most it can do in exhalation is to oppose the other muscles in their effort to expel the air and thus help to control the outgoing air stream.

### PHONATION

The vocal folds are housed in a structure called the larynx. It is situated at the top of the windpipe, or trachea, and is clearly evidenced in men by the protrusion in the neck commonly called

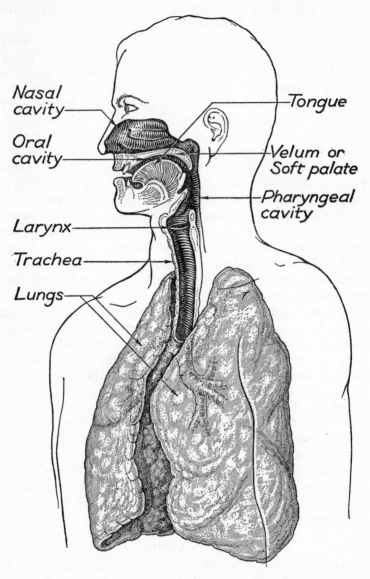

FIGURE XIV-3. THE PRINCIPAL ORGANS OF SPEECH. THE
RIBS, DIAPHRAGM, AND THORACIC MUSCLES ARE NOT SHOWN.

the "Adam's apple." What we refer to as the "Adam's apple" is
in reality one of the nine cartilages that make up the larynx.
These cartilages are joined together and to the body by ligaments
and are operated by a nicely balanced set of opposing muscles.
Two of the cartilages of the larynx are called the *arytenoids.*
These are shaped somewhat like pyramids and are arranged so
that they can pivot on their base. Connecting the arytenoids and
the thyroid cartilage (the "Adam's apple") are two muscles
called the *thyro-arytenoids.* It is the thyro-artyenoid muscles that
form the major portion of the body of the vocal folds. When
certain other muscles (mainly the crico-arytenoid and the arytenoid muscles) are tensed, they pivot the arytenoid cartilages and
bring them closer together. In this manner the thyro-arytenoid
muscles are also brought together. (See Figure XIV–4.) This
action closes off the passage that leads from the lungs to the outer
air and impounds air in the lungs. When the muscles of exhalation force air out of the lungs, the pressure that is built up under
the vocal folds forces them aside so that a puff of air escapes. As
the air escapes pressure is reduced. Elasticity and muscular ten-

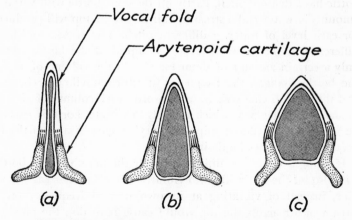

FIGURE XIV–4. THE VOCAL FOLDS AND THE ARYTENOID CAR-
TILAGES. *Diagram a:* THE VOCAL FOLDS CLOSE TOGETHER, AS IN
PHONATION. *Diagram b:* THE VOCAL FOLDS PARTLY OPEN, AS
IN WHISPERING. *Diagram c:* THE VOCAL FOLDS RELAXED AND
ENTIRELY OPEN, AS IN DEEP BREATHING.

sion in the folds causes them to close off the passage again. Immediately pressure builds up and the folds are forced aside. This open-and-close action sets the passing stream of air into vibration and produces vocal sound. The speed at which the vocal folds vibrate can be seen from the fact that to produce the pitch A above middle C they would have to open and close 440 times a second.

A complete theory of vocal-fold vibration has yet to be developed and there have been for many years widespread differences of opinion about the exact nature of their movement. It is clear, however, that the vocal folds are not to be visualized as strings similar to those of a violin. Nor are they to be likened to the reed of a clarinet. A much closer analogy is to be found in the lips of a trumpet player when he sets into vibration the column of air in that instrument.

## RESONATION

A simple experiment will help to explain resonance.

The sound produced by blowing across the top of an empty bottle has a definite pitch. Partly fill the same bottle with varying amounts of water and a stream of air across the top will produce, for each level of water, a different pitch. The reason for these differences is that at each level, the liquid in the bottle leaves only a certain amount of room for air. As the volume of air in the bottle changes, the frequency at which it vibrates changes and the pitch is changed. In other words, each column of air has a natural frequency at which it tends to vibrate. For this reason, an organ maker chooses pipes of varying lengths and girths to produce the pitches he desires.

Holding a vibrating tuning fork over the mouth of the bottle will also set the air inside into vibration. In this latter case, however, instead of vibrating at its own natural frequency (as a stream of air across the top would cause it to do), the air will vibrate in the bottle at the approximate frequency of the tuning fork. The sound of the tuning fork thus is amplified (made louder) because the sound from the vibration of air in the bottle is added to it. By using tuning forks of different pitches, it can be shown that the more closely the tuning fork matches the natural frequency of the column of air in the bottle, the louder the resultant sound becomes. This amplification of sound is called *resonance,* and the bottle acts as a *resonator.* The specific instance described is an example of *cavity* resonance. Putting the handle of a vibrating tuning fork against a table top will produce an example of what is called *sounding-board* resonance. Here again, the more closely the tuning fork approximates the natural frequency of the surface, the louder will be the total sound produced. Through cavity resonance, and to some extent through sounding-board resonance, the voice is amplified as it passes from the vocal folds through the throat and mouth.

Resonance is not to be confused with reverberation. Reverberation occurs when sound is reflected from a surface such as the wall of a room. It is, in other words, an echo. When you stand at some distance from a surface that reflects sound and shout, or clap your hands, you can hear the sound coming back to you after it has bounced off the reflecting surface. In a room, reverberations are usually undesirable because the reflected sound is mixed in with the original and distorts its quality. The booming sounds one hears in a large church with a vaulted ceiling, which distort the music of the choir and make it difficult to understand the words of a sermon, are examples of the disrupting effect of reverberation. Resonance, on the other hand, takes place mainly within the cavities formed by a speaker's throat, mouth, and nasal passages. Instead of distorting the sound, resonance gives the speaker's voice its characteristic quality.

## ARTICULATION AND PRONUNCIATION

Once the processes of respiration, phonation, and resonation have been accomplished, a speaker has (at the tip of his tongue, literally) the raw material of speech. Vocal sound does not become connected discourse until the speaker has modified the vocal tone into the sounds that make up whatever dialect he speaks. Articulation and pronunciation, then, are significant in the production of good speech. *Pronunciation* is the sum of all the audible characteristics of a word: the individual sounds, the

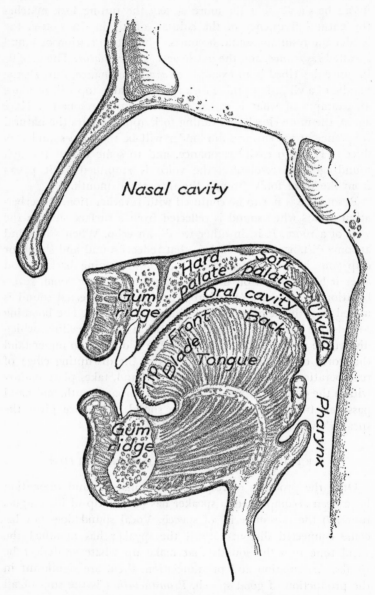

FIGURE XIV-5. THE ARTICULATORS AND RESONATORS.

order in which they occur, their duration, the stress given to syllables, and so on. *Articulation* is the process by which the individual sounds are formed and connected into speech. Decisions about what sounds should make up a word must be made before the sounds can be formed. Therefore, let's consider pronunciation first, and then examine briefly the process of articulation.

**Pronunciation.**    Good pronunciation is achieved when the sounds a speaker articulates are acceptable in the standard version of the dialect he speaks. In other words, it is quite possible for a speaker to have very precise articulation and still be guilty of poor pronunciation. If, for example, he pronounces the word *can't* as "cain't," even though his articulation of each sound in the word is quite accurate and precise, and though the word is clearly understood by all who hear him, his pronunciation of this word should be considered poor, because it is not the one accepted by the vast majority of educated Americans.

Dictionaries are the most obvious authoritative source of information about the accepted or agreed pronunciation of words. Notice, though, that we do not speak of "correct" pronunciation. As long as a language is spoken, it changes. Dictionaries can only report what is current usage at the time they are printed and printing a word does not freeze its pronunciation for all time. But since language changes occur slowly, a dictionary's report of standard pronunciation may be safely accepted.

English is spoken in a large number of dialects throughout the world. Speakers from England, Canada, Australia, New Zealand, and other parts of the English-speaking world are clearly distinguishable one from the other. Persons who learn English as a second language will also ordinarily use a distinguishable pronunciation.

Not only will English be pronounced differently in different parts of the world, but within the borders of one country a variety of dialects will be heard.

In the United States, there are many dialect regions. Three of these include a large enough portion of the population to be considered the major dialect regions of this country. The three major dialects of the United States are Eastern, Southern, and General American English. Each of these is recognized as a "standard" dialect, and is considered to be preferable to any other speech pattern in the area in which it is used. Deviations from the standard dialect of the region in which a speaker lives are generally considered "substandard" and ought to be avoided.

***The speech alphabet.*** To study the sound system of any language, or any dialect of a language, some accurate method of notation is necessary. English spelling is notoriously untrustworthy as a means of indicating the pronunciation of a word. A single letter of the alphabet may be used to spell a variety of sounds. The letter *a,* for example, spells a different sound in each of the following words: *hat, late, calm, above, courage.* The same sound, on the other hand, may be spelled in several different ways. Look at the word *courage,* for instance. The letter *a* in this word spells the same sound as the *i* in *hit,* the *o* in *women,* the *e* in *exist,* and both the *u* and the *y* in *busy!*

A very useful system for circumventing the vagaries of spelling is found in the International Phonetic Alphabet, a set of symbols that may be used to indicate with precision and uniformity the sounds that appear in spoken language. Using symbols from the I.P.A., one may put into written form the essential elements of any word in English.

Many of the symbols in the phonetic alphabet appear exactly like the letters you are familiar with in the printing of an ordinary book. Several others are likely to be unfamiliar. These are taken from the alphabets of other languages such as Greek, or are arbitrarily created, or are variations of familiar symbols. ˈn any case, the symbols are easy to understand, easy to learn, and asy to use. Their most important usefulness lies in the fact that each symbol has a uniform meaning. A given sound, no matter how it may be spelled in a word, is always indicated by the same symbol in phonetic transcription; and a given symbol, no matter where it appears in a phonetic transcription, always stands for the same sound.

The following list includes the symbols that are used to tran-

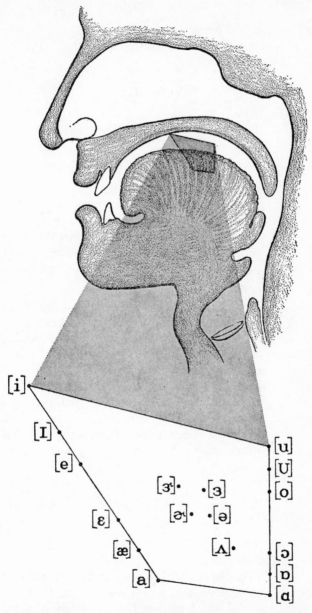

FIGURE XIV-6. TONGUE POSITION IN FORMING CERTAIN VOWELS. (*adapted from Eisenson*)

scribe the standard sounds of American English. The symbol [']
in a phonetic transcription means that the syllable which
*follows* it should be stressed.

## VOWELS

| Phonetic Symbol | Key Word | Phonetic Transcription |
|---|---|---|
| i | meet | [mit] |
| ɪ | hit | [hɪt] |
| e | chaotic | [ke'atɪk] |

Depending on such factors as its position in a
syllable, stress, and duration, the vowel [e] in
English words frequently becomes the diphthong
[eɪ]. See the list of diphthongs that follows.

| | | |
|---|---|---|
| ɛ | net | [nɛt] |
| æ | bad | [bæd] |
| a | | |

A satisfactory key word for this vowel is hard to
find. It may be considered an intermediate sound
between [æ] and [ɑ]. Some Eastern speakers use
[a] instead of [æ] or [ɑ] in "broad a" words. For
example, path is [paθ] instead of [pæθ, pɑθ]. Perhaps you have heard President Kennedy's pronunciation of the words *last* [last], *path* [paθ], or
*grass* [gras]. The sound [a] is most commonly
heard in the standard diphthongs [aɪ] and [aʊ]
which are listed below.

| | | |
|---|---|---|
| ɑ | calm | [kɑm] |
| ɒ | hot | [hɒt] |

(as pronounced by Southern British and some
Eastern American speakers)

| | | |
|---|---|---|
| ɔ | ball | [bɔl] |
| o | location | [lo'keɪʃən] |

Like the sound [e], and under the same general
conditions, this vowel also frequently becomes a
diphthong [oʊ]. See the list of diphthongs that
follows.

| Phonetic Symbol | Key Word | Phonetic Transcription |
|---|---|---|
| ʊ | look | [lʊk] |
| u | pool | [pul] |
| ɝ | bird | [bɝd] |

(as heard in General American English)

| | | |
|---|---|---|
| ɜ | bird | [bɜd] |

(as heard in the East and South)

| | | |
|---|---|---|
| ɚ | father | ['fɑðɚ] |

(as heard in General American English) . [ɚ] is always an unstressed vowel.

| | | |
|---|---|---|
| ə | father | ['fɑðə] |

(as heard in the East and South) Like [ɚ], the vowel [ə] is always unstressed. Not only is [ə] the Eastern and Southern variant of [ɚ], it is also one of the most frequent vowels in English. It appears as the pronunciation of many vowels in unstressed syllables.

| | | |
|---|---|---|
| ʌ | love | [lʌv] |

## DIPHTHONGS[1]

| | | |
|---|---|---|
| aɪ | kite | [kaɪt] |
| aʊ | cow | [kaʊ] |
| eɪ | gay | [geɪ] |
| oʊ | go | [goʊ] |
| ɔɪ | boil | [bɔɪl] |

## CONSONANTS

| | | |
|---|---|---|
| b | be | [bi] |
| p | pit | [pɪt] |

[1] A diphthong is a complex of vowel sounds within the same syllable. It begins with a recognizable vowel sound, glides through several intermediate positions, and ends with another recognizable vowel. The average listener usually hears a diphthong as a single sound. There are many diphthongs in American English. The five listed here are considered major.

| Phonetic Symbol | Key Word | Phonetic Transcription |
|---|---|---|
| t | tag | [tæg] |
| d | dog | [dɔg] |
| k | cake | [keɪk] |
| g | go | [goʊ] |
| m | meat | [mit] |
| n | no | [noʊ] |
| ŋ | sing | [sɪŋ] |
| f | fun | [fʌn] |
| v | vain | [veɪn] |
| s | six | [sɪks] |
| z | zoo | [zu] |
| θ | thin | [θɪn] |
| ð | then | [ðɛn] |
| ʃ | ship | [ʃɪp] |
| ʒ | measure | ['mɛʒɚ, 'mɛʒə] |
| h | hit | [hɪt] |
| ʍ | white | [ʍaɪt] |

This sound is sometimes transcribed as [hw], thus [hwaɪt].

| | | |
|---|---|---|
| tʃ | chin | [tʃɪn] |
| dʒ | judge | [dʒʌdʒ] |
| l | lull | [lʌl] |
| r | red | [rɛd] |
| w | wet | [wɛt] |
| j | yes | [jɛs] |

Many of the symbols in the phonetic alphabet are familiar to you, while several of them are quite strange. Get to know all of them. Try writing words, phrases and sentences in phonetic symbols. The more aware you become of the sound system of English, the more conscious you will be of your own speech and of the precision with which you pronounce your words.

***Articulation.*** Articulation has been identified as the process whereby vocal tone is modified into the sounds of oral communication. Figure XIV-5 shows what the articulators are. Let's see briefly how they help to produce clear speech.

The major factor in the articulation of vowel sounds is the position of the tongue in the mouth. The best illustration of this position effect is the vowel diagram, a formalized, schematic representation of the interior of the mouth with the lips to the left and the pharynx to the right as indicated in Figure XIV-6.

The dots on the diagram suggest for each vowel the approximate position of the highest part of the tongue when the vowel is pronounced. Look, for example, at the four words *seat, sit, set,* and *sat.* The spellings, of course, are all different. When you listen to each word, however, you can tell that what distinguishes one from another is the vowel sound. The initial and final sounds, [s] and [t], are the same for all. Say each of the words and notice carefully how you cause this difference. You will observe that in each case the vowel sound is different for one main reason —you change the position of your tongue. The vowel [i] in *seat* [sit] is distinguishable from [ɪ], [ɛ] and [æ] because the position and tension of your tongue are different from what they are when you say the other vowels.

The lips become significant in forming the back vowels [ɒ], [ɔ], [o], [ʊ] and [u] because the lips are normally rounded in the proper articulation of these sounds. In a sense, the lower jaw may be considered an articulator as well. It would be difficult to produce a good [ɑ] or [ɔ] sound without dropping your lower jaw to give room in your mouth for proper articulation of these vowels.

All parts of the articulatory mechanism help to fashion the consonant sounds. A few simple examples will show how each of these works. When you say a [b], an [m] or a [p], your lips are lightly pressed together to give each of these part of its characteristic sound. Thus the lips are important. [θ] and [ð] are made with the help of the tongue and the teeth, and the lower lip and the teeth co-operate on [f] and [v]. The teeth, then, are important. The gum ridge becomes an articulator when the tip of the tongue touches it in [t], [d], [n] and [l]. For [m], [n] and [ŋ], the soft palate (velum) must be relaxed so that air can pass through the nose. In all other English sounds, the soft palate should be raised to close off the nasal passage. Finally, the vocal folds themselves are important articulators. Except for factors not important here, the only significant difference between [s] and [z] or between [f] and [v] is that the [s] and [f] are produced without vibrating the vocal folds, whereas the [z] and the [v] require that the vocal folds vibrate. The same is true of several other "voiced" and "voiceless" pairs of consonants:

Think for a moment about the total physiological process of voice production. Muscles of the chest and abdomen must be tensed and relaxed at the proper moment and for just the right sustained period of time to provide air at just the proper pressure. The vocal folds must be lengthened and shortened, tensed and relaxed discretely to produce desired pitches. The resonating cavities must be modified in shape by the articulators at a rapid rate and at precisely the right moment to form accurately the different sounds of speech. The fact that intelligible speech can occur at all seems almost miraculous.

Actually, this complex mechanism works so rapidly and each part is so thoroughly integrated with every other that an attempt to isolate and improve any single part of the process should be guided by a highly skilled professional. A knowledge of the physiology of the vocal mechanism is of value in the classroom primarily in order to dispel some of the untrue notions about speech. It is easy to see that a speaker seriously oversimplifies the process when he looks for the solution to speech problems in "diaphragmatic breathing," "lower pitch," or "more careful articulation." In a public-speaking class, only the most general problems can be solved.

## Elements of Voice

All judgments about a speaker's voice are limited by the ear of the hearer. Since, as we have said, the ear hears a voice in terms of its pitch, force, time, and quality, any meaningful consideration of the voice must be in terms of these four elements. Thus in talking about the voice in isolation from other factors in delivery, it is perhaps best to think of the vocal mechanism not only as a means of producing sound, but also as an instrument admirably suited to controlling variation of pitch, force, time, and quality in the sounds it produces. Let us examine each of these elements in order to define it and to discover the part it plays in effective communication.

## PITCH

We have said that when an elastic system is set into vibration by some outside force, sound results. The rate at which the vibrations occur (number of vibrations per second) is called the frequency. It is the frequency of vibration which is interpreted by the ear as pitch. To produce the pitch A above middle C, the sound source must vibrate 440 times per second. The faster the sound source vibrates (that is, the higher the frequency), the higher the pitch sounds. As the frequency increases or decreases, the pitch rises and falls. Thus pitch can be defined as the relative highness or lowness of a sound in terms of some musical scale. By using the muscles in the larynx a speaker controls the length and tension of the vocal folds in order to produce variations in pitch.

In order for a sound to be audible to the normal ear, the frequency must be within certain limits. If there are too few or too many vibrations per second, the human ear cannot hear the sound. This principle is utilized in "silent" whistles that are used for signaling to dogs. These are so high in pitch that a man cannot hear them, but a dog's ears respond to such high pitches that the whistle is plainly audible to him.

## FORCE

Perhaps the easiest element of voice to understand is force. For our purposes, we can use this term to refer simply to the loudness of a sound. It is mainly determined by what is called the *amplitude* of the vibration. When the stream of air that vibrates the vocal folds is not strong, the vocal folds move but little and only relatively slight disturbances are set up in the air that transmits the sound to the ear. Consequently, the ear is not strongly stimulated and the sound is heard as a soft tone. When the breath is more strongly expelled from the lungs and the vocal folds are caused to vibrate more vigorously, greater disturbances are set up in the air. These strike the ear more forcibly and the ear records the sound as being loud. There is no necessary connection between force and pitch. Each can vary independently of the other. There is a tendency, however, for pitch to rise as force increases.

## TIME

There are three ways the ear recognizes time in speech. The first of these is through *duration*. This term refers to the length of time any given sound is made to last. For an example, look at the two words *leap* and *gleam*. The letters *ea* are used to spell the same vowel sound [i] in both words. The vowel is quite short in the word *leap* but in *gleam* the vowel lasts a noticeably greater length of time.

The second factor of time is *rate,* or the number of words spoken per minute. There is no necessary connection between rate and duration any more than there is between pitch and force. The two are independent of each other. That is, the rate of speech can be slow, even though the individual sounds are given short duration. The result is a choppy, staccato delivery. On the other hand, when rate is slow and duration is long, a form of drawl results. By the same token, the duration of individual sounds can be long or short when the rate is fast.

The third factor of time is *pause:* the moments when sound ceases. Pauses are an essential part of speaking: a speaker must breathe, he must rethink his ideas, and he must allow the audience to grasp what he has said before he goes on. The most efficient use of pauses takes place when a speaker makes all three of these objectives coincide. That is, the speaker should pause to breathe and to think at points where it will most benefit his listeners to have an interval for assimilating an idea.

Frequently nervousness will interfere with an effective use of pauses. When a speaker rushes ahead to get the speech over with in the shortest possible time, none of his pauses, for breathing, for thought, or for audience assimilation, will make much sense.

Often a speaker feels that if he isn't talking all the time, the audience's impression of his fluency will suffer. Many speakers, oppressed by this notion, will fill what should be pauses with meaningless vocalization, a continued nervous insertion of "er" and "uh" that not only distract from what is being said but also make the speaker appear to be at a loss for ideas and words.

The length of a pause can indicate the importance of a point the speaker has made. In a sense, it tells the listeners how long the speaker wants them to "think that one over." By pausing when he has completed a main point, a speaker can tell the listeners how important the point is; at the same time, he lets them think the idea over, thinks for himself about what he is going to say next, and draws in a good breath of air. When pauses are properly used, they do much to clarify the phrasing in a sentence; they add emphasis to ideas; and they contribute greatly to the audience's impression of the speaker as a mature, thoughtful, and secure person.

## QUALITY

There is a wide variety in the sounds produced by different kinds of vibrating bodies. Among musical instruments, for example, it is easy to distinguish one from another because no two different kinds of instruments sound exactly alike. It is not necessary to know the name of a marimba or a glockenspiel to tell them apart even when they play the same notes. The difference lies in the quality of the sounds they produce. Similar quality differentiations can be made among human voices. Even over the telephone, an instrument designed for intelligibility of transmission rather than fidelity, a voice can usually be recognized. Characteristic articulations as well as pitch and time patterns help to identify it, but its unique quality also helps to single it out. Let's see briefly how vocal quality is determined.

You will remember from an earlier part of this chapter that cavities and sounding boards will best resonate pitches that match their own natural frequencies. This fact helps to explain vocal quality. In voice production, cavity resonance is more significant than sounding-board resonance. Thus the cavities of the throat, mouth, and nose are the most important resonators of the voice.

The sound produced by vibration of the vocal folds is very complex. That is, it has not only a fundamental pitch, but contains many overtones as well. It differs, for instance, from a tuning fork, which produces a pure tone, a fundamental pitch with no overtones. Each of the overtones in the voice is acted upon by the resonating cavities of the throat and head so that it is either increased or decreased in strength depending upon whether the cavities respond to its particular pitch. The result is that each voice acquires its own peculiar characteristic quality or timbre. We can thus say that quality is determined by the number, the frequency, and the relative strengths of the overtones in the voice.

# Using the Voice to Communicate Meaning

A speaker must make his ideas immediately intelligible. Listeners cannot stop to mull over a speaker's idea as they might re-examine an obscure paragraph in an essay. Neither informative nor argumentative discourse can be meaningful and compelling without the kind of delivery which brings the speaker's ideas sharply and immediately into focus. Here are some of the ways a good speaker uses his voice to give clarity to his ideas.

### Emphasize the Important Words

Although a speaker gives up the writer's advantage of allowing a reader to understand ideas at leisure, the speaker has an advantage which a writer does not. He can use his voice to say instantly what he means. He does not have to depend on such crude symbols as commas, periods, exclamation points, and question marks to carry shades of meaning. If he has good control of his voice, a speaker can give a whole complex of different emphases to a single phrase.

In almost any sentence, some of the words are more important than others, the less important ones can, in fact, often be omitted without loss of the basic meaning. Because reader time and newspaper space are both at a premium, newspaper headlines are usually telescoped to as short a form as the writer feels he can use and still accurately communicate meaning. Sometimes an obvious verb will be left out. "Legislative Session Near Close." Such words as *a, and, the* are seldom used. "Clouds, Fog Lift for Pleasant Day." To say more is unnecessary; to say less would destroy the meaning.

Even in the case of newspaper headlines, however, the words that remain are not of equal importance. A news item may be headed "Pilgrims for Holy Week Come to Old Jerusalem." While all of the words may be needed, some carry a larger burden of the meaning than do others. The word *Pilgrims,* for instance, not only cannot be omitted, but it is obviously more important than the words *for* and *to*. If this headline is read aloud, the word *Pilgrims,* then, must be given somewhat greater stress than either *for* or *to*. The phrase *for Holy Week* means not just any week in the year, but a very particular one. Thus the word *Holy* would be given more stress than either of the other two words. Further, the word *Week* is of greater relative importance than *to*. In terms of emphasis, then, the words in the headline call for something like the following degrees of relative emphasis. "PILGRIMS for HOLY *Week Come* to OLD JERUSALEM."

In the most rudimentary sort of language use, nouns and verbs do the real work. As ideas become more complex, other kinds of words are used to add subtlety to the meaning. A speaker is the only one who knows exactly what he means; he is the one who must decide which of his words carry the burden of his meaning. In every case, he must select these important words that carry his meaning and give emphasis to them.

Emphasis is likely to be identified at first thought with loudness. One way to let an audience know what is important is to make it loud. This is the parent's tried and true method with young children. When mother says, "Come at once," children will frequently wait until the call becomes loud enough to indicate that mother means business. However, the speaker who deals with sophisticated people learns that loudness is the crudest form of stress. The most effective emphasis is created through *variety,* in *all* the elements of vocal delivery: pitch, force, time, and quality.

## MAKE CLEAR DISTINCTIONS AMONG THE IDEAS

"Catholics make up approximately five per cent of the population in West Virginia compared with thirty per cent in Wisconsin." In this sentence there are at least two and possibly three opposing sets of ideas that must be made separate and distinct. Clearly, *five* per cent is different from *thirty* per cent and this difference should be made clear by the voice. Moreover, West Virginia is not to be confused with Wisconsin. And by the attention to Catholics, a distinction is implied between Catholics and non-Catholics among the populations of the two states. Variety in pitch, force, time, and quality must make audible for the listeners such distinctions among the speaker's ideas.

The same principle applies not only to words that communicate a contrast but also to those that express ideas in a series. Lack of variety in the speaker's voice makes them all sound alike. In a West Coast area the Weather Bureau once made a most unfelicitous assignment of a representative to read the midday forecast. He was well aware of the different words for meteorological phenomenon, but his speech habit prevented his listeners from hearing these words clearly. Through its lack of variety, his voice made "clouds," "fog," "rain," "clear," "warm," sound the same; the words might almost as well have *meant* the same. Because they are not the same, variation in pitch, force, time, and quality should have been used to suggest that each of the words in this series was to be distinguished from the others.

## MAKE WORDS SOUND LIKE WHAT THEY MEAN

There are many words which are an imitation of the sound they name. This is true, for example, in naming the sounds made by birds: ducks quack, geese hiss, sparrows chirp, hens cluck, and so on. Insects buzz and hum. The word *boom* imitates the sound it means. The fact that words often imitate sounds can add color to speech.

The imitation of the sound indicated by a word, however, is only a part of what we are talking about when we say that a word should be made to sound like what it means. One of the major functions of a speaker's words is to communicate not only the factual and logical notions he has in mind but an emotive qualitative content as well. He can convey attitudes towards the ideas he discusses more clearly if he uses his voice to carry to his listeners the emotional qualities he wants in his words. The speaker can, for example, make *war* sound heroic or unpleasant, *peace* pleasant or weak. His voice, by the vocal quality he gives to his words, can help him to show the goodness or badness in ideas, their rightness or wrongness, their beauty or ugliness, their merit or lack of it.

## SPEAK IN A CONVERSATIONAL MANNER

Probably nothing in speaking contributes more importantly to effective delivery than a conversational style. A speaker can conceivably use bad diction or even bad grammar, yet if his delivery is spontaneous, direct, and conversational, his chances of effective communication are better than if he had beautiful diction and perfect grammar but lacked a conversational delivery.

Most Americans do not, as a rule, read aloud very often or at any great length. When they do, they sound much like the child first learning to read. Even when he reads fluently, the words of an inexperienced or untrained reader will most likely sound crated for delivery, boxed in with a variety of stiff patterns, repetitions of pitch cadences, an unvaried tempo, an unchanging degree of force, and a dull quality of monotony that destroys much of the meaning of what is being read. Reading patterns often attach themselves to the speaking of memorized words as well. One mark of a poor actor is his inability to speak in a spontaneous, conversational mode.

A good speaker uses all the means of emphasis at his command and the amount of emphasis he can create through variety is enormous. Considering this fact, it is amazing that so many speakers talk as if they were reading a series of words from a paper. Through monotony and dullness, they throw away one of the most important advantages a speaker has over a writer— the ability to give instantaneous clarity to ideas through variety in the elements of speech.

## SUMMARY

Speech is brought about by the operation of four bodily processes: respiration, phonation, resonation, and articulation. Respiration supplies the force for phonation. Phonation produces vocal sound. This sound is resonated by the cavities of the throat, mouth, and head to give each voice its characteristic quality. Finally, the indeterminate vocal sound is transformed into speech by the articulators: lips, teeth, tongue, lower jaw, hard palate, and velum.

Speech is heard by the ear in terms of its four variable characteristics: pitch, force, time, and quality. By controlled variation of these elements, a speaker gives emphasis to his ideas and helps bring clarity to his speech.

In using his voice, a speaker should be guided by four principles:

1. Emphasize the important words.
2. Make clear distinctions among the ideas.
3. Make words sound like what they mean.
4. Speak in a conversational manner.

## QUESTIONS

1. Explain the two conditions necessary for the production of sound.
2. How is the diaphragm used in speech?
3. Explain how the vocal folds function to produce a sound.

**4.** What is resonance?

**5.** What are the articulators? What do they do?

**6.** Would you agree that a person with good articulation would have good pronunciation?

**7.** How is acceptable pronunciation determined?

**8.** Should a Southern dialect be considered a substandard form of American speech?

**9.** What are the four elements of sound which the ear hears?

**10.** Discuss how the pause is used in speech.

**11.** What must the speaker substitute in his speech for the punctuation marks used in writing?

**12.** What is the significance of the conversational mode in speech?


# SPECIAL READINGS IN VOICE

Little can be done in a public-speaking course to correct specific problems in vocal delivery. If you have such problems, your instructor may refer you to the speech clinic of your college. If there is no clinic on campus, he may want to recommend practice materials that will be of help. There are many good and quite readable books in voice and diction. Each one will have a variety of practice materials. We list a few of these here. Some of them are almost sure to be in your library.

Anderson, Virgil A. *Training the Speaking Voice*. New York: Oxford University Press, 1954.

Eisenson, Jon. *The Improvement of Voice and Diction*. New York: The Macmillan Company, 1958.

Fairbanks, Grant. *Voice and Articulation Drillbook*. New York: Harper and Brothers, 1960.

Hahn, Elise, Charles W. Lomas, Donald E. Hargis, and Daniel Vandraegen. *Basic Voice Training for Speech*. New York: McGraw-Hill Book Co., Inc., 1957.

Karr, Harrison M. *Developing Your Speaking Voice*. New York: Harper and Brothers, 1953.

# DELIVERY: VISUAL ELEMENTS

   I. The uses of the body in speech
      A. Eye contact
      B. Posture
      C. Movement
      D. Gesture
  II. The use of visual aids
      A. Types of visual aids
         1. Diagrams and graphs
         2. Maps and globes
         3. Pictures
         4. Models and actual objects
      B. Principles for the use of visual aids
 III. Summary, questions, and exercise

*Chapter* **XV**


# DELIVERY: VISUAL ELEMENTS

## The Use of the Body in Speech

Everything a speaker does, in public or private address, on or off the platform, helps to communicate something. "Everything" includes especially his language, his voice, and the way he uses his body. Not everything that these communicate, however, is necessarily what he intends. Listeners get very strong impressions about speakers and about what they say from all sorts of visual cues. These cues cannot always be identified, nor their specific effect, but they are present and have an effect for good or ill. It is up to a speaker, then, to see to it that the communication of his ideas is not hampered unnecessarily by the way in which he uses his body when he speaks. That he uses his body implies that he must have his body under control.

### EYE CONTACT

When one speaks, he should *look directly at the audience*. This means something more than not looking at the floor, at the walls, out the window, or head-down into his notes. It means more than sweeping the audience with an occasional glance. It means looking directly and personally into the faces of individual members of the audience, moving the look from person to person in the group, making personal eye contact with everyone to whom he speaks. Now, when a speaker addresses a very large crowd, or speaks in a large auditorium where he is removed from his audience at some distance, looking directly into the eyes of each listener becomes difficult or impossible. He must nevertheless give the impression as best he can that he is doing just that.

Your own experience will tell you that listeners do not respond well to a speaker in public or private who does not look at them. Some people are not aware of this reaction because their own habits of eye contact are poor. But you have met people who avoided your glance. What was your reaction to them? There is no point in trying to make a case for the notion that the man who refuses to look you in the eye is himself shifty or untrust-worthy; the important idea here is that you react badly to him when he does.

There is one more important reason for the speaker to look directly at his listeners. A speaker should take advantage of every bit of help he can get. The audience itself is an important source of help. As a rule, people respond to what they see and hear, and their responses tell the speaker what effect he has on them. It would be extravagant for the speaker not to use to advantage the audience's reaction to his speech. Only by making direct visual contact with individual members of the group can the speaker tell who is alert and friendly, who is bored, who is unconcerned, or who is just not listening.

## POSTURE

A speaker's posture probably does more to give effectiveness to him as a person than it does to give effectiveness to his ideas. But listeners are moved to accept or reject ideas on the basis of merit in the speaker as well as merit in his ideas. Consequently, the speaker should stand before his audience in a manner that indicates stability and assurance. His posture should be poised but not stiff, relaxed but not sloppy.

Experienced speakers sometimes lean on a speaking stand, put their hands in their pants pockets, or even sit on the edge of a table. Whether such posture is acceptable depends more on the degree of formality in the speaking situation than it does on "rules" of public speaking. Such obvious casualness is likely to work to the disadvantage of a beginning speaker, for many audiences tend to expect speakers to treat them with a kind of formal respect. Correctly or incorrectly, they consider the speaker who is too relaxed in his posture to be taking liberties with them. A second and perhaps more important reason for not being too casual is that an inexperienced speaker is likely to dramatize his relaxation in the effort to dispel or disguise stage fright. Instead of covering up his nervousness, he points it up. This does his speaking more harm than good.

Even so, a speaker can achieve and communicate assurance through control over his body and its posture. Though he may not control the trembling in his muscles, he can control the things he does to try to hide it. If you have any such need, stand straight, balance your weight on both feet, and look directly at your audience. The results will be far better than anything you can do by way of draping yourself over the lectern, crossing your ankles, slouching with your hands in your pockets, sitting on the edge of a desk, or pacing back and forth in front of your audience. Granted, this posture won't do much to keep your hands and legs from quivering, but it will help to keep your nervousness from interfering with your communication. You may not think so but your audience will. And that is the important point. Put the stress where the stress belongs. Remember that you are there to *talk;* to talk about *ideas,* not to model clothes or to make a pretty picture for the audience.

## MOVEMENT

In general, a speaker should avoid making any movement which is not necessary. Moving from one place to another in the room, pacing back and forth on the platform, are seldom necessary. Many an anxious speaker has used such wandering as a means of working off some of the excess energy that builds up before he begins to speak. But when there is nothing in the *speech* to motivate his pacing, when the motivation is in the *nervousness of the speaker,* his walking around during the speech serves no real purpose as far as the audience is concerned and is therefore only distracting.

A highly important detail of movement is the manner of getting to your designated speaking position and back to your seat when you have finished. An audience will consider these acts a

part of your speech and will hold you responsible for everything
you do from the time you leave your seat until you sit down
again. Your speech begins not when you utter your first words,
but when you first stand up. Similarly, your speech is not over
with your conclusion; it goes on until the attention of the audience is no longer on you. It is quite conceivable that you will
hold the attention of your listeners even after you sit down and
until something actually distracts them from you.

Under these conditions, it is only reasonable to conduct yourself in a manner that will not detract from the general effectiveness of your speech. Walk to and from the platform with firmness
and poise. A large part of the ethical proof discussed in Chapter
XI comes from your giving the audience the impression that you
are prepared to speak and that you welcome the opportunity.
Preserve your dignity by neither racing nor shuffling to the front
of the room. When you have finished speaking, maintain the
atmosphere of competence and authority you have built up by
returning to your seat quietly and deliberately.

## Gesture

Another kind of bodily activity in speech is gesture. Gesture is
distinguished from the kind of movement just discussed by the
fact that it involves the hands, arms, and head, but does not
carry the speaker from one part of the room to another.

If they are to be effective, gestures must appear to be natural
and spontaneous. When a speaker is criticized for lack of physical activity, he will often comment that gesturing is not "natural"
for him. More often than not, the very remark will be accompanied by an emphatic and decisive gesture. The point is that
gesture is quite *natural,* but it is not *habitual* for the beginner in
a formal speaking situation. The problem is to carry over into
public speech the same freedom of movement the speaker
normally gives to hands, arms, and head, and the same mobility
of facial expression he uses so naturally in private speech. Obviously, some speakers quite naturally gesture more than others.
But every speaker should use gestures at least as extensively as
he does in private conversation. Those rare persons who do not

gesture at all, even in private speech, should maintain the poise of private speech even in public. They should have no difficulty in finding a place to put their hands. The usual experience has been, however, that most speakers have some movement of the hands and arms but these movements are choppy and incomplete. Beginning speakers frequently have slight movement of the hands as their hands rest at their sides or on the rostrum. The speaker in such cases feels the need for movement but is inhibited from making meaningful gestures. If involuntary or inhibited gesturing is your problem, give some conscious attention to bringing your gestures up and making them deliberate, complete, and forceful.

Gestures made with the hands and arms are of two kinds: those that are used to point up ideas by giving emphasis to the words that carry the ideas, and those that are used for description. There is no set vocabulary of gestures. You may point up an idea with your finger or pound a word home with your fist. You may spread your hands to show size or extend your arm to show place. You will find that when you are enthusiastic about your own ideas and when you have the will to communicate those ideas, your own personal speaking habits will supply you with a spontaneous and varied group of gestures that belong to you.

Facial expression is as significant in delivery as gestures made with the hands and arms. When you speak, your face gives your listeners very clear cues on your own reactions to what you are saying. Audiences tend to read your face as closely as they listen to your words. Therefore, it is up to you to give them accurate cues. A lively mobility of facial expression is such a natural part of spontaneous oral communication that even though the speaker with the stiff, dead-pan face may be thoroughly engaged in what he is saying, the audience tends to interpret his lack of facial expression as a lack of enthusiasm for his own ideas.

## The Use of Visual Aids

We conclude these chapters on delivery with a brief section on the use of visual aids. These mechanical aids which a speaker brings to the speaking situation are sometimes quite useful in making an idea clear. It is our intention only to mention the various types of aids which are available and to indicate some common-sense rules for using them.

## TYPES OF VISUAL AIDS

Most visual aids can be classified into four categories: (1) diagrams and graphs, (2) maps and globes, (3) pictures, and (4) models and actual objects.

***Diagrams and graphs.*** Diagrams are useful when the speaker wishes to explain some process. When a speaker talks about the basic operation of a spring motor or an internal-combustion engine, a schematic diagram will help him to show the relationships among the various parts and functions of the object under discussion. See Figure XV-1.

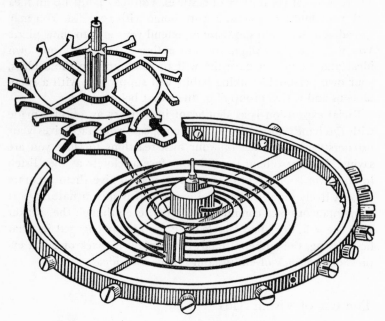

FIGURE XV–1. A SIMPLE DIAGRAM THAT CAN BE ENLARGED
FOR VIEWING BY AN AUDIENCE OR SHOWN BY A PROJECTOR.
*(Hamilton Watch Company)*

Graphs provide a means for showing relationships among statistical data, such as the yearly crime rate, the federal government's tax collections, or the increasing school population. Such graphs are generally of three types. A *line graph* will give the viewer an idea of a general trend over a period of time. A *bar graph* shows comparative quantities clearly where the comparison is among a relatively small number of years, companies, nations, or what have you. It is simple to make. Figure XV-2 shows a bar graph and line graph combined.

A *pie graph* is useful for showing how the parts of a whole are divided. See Figure XV-3.

***Maps and globes.*** Maps will frequently help a speaker to explain geographical relationships. Globes are ordinarily less use-

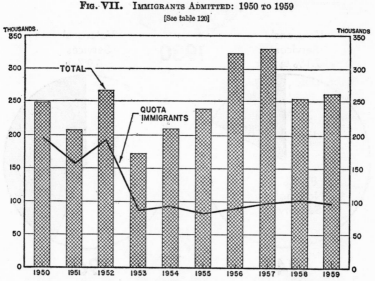

Fɪɢ. VII. Iᴍᴍɪɢʀᴀɴᴛs Aᴅᴍɪᴛᴛᴇᴅ: 1950 ᴛᴏ 1959

[See table 120]

Fɪɢᴜʀᴇ XV–2. A ɢʀᴀᴘʜ ꜰʀᴏᴍ ᴛʜᴇ *Statistical Abstract of the United States.* Iᴛ sʜᴏᴡs ᴛᴡᴏ sᴇᴛs ᴏꜰ ᴅᴀᴛᴀ, ᴏɴᴇ ᴀs ᴀ ʙᴀʀ ɢʀᴀᴘʜ ᴀɴᴅ ᴏɴᴇ ᴀs ᴀ ʟɪɴᴇ ɢʀᴀᴘʜ. Mᴏsᴛ ɢʀᴀᴘʜs ᴘᴜʙʟɪsʜᴇᴅ ɪɴ ʙᴏᴏᴋs, ʀᴇᴘᴏʀᴛs, ᴀɴᴅ ᴍᴀɢᴀᴢɪɴᴇs ʀᴇǫᴜɪʀᴇ ʀᴇᴅᴇsɪɢɴ ᴛᴏ ᴍᴀᴋᴇ ᴛʜᴇᴍ sᴀᴛɪsꜰᴀᴄᴛᴏʀʏ ᴀs ᴠɪsᴜᴀʟ ᴀɪᴅs ꜰᴏʀ sᴘᴇᴀᴋᴇʀs. Tʜɪs ᴏɴᴇ ɪs ʀᴇʟᴀᴛɪᴠᴇʟʏ sɪᴍᴘʟᴇ ᴀɴᴅ ᴄʟᴇᴀʀ. Iᴛ ᴄᴏᴜʟᴅ ʙᴇ ᴇɴʟᴀʀɢᴇᴅ ꜰᴏʀ ᴇᴀsᴇʟ ᴅɪsᴘʟᴀʏ ᴏʀ ᴘʀᴏᴊᴇᴄᴛᴇᴅ ᴏɴ ᴀ sᴄʀᴇᴇɴ.

# FEDERAL GOVERNMENT EXPENDITURES
# FOR NATIONAL SECURITY AND VETERANS' SERVICES
# IN RELATION TO TOTAL EXPENDITURES

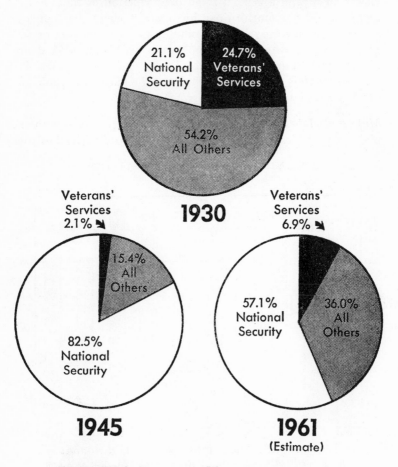

FIGURE XV–3. PIE GRAPHS. WHEN THESE ARE USED FOR WALL DISPLAY OR PROJECTION, THE SECTORS SHOULD BE CLEARLY DISTINGUISHED BY COLOR OR BY STRONGLY CONTRASTING SHADING. THIS GRAPH WAS PREPARED FROM DATA IN A TABLE IN THE *Statistical Abstract of the United States.*

ful to a public speaker than maps because of the distance that is likely to separate the speaker from his audience. If listeners are gathered about a speaker, a globe may be useful; otherwise, a globe is difficult for all to see and for the speaker to use. When a speaker needs to give particular emphasis to the shape of the earth and to the relationships which are brought about because of that shape, a globe becomes a functional visual aid.

*Pictures.* It is not always true that "a picture is worth a thousand words" because a picture has a particular disadvantage which graphs and maps do not have. Whether it is a drawing, a painting, or a photograph, a picture necessarily encompasses a narrower scope of material than a graph or diagram. Furthermore, it does not make comparisons and contrasts immediately comprehensible as do graphs. A picture becomes most useful when it portrays an object that is unfamiliar to an audience.

*Models and actual objects.* When a speaker wishes to explain some object, displaying the object itself or a model of it during the speech will help an audience visualize what the speaker is saying. Like pictures, however, these visual aids often seem more useful than they actually are. The mere presence of an object does not make its explanation more clear. To explain the aerodynamic principle of lift, a diagram of an airplane wing showing lines of air flow is probably more illustrative than a small model of an airplane. If a speaker wanted to explain the functioning of the $f$ stop and the time mechanism on a camera, he could do a better job with a diagram than with the actual camera because the latter is so small that the members of the audience couldn't see it nearly as well.

## PRINCIPLES FOR THE USE OF VISUAL AIDS

A little common sense is about all one really needs to use visual aids properly. Here are some common-sense principles to keep in mind when you design and use visual aids.

1. The visual aid must be large enough to be easily seen by all the members of the audience. If it is too small it is of no help.
2. The speaker should talk to the audience and not to the aid.
3. The speaker's language should be as vividly descriptive as if there were no model, map, or diagram. The visual aid should support the language of the speaker and not be a substitute for language.
4. The speaker should avoid blocking the audience's view of the visual aid.
5. The speaker should be sure that his visual aid has only enough detail to make his point. The visual aid should be as simple as is practical.
6. The visual aid should be at the intellectual level of the audience. Clarifying notations which the audience would already know should be omitted.
7. The relationships among various items on the visual aid should be clearly indicated.
8. The visual aid should be an integral part of the speech. The speaker should avoid using pictures, models, and the like unless they clearly add to his main idea. Remember, an attractive visual aid which is not related to the main purpose of the speech will do as much to draw attention away from the speech as an amusing but unrelated anecdote.
9. In using a blackboard for diagrams to be made during the speech, the speaker must draw well enough to get a favorable response from his diagrams and he must be sure that he doesn't take too much time doing it.
10. When the speaker is finished with his visual aid he should put it out of view of the audience. Otherwise, it will be a continuing distraction.

## SUMMARY

A speaker's physical action is as much a part of the speech as his ideas or his vocal delivery. An audience judges a speaker and his ideas by what it sees almost as much as by what it hears. Consequently, controlled physical action is an important part of effective delivery. Perhaps the most significant visual aspect of communication is eye contact; a speaker should look directly at his audience. He should stand before the audience with a relaxed yet not too casual posture. The movement of the speaker to and from the speaking position helps to manifest his vitality, but he should not pace around the room during his speech. The gestures he uses should be full and complete rather than choppy and underdeveloped, definite rather than vague.

A speaker may also add to his speech effectiveness by visual aids. Most visual aids can be classified as diagrams and graphs (among which are the line, bar, and pie graphs), maps and globes, pictures, and models and actual objects. The rules for using visual aids are largely matters of common sense. Keep these points in mind:

1. Make the aid large enough.
2. Speak to the audience, not to the aid.
3. Continue to use descriptive language; the aid is not a substitute.
4. Avoid blocking the view of the members of the audience.
5. Try to keep the aid as simple as possible but be sure to use enough detail to cover all the points which must be covered.
6. Keep the aid at the intellectual level of the audience.
7. Indicate relationships clearly.
8. Make the aid an integral part of the speech.
9. Take special care with preparation and practice if you plan to use the blackboard for visual aids.
10. When you are finished with the aid, put it out of sight of the audience.

## QUESTIONS

1. Why is eye contact important?
2. How much should a speaker gesture?

3. Explain the nature of the different kinds of diagrams and graphs mentioned in the text.

4. What is the potential disadvantage to using models?

5. The text lists ten principles for the use of visual aids. Which five do you consider most important?


## EXERCISE

1. Prepare a five-minute informative speech in which you use visual aids to clarify the main purpose of the speech. Be sure that the speech you choose needs visual aids and that the aids are essential to the whole speech, not to just a part of it.

# SPEAKING TO ENTERTAIN

# Chapter XVI

## SPEAKING TO ENTERTAIN

Every effective speech, regardless of the ultimate response the speaker wants, must be clear and interesting to his audience. The two-fold requirement of clarity and interest has been recurrently and repeatedly stressed in this book. The present chapter and the three following will show how this requirement may be satisfied in working toward each of the four general ends of speaking. Our specific subject now is speaking to entertain.

On many occasions, a speaker's sole purpose is to interest, divert, or amuse his audience. A fairly obvious example of such an occasion is the after-dinner speech. Someone once introduced an after-dinner speaker by asking the audience to divert its attention from a turkey stuffed with sage in order to hear a sage stuffed with turkey. It would be a brave man who dared approach that audience looking for serious consideration of a weighty topic. But what kind of topics are suitable for you when you want to entertain?

## Topics

In choosing the subject for a speech to entertain, look primarily to personal experience for a topic. Nearly everyone has had adventures, exciting experiences, or just experiences that will make good speech subjects. You may have made trips to interesting parts of the country, or to foreign countries. You may have had interesting jobs, met unusual people, developed unique hobbies, done exciting things. Any of these activities is a potential subject for an interesting and entertaining speech.

To be entertaining, a speech need not be devoid of meaningful ideas. It can have a very real and useful point to it. The speaker who talked about the glories of growing up and described the dubious advantages of maturity—with its responsibilities, debts, taxes, and the like—did have something of a point. But because he had no problem to solve, no proposition to prove, and no lesson to teach, he amused and diverted his audience with an offbeat, deliberately eccentric discussion of the subject. What distinguishes a speech to entertain from one to inform or to persuade is the light touch with which the speaker takes up his subject.

Even if we were to suppose that you had never had any exciting or interesting experiences, you would still not lack an abundance of suitable topics. Being able to entertain others lies not so much in the excitement or amusement inherent in what you have to say as in the exciting or amusing way you look at things and make others see them. If you have never traveled, here or abroad, or fought a war, or had a hobby, you can still find entertaining subjects provided you have a sense of humor. Of course, if you have done nothing, seen nothing, felt nothing, never have been amused or excited, and have no sense of humor, we must admit you face something of a problem. But certainly you don't consider yourself an amoeba. As long as you are alive, you are in a world filled with situations and people—and these are the basis of entertainment. They are the subjects of speeches to entertain.

## Organization

A speech to entertain is not merely a collection of funny stories. It is a speech and, as such, must have at least a semblance of order. The speaker devises a central idea and then proceeds to "develop" it. Some of the audience's pleasure may come from the insane way the idea is developed, but the speaker must give the appearance of starting from a logical base. Digressions need only seem to be appropriate in order to be perfectly acceptable.

But the speaker should be aware of his diversions. Then he can use them as a source of humor.

A lawyer gave a speech that offers a good example of this point. He talked about the problems of forming the then new American Football League. His starting point was that the initials of the group, AFL, had led to all kinds of confusions—including labor problems. He moved next to the fact that forming the League required the work of many lawyers. Having thus mentioned lawyers, he digressed purposely into a discussion of the evils of having too many lawyers around. As he neared the end, he paused, looked at his audience and said, "I seem to be talking too much about lawyers. I wonder why that is." His audience, knowing that he was a lawyer, laughed with him as he moved into the conclusion of his speech.

Good transitions are a useful device for imposing a sense of order on a speech to entertain. The temptation to say, "That reminds me of a story," is a strong one. Resist it. Look instead for transitions which move the speech from point to point, not from joke to joke. The stories and quips then fall into place with the force of properly used supporting material. If your transitions emphasize the gist and not the jests, the audience will see in your speech a plausible (though perhaps zany) coherence.


## Humor

There has been strong implication in what we have said so far that much of a speaker's success in entertaining speeches springs from his ability to use humor well. It does, indeed. Therefore, we must say something about the use of humor.

Humor is as universal as language. It is found in the gentle teasing of a friend; in subtle quips understandable only to a few; in bitter satire that strikes at folly and vice. The things that cause amusement range widely from the most highly intellectual delicacies of wit to the broadest sort of slapstick, custard-pie comedy. In life's most serious moments, laughter intrudes to break tension. The grim jests of war are clear proof that individuals need release and frequently seek it in humor.

Just what it is that makes humor has often occupied the thoughts of psychologists, rhetoricians, philosophers, and philosophical comedians. Quintilian, who taught speech at Rome in the first century of the Christian era, said,*

I do not think that anybody can give an adequate explanation, though many have attempted to do so, of the cause of laughter, which is excited not merely by words or deeds, but sometimes by touch.

And further:

There are no specific exercises for humor nor professors to teach it.

But if there are no professors of humor, there are students of humor, or at least students. And professors can offer an introductory discussion and suggestions that may move the students to reflection about humor and to further study.

## SOURCES OF HUMOR

Whatever other points may be at issue about the nature of humor, one must agree that it is exclusively a human characteristic. Only men among all living creatures laugh. Human beings have even been defined as "animals that laugh." Upon no more than casual examination, it becomes evident that what seems to be laughter in animals is only a caricature of human amusement. Probably the simplest explanation for man's sole proprietorship over laughter lies in the fact that it requires intelligence somewhat above that of a chimpanzee, a horse, or a dog to understand the things that cause amusement.

It has also been said that the comical does not exist outside of what is strictly human.† To borrow examples from Bergson, landscapes may be dull, or beautiful; they are never laughable.

---

* *Institutio Oratoriae,* VI, 3. Translated by H. Rackham. Loeb Classical Library.

† For a more thorough discussion of ideas merely sketched in this paragraph and the next, see Henri Bergson, *Laughter* (New York: The Macmillan Company, 1911).

Human beings laugh at animals only when the latter exhibit some human characteristic, attitude, or expression. A hat is "funny" not of itself but because of the human whimsy that gave it a shape out of the ordinary.

Bergson's observations lead him to two other conclusions which are of interest here. First, emotions tend to silence laughter. Disinterestedness, emotional detachment, seems to be a necessary condition for amusement. The comical appeals only to intelligence. Bergson points out, secondly, that laughter needs an echo. It is social; it occurs in a *group*. Regardless of how large it may grow, the circle of those who laugh is a closed one. Those not privy to a joke feel no desire to laugh.

There seem to be many different kinds of laughter, only one of which is the sort that arises out of amusement. J. C. Gregory has attempted to show that laughter of all kinds springs from one form or another of relief.* Among these is the laughter caused by tickling, said to be relief springing from the recognition that an attack on the sensitive areas of throat or ribs is not made by fangs but by friendly fingers. Again, there is the laugh of greeting, which arises from relief felt when a potential enemy is seen to be a friend. Laughs of contempt, superiority, and self-congratulation may arise out of relief one feels at victory and an end to danger, or at escaping the misfortunes that befall another. Gregory rather pointedly denies Bergson's contention that emotion is absent from the reaction to what is comical. It need not be of great concern which of the two theories is correct. If emotion accompanies laughter, it is human emotion and it is clear that intelligence is needed to appreciate humor.

Despite the modesty with which students of humor approach an attempt to isolate the sources of humor and its constituents, there is some agreement as to what these are. Whether other elements may be present in comic situations, in amusing language, or in droll characters, *incongruity* and *surprise* seem to be sufficient to cause laughter. The humor springs from recognition of the incongruity or from the failure of an expected outcome to be realized.

* J. C. Gregory, *The Nature of Laughter* (New York: Harcourt, Brace & Co., Inc., 1924).

It is not always possible to judge what will cause amusement in an individual. The great German philosopher Schopenhauer is said to have chuckled when he saw a tangent to a circle. The straight line of the tangent led him to expect it to meet another straight line at an angle but the curving circumference of the circle failed to follow through. To Schopenhauer, this unexpected geometry seemed ludicrous. Who could anticipate this reaction?

A speaker faces a somewhat analogous situation. The specific instances of circumstance or language that will amuse an audience are not always anticipated by the speaker. A young lady launching a vigorous attack on the foreign-aid policy of the United States offered evidence of its wastefulness by citing the amount of money spent in India to build grain elevators that are "better than our own." "But," she said, "they are empty." When her audience laughed, a look of surprise crossed her face. She seemed a little vexed to find such levity in the audience. She was talking about *quite* serious matters. Recovering her poise, she went on to show that money had also been spent "to build elaborate cotton mills in Korea. But cotton doesn't grow there." When the audience laughed again, she was quite disconcerted. She looked out over the group with a puzzled frown, and then as she realized the incongruity in the conditions she described, her expression gave her listeners still another moment of unintended delight. Had she seen the incongruity in the situation sooner, she could have used it to advantage.

## FORMS OF HUMOR

The list of things that bring laughter is long and varied. We will mention here six types of humor that seem especially useful in speaking to entertain.

**Overstatement.**    Stories about the New Jersey mosquito are as numerous as the little monsters which inspire them. But no New Jersey mosquito can compete with the variety that inhabit Minnesota.

A party of campers were sleeping in the Minnesota woods. One of the group, Harold Erickson, heard a commotion near him as he dozed in his sleeping bag. Then he realized that someone or something was pulling one of his companions, sleeping bag and all, off into the brush. Erickson crawled after the retreating sleeping bag some hundred yards. He reached a rise and looked down into a gully to see two mosquitoes standing over his friend.

"Let's drag him back a little further," said one.

"No," said the other, "let's eat him here before the big ones come and take him away from us."

It is well to understand that humor is not always pleasant or funny. Recognizing incongruity or being surprised by an unexpected outcome can cause laughter under grim conditions as the following example of overstatement shows.

A young man driving a car around Rim of the World Highway near Crestline, California, drove off the road and down the side of the mountain. When the accident was discovered, a police car and an ambulance were dispatched to the area. While the ambulance attendants were giving what comfort they could to the battered young man, a zealous policeman badgered the poor fellow with questions. The officer seemed to be particularly concerned about speed and kept forcing the question, "How fast were you driving when you went over the cliff?" Finally the injured man looked up at the policeman and said, "Three hundred and seventy-five miles an hour."

*Understatement.*    If one may believe them, the stories that are told about President Calvin Coolidge make him the champion understater of all time. "Silent Cal" wasn't much of a talker anyway and what little he had to say didn't tend toward elaboration.

Mr. Coolidge returned home from church one Sunday morning and was asked by Mrs. Coolidge what the minister had talked about.

"Sin."

"Well, what did he have to say?"

"He's against it."

**Irony:** *Intending a meaning which is the opposite of the literal sense of the words.* According to Abraham Lincoln:

A politician of less than ideal quality so aroused the citizenry of a small midwestern town that they decided to tar and feather him and ride him out of town on a rail. As they put him on the rail, he remarked, "It it weren't for the honor of the thing, I would just as soon walk."

**Unexpected turns.** A Texan and an Ohioan were riding through the Middle West on a train. The Texan spent considerable time telling his fellow passenger about the vastness of the state of Texas. "Why" he said, "do you know that in Texas you can ride all day and all night and all the next day and never leave the state of Texas?"

"I know what you mean," said the Ohioan, "the trains are terribly slow in Ohio, too."

**Play on words.** One evening during a terrible storm on the English countryside, a knight rode up to an inn on a greyhound dog. He inquired of the innkeeper whether he could find a place to sleep. The innkeeper at first told him that there was no more space. It looked as if the knight would have to go back out into the storm. But then the innkeeper noticed that the greyhound was sorely fatigued and in general quite the worse for wear. So he changed his mind, saying, "I wouldn't send a knight out on a dog like this."

"Oh Mr. Gilbert," said a wealthy lady to William Gilbert at a dinner party, "your friend Mr. Sullivan's music is really too delightful. It reminds me so much of dear Baytch [Bach]. Do tell me: What is Baytch doing just now? Is he still composing?"

"Well, no, madam," Gilbert returned, "just now, as a matter of fact, dear Baytch is by way of decomposing.*

**Burlesque:** *Ludicrous treatment of the sensible and sensible treatment of the ludicrous.* Ambrose Bierce† had this way of dealing with Ben Franklin's sayings from *Poor Richard's Almanac.*

* Hesketh Pearson, *Gilbert and Sullivan,* Penguin Books, 1950, p. 93.
† As quoted in R. P. Falk, *The Antic Muse,* Grove Press, 1955, p. 27. This book is worth consulting.

A penny saved is a penny to squander.

A man is known by the company he organizes.

A bad workman quarrels with the man who calls him that.

What is worth doing is worth the trouble of asking somebody to do it.

Think twice before you speak to a friend in need.

## MAKING HUMOR EFFECTIVE

The following suggestions will help you to get the best results from your use of humor in speaking.

*Be objective.*  Overriding all use of humor should be a sense of the speaker's objectivity toward the situations and people he pokes fun at. Listeners must feel that the weaknesses a speaker sees in them and others are the normal weaknesses of human beings. Outlandish techniques may be used to point up these foibles, but listeners can laugh more freely if they are confronted with what is at base a true picture (though drawn in caricature), presented impartially and without prejudice.

*Show kindliness.*  Speakers are constantly tempted in using humor to be sarcastic, to ridicule some person, group, or idea. Sarcasm and ridicule are properly classed as forms of humor and they are effective weapons in the arsenal of a persuasive speaker. But in a speech meant to entertain, they strike a sour note. Barbed attacks may seem to find favor with an audience, but the truth is that though they may please they do so by inviting the audience toward smugness and the speaker toward insolence. The speaker also runs the danger of offending his listeners or of having them realize that they have been cheapened by their part in the act. Pointing out incongruities is not in itself an act of un-kindness. But to do so with bitterness is out of place in a speech to entertain. Raillery and banter lack the bitterness of sarcasm and ridicule. These may be used in a spirit of good will.

*Use good taste.*  Good taste is difficult to define and audiences differ in what they consider to be acceptable. Therefore, arbitrary prescriptions to avoid jokes about nationality, race, religion, and sex do not always hold true. A good rule to follow is that if any bit of humor is at all likely to offend, avoid it. On the public platform, therefore, avoid any humor which even hints at vulgarity or obscenity. The stock in trade of the burlesque-stage comedian has no place in the kind of speaking that is of interest to us here. The world is full of fine humor which can be drawn upon without invading areas which may give offense. The cost of a laugh is too high if the price you pay for it is making yourself offensive.

***Learn to laugh at yourself.***     One way a speaker reveals both objectivity and kindliness in humor is to laugh at himself. Before he can find effective humor in the weaknesses of others he must first sense the foibles in himself.

***Let the humor label itself.***     There is no joke that has to work so hard for a laugh as the one that is introduced with the suggestion that it is intended to be funny. If a speaker lets it appear that he is working at being witty, he will never make it. The humor that is worth using needs no identification by the speaker. Then, too, some audiences are strangely perverse in that if a speaker tells them he has an amusing incident to recount, they either expect too much or set themselves (unconsciously or no) to resist. The most effective humor slides into the mind without announcement or fanfare.

***Stop when you're ahead.***     There are few things for which people develop a taste more easily than applause. And the taste for applause is virtually insatiable. It is difficult to stop when you know you are doing a good job, when an audience is responsive and you feel that you could hold it indefinitely. There is always a tendency to exploit the favorable reaction of the audience just a little more. But just those few extra stories or jokes may be all it takes to push the speech past its peak of effectiveness. From then on, it goes downhill. It is much better to quit while you're winning. Paradoxically, your listeners will be better satisfied if you leave them feeling that they still want more.

# Heightening the Interest

Humor is only one of the sources from which entertainment is derived. Any device a speaker uses to heighten the interest of his audience in what he says can contribute to the success of a speech to entertain. Some of these devices demand brief mention now. Several of them have already been noted either in Chapter IX (Attention and Interest) or in Chapter XII (Language and Style). It is proper that they should have been, for there is no way of separating these methods of heightening the effect of a speech from the principles of attention and interest or from the element of language.

## SUSPENSE

Curiosity, the desire for information, is not the exclusive property of monkeys, cats, and children. Every normally alert person has some degree of inquisitiveness. In human beings, curiosity evidences an eagerness to learn. This fact can be used by a speaker to catch and hold the attention of an audience and to heighten its interest in what he has to say. If listeners want information, they will be interested in the source from which it may come to them: the speaker and his speech. The "information" they want can be about the outcome of some point at issue, the identity of the murderer in a crime story, or the punch line of a joke.

Suspense is created when the speaker withholds from the audience for a time the information required to forecast the final outcome of what he is talking about. As long as he can keep his listeners guessing, he can keep them interested. Suspense is thus a means of heightening their interest.

## CONFLICT

An interest in conflict seems to be natural. The enormous popularity of westerns on television is a case in point. All sports involve competition in one form or another and the essence of competition is conflict, hence the popularity of sports. The more obvious competition is, the greater the interest becomes. Anything

that suggests a fight draws interest whether it is a schoolyard
brawl, a chess game, professional boxing, or athletic teams in
competition. The interest of plays and stories is almost always
in some kind of conflict. A similar interest can be created by a
speaker when the materials he uses suggest conflict or struggle.
A conflict has an outcome; listeners want to know the outcome
of stories and situations a speaker uses. Thus conflict heightens
the audience interest in a speech. Moreover, by timing his
revelation of the outcome to create suspense, the speaker can
heighten the interest still further.

## VIVIDNESS

The more vividly a scene or incident can be visualized, the
more colorful it becomes. Adding concrete details to the telling
of a story heightens interest by making the ideas immediately
clear and easy to grasp. Language that is vague, general, and
abstract makes audiences struggle for the ideas it is supposed to
communicate; and they quickly cease to struggle. Specific language, on the other hand, builds images that make the ideas
sharp and clear.

Dialogue and dialect also lend vividness to the telling of a
story. If, instead of translating what is said, a speaker lets his
characters talk in their own words, they come alive in a way they
otherwise would not. If the characters speak in a regional or
other dialect, the speaker can use it to add another dimension of
reality and vividness to the telling—*provided* his rendition of
the dialect is accurate enough to be believable. Using dialects
well is not a skill that comes naturally; it must be developed
through practice. Moreover, it requires a good ear for the sounds
of language and for the tone and the tempo patterns of speech.
Lacking this, a speaker will do better to ignore a dialect rather
than imitate it poorly.

The use of dialect is also a matter of good taste. It may offend
some listeners.

## NOVELTY AND FAMILIARITY

New ideas lose their strangeness and become welcome when
they are associated with ideas that are familiar. Something one

has never seen or even heard of makes no sense to him until he can join it to something familiar. A distributor for one of the major oil companies, an engineer and a graduate of Princeton University, said that when he first went to a small town in southwest Texas to represent his company, he found it difficult to overcome barriers between himself and the dealers who retail his company's petroleum products. As soon as he learned to talk their kind of language, however, his problem dissipated. At first he had been something wholly novel to their experience; now his language had become a linking familiarity.

Interest in new ideas comes from finding something known in what is unknown. Novelty is effective for heightening interest only when there is a familiar peg to hang it on. Illustrative analogies and apt examples can be used to help listeners see the familiar in novel ideas and situations.

Speakers often have the reverse opportunity: to heighten interest in familiar ideas by giving them a novel treatment. No matter how stale a subject is, a clever treatment and fresh materials can give it a slant that will delight an audience. Here again, as we said earlier, the way a subject is handled is what determines its ability to entertain.

## SUMMARY

Virtually any topic that would be suitable and in good taste in a friendly conversation can be converted into an entertaining speech. The central idea may be organized in either a conventional or unconventional way, but the development of the speech should emphasize the central idea rather than lose it among jokes or stories.

The major emphasis in speeches to entertain is ordinarily put on humor. This is found in the recognition of incongruity or in the surprise that springs from an unexpected outcome. Humor takes several forms, among them, overstatement, understatement, irony (saying one thing but meaning the opposite), unexpected turns, plays on words, and burlesque (giving ludicrous treatment to sensible subjects and sensible treatment to ludicrous subjects).

For greatest effectiveness, a speaker's humor should be objective, without malice, and in good taste. If he learns to laugh at himself and his own shortcomings, the speaker will be better able to enjoy and help audiences enjoy the foibles of others. Humor that is labeled as such will tend to have less effect. The best humor will identify itself without being labeled. Plan the speech to entertain so that it reaches its peak of reaction in the audience very near the end. Letting a humorous speech drag on after this peak has been reached may destroy the whole effect.

Other than humor, there are several devices that one may use to heighten the effectiveness of his speaking. These devices stimulate the interest of an audience: suspense, conflict, concreteness, novelty, and familiarity.

## QUESTIONS

1. What is the purpose of an after-dinner speech?

2. What is the primary source for topics for the speech to entertain?

3. Comment on the notion that the speech to entertain should avoid the discussion of meaningful ideas.

4. What is the function of the transition in a good speech to entertain?

5. Comment on the idea that "the comical does not exist outside of what is strictly human."

6. Do you believe that humor is an intellectual and not an emotional experience?

7. What are two basic constituents of humor?

8. Define the six forms of humor discussed in the text.

9. Why should sarcasm be avoided?

10. Should a speaker let an audience know he intends to be humorous? Explain your answer.

11. Comment on the idea that a speaker should exhaust the humor in a situation before closing his speech.

12. Explain three of the four methods discussed in the text for heightening interest.

## SPEAKING TO INFORM

I. Determining the specific subject of the speech
   A. Limiting the subject
      1. Narrowing the scope to limit a subject
         a. Limit the subject in time
         b. Limit the subject in space
         c. Narrow the subject to a subproblem
         d. Discuss a portion of a process
      2. Treating a series of narrowed aspects of a subject
   B. Formulating a statement of purpose
II. Organizing the body of the speech
   A. Patterns of arrangement
      1. Chronological pattern
      2. Geographical or spatial pattern
      3. Topical pattern
      4. Pattern of definition
      5. Pattern of comparison and contrast
      6. Pattern of cause and effect
   B. Using multiple patterns of arrangement
   C. Number of points in the body of the speech
III. Adding supporting detail
IV. Preparing the conclusion
V. Preparing the introduction
   A. Gaining attention
   B. The subject sentence
   C. Background material
VI. Practicing the delivery
VII. Summary, questions, and exercises

*Chapter* **XVII**

## SPEAKING TO INFORM

Of all the talking that goes on in the world, an enormous part of it is done to accomplish such ends as clarifying ideas, transmitting facts, or giving instructions. At home, at school, and at work, as well as on the public platform, much communication has as its purpose giving information to others. If information is to be given with clarity and received with accuracy, it should be carefully prepared and presented.

Preparing an informative speech involves six steps. When these are properly taken, a speaker may be reasonably sure his communication will be effective. In the order they are carried out, these steps are:

1. Determine the specific subject of the speech.
2. Organize the body of the speech.
3. Add supporting materials.
4. Prepare the conclusion.
5. Prepare the introduction.
6. Practice the delivery.

## Determining the Specific Subject of the Speech

Before he can make an outline, and even before he can begin to gather materials, a speaker must do two things: first, he must determine the scope or breadth of his subject and, second, he must formulate a precise statement of what his specific subject will be.

## LIMITING THE SUBJECT

*Narrowing the scope to limit a subject.*    More often than not, determining the scope of a speech means limiting or narrowing the subject so that the speaker can develop his ideas in sufficient detail within the time limit of his speech. There are several means of narrowing a topic:

1. Limit the subject in *time*. Such a general subject as "American Presidential elections" might be restricted to a discussion of "The disputed election of 1876," or "The war-time elections of 1864 and 1944."

2. Limit the subject in *space*. A speech on American foreign trade could be narrowed to a consideration of trade with a selected country or to the most significant foreign products which enter through the Port of New York.

3. Narrow the subject by selecting as the specific topic of the speech a *subproblem* of some larger question or controversy. Instead of discussing the general question of labor-management relations, for example, isolate the subproblem of labor difficulty on the Los Angeles or New York waterfront and deal only with this.

4. Discuss a *portion of a process*. The unloading of a cargo ship on the New York waterfront is a topic restricted in scope to give the speaker ample time for detailed development of the subject.

Overambitious students frequently complain that an adequately limited subject isn't broad enough, that nothing can be said about topics that are so narrow. Industrious and imaginative research, however, will discover a variety of instructive ideas in the most narrowly restricted subject. The speaker who begins by thinking a subject is too narrow appears on the day he is to speak with the concern that he has too much material.

The kind of limitation you give to a subject must be decided in terms of the subject itself; choose the narrowing principle that will best clarify the ideas. While you might use no more than one of these methods in limiting many subjects, in restricting others you will want to use more than one. It is not necessary to narrow a subject by all of these methods, but let's see what might be done with a single topic, using all four methods of limitation.

*General Subject:* "Combat Landings"
*Narrowed in time:* "Combat Landings in the Korean War"
*Narrowed in space:* "The Landing at Inchon in the Korean War"
*Narrowed to a subproblem:* "The Parts Played by the Three Services in the Combat Landing at Inchon in the Korean War"
*Narrowed to a portion of the process:* "The Preparations Made by the Three Services for the Inchon Landing."

Because every speech must ultimately come to an end, even if the only limitation is the physical endurance of the speaker, we have stressed the desirability of narrowing the subject so that the ideas may be developed in whatever detail is warranted.

But a naval officer, assigned to brief a group of civilian government officials on combat landings, obviously could not restrict the scope of his talk by any of the four methods suggested. Sometimes, then, an audience or occasion can prevent a speaker from narrowing his subject in this conventional manner. Nevertheless, the same demands for clear exposition must be met in these circumstances as in those that permit subjects narrower in scope.

***Treating a series of narrowed aspects of a subject.*** When a speaker must cover a broad subject, he can do it successfully by putting together a series of treatments of *narrow aspects* of the broader subject. An example will help to clarify the distinction between the two methods of limitation. A student wanted to select a speech topic from the general subject the Catholic Church. Using conventional methods of narrowing the scope of his subject, he might have arrived at this topic: "The rites of ordination to the priesthood of the Catholic Church." Instead, this speaker chose to present the Church in a much broader aspect. In his speech he maintained the over-all broadness of view of the general subject, but selected three specific points which he felt would not only increase his audience's knowledge of the

Church but would also be of interest to a group of non-Catholic
listeners: the Mass as the central act of worship, the practice of
confession, and the doctrine of papal infallibility. His speech
was interesting and clear, and the three points had adequate
attention.

## FORMULATING A STATEMENT OF PURPOSE

The general end of an informative speech is, as was said in
Chapter III, to bring about understanding of something. Before
you can begin to organize the speech, however, and even before
you begin to gather materials, you must make for yourself a
clear statement of precisely what this something is. The most
common procedure for making such a statement is to formulate
an infinitive phrase which says clearly what response you want
from your audience. Such a phrase simultaneously identifies the
general end of the speech, specifies the subject of the speech, and
sets its precise scope. The resulting expression of what you intend to accomplish in your speech is called a statement of specific
purpose or, more simply, a statement of purpose. It identifies for
you exactly what idea you want to clarify for your audience.
Going back for a moment to the subject of combat landings as it
was limited in the example on page 327, here is the statement
of purpose for a speech on that topic:

> To inform the audience of the actions taken by the
> air, sea, and ground forces of the United States in
> preparation for the Inchon Landing in the Korean
> War.

The statement of purpose should be put in writing so that
you can refer to it as a guide for your speech. It will serve as a
test to help you decide what material belongs in the speech and
what does not. Every speaker can find many interesting ideas and
tempting pieces of material to put into a speech. His great
problem is one of selection: admitting those items which are
essential to the specific purpose and rejecting those which are
not. Sometimes even the most interesting material must be
omitted, if the essential unity of the speech is to be preserved. A

carefully drawn statement of purpose is essential to guide selection.

Recently, a student gave a speech with the specific purpose of informing his audience about the basic teachings of Siddhartha Gautama, founder of the religion now known as Buddhism. The speech was developed through four main points: (1) Hindu influence; (2) the "Four Noble Truths" that explain the cause and cure of human suffering; (3) the "Noble Eight-Fold Path" by which the cure of human suffering can be established; (4) the concept of Nirvana. Unfortunately, in the course of the speech the speaker allowed himself to drift into a lengthy discussion of Gautama Buddha's life. Now, there is without doubt a close connection between the life history of a man and the religious-philosophical system he establishes. Nonetheless, in this instance it was apparent that the speaker included this material because it was *interesting* and not because it was *necessary* to accomplish the specific purpose of the speech.

To be useful, speech materials must be more than interesting; they must be directly related to the central idea of the speech as expressed in the statement of purpose and they must serve to make the idea clear. Once it is formed, the statement of purpose should be used as a rigorous standard by which to eliminate unneeded materials. In the case just cited, the statement of purpose was not so used.

## Organizing the Body of the Speech

From the days of the earliest writers on public speaking, order has been recognized as an essential ingredient in good communication. If a speech is to make the impression the speaker desires, its parts must be so related that the speech as a whole is easy to understand and easy to remember. A well-ordered speech has three basic divisions: introduction, body, and conclusion. These have been referred to in earlier chapters. All the essential material implied in the statement of purpose is contained in the body of the speech. The introduction and the conclusion help to make the body effective. Since the body is the essential part of a speech, it is organized first.

## PATTERNS OF ARRANGEMENT

In deciding what will be the main points in the body of your speech, look for the organizational pattern which will best help your audience understand and remember what you say. There are several methods of arranging an informative speech to achieve clarity and retention. We will comment on the chronological pattern, the geographical or spatial pattern, the topical pattern, the pattern of definition, the pattern of comparison and contrast, and the pattern of cause and effect. Select for your speech the pattern which best fits your subject.

***Chronological pattern.*** Many subjects will yield easily to a historical or chronological sequence of presentation. In the following example, the basic steps in the development of the table of atomic weights are clarified by using a chronological partition as the means of ordering the main ideas.

> *Statement of purpose:* TO INFORM THE AUDIENCE ABOUT THE BASIC STEPS IN THE DEVELOPMENT OF THE PERIODIC TABLE.
> I. Scientists observed certain similarities in the behavior of groups of elements.
> II. Mendelyeev found that the elements could be arranged in an order of increasing atomic weight to bring the elements of these groups into columns.
> III. Ramsey completed the organization by assigning atomic numbers.
> IV. Later atomic chemists related the atomic numbers to the distribution of electrons in the shells of the various atoms.

***Geographical or spatial pattern.*** Another common pattern of arrangement is by location. Such an order provides the opportunity to develop a subject in terms of the relation of one point to another in space. In explaining what functions are carried on in the administration building of your college, you may find it convenient to move in order from one floor to another. Let us suppose that you are to tell a group of freshmen about the offices in the administration building.

> *Statement of purpose:* To INFORM THE AUDIENCE ABOUT THE OFFICES WHICH CAN BE OF SERVICE TO NEW STUDENTS.
> I. The first floor
>   A. Business Office makes loans to students.
>   B. Registrar's Office handles all student records.
> II. The second floor
>   A. Dean of Men gives personal and academic advice to men students.
>   B. Dean of Women does the same for women students.
> III. The third floor
>   A. Student Body offices regulate extracurricular activities.
>   B. Religious Counselor's office assists with spiritual problems.

Obviously, if all the offices were on one floor, you might still show the spatial relationship of one office to another as you move down the hall. You would use this order if you wished to impress upon your audience the places where things are to be found.

***Topical pattern.*** Any method of partitioning which divides a subject into its component parts can be called a topical pattern. In this sense, both the chronological and the geographical patterns or organizations are forms of topical arrangement. The latter is considered as a separate method of organization to accommodate natural or traditional classifications that are neither chronological nor geographical. Many such classifications are familiar to you: animal, vegetable, and mineral; political, social, and economic; strings, percussion, woodwinds, and brass. Any subject which can be analyzed into component parts can be organized by the method of topical arrangement. Let's look again at the Inchon landing and see what might be done here.

*Statement of purpose:* TO INFORM THE AUDIENCE OF
   THE PART PLAYED BY EACH OF THE THREE SERV-
   ICES TO MAKE THE INCHON LANDING A SUCCESS.
   I. The Air Force of the United States softened up
      the area and protected the troops.
  II. The Navy guarded the troopships and softened
      up the beach.
 III. The ground forces went ashore to take and hold
      the city.

**Pattern of definition.**     A fourth method of division is definition. Speeches intended to answer such questions as "What is
radioactivity?" or "What is a depression?" or "What is a Socialist?" can often be made meaningful by using both logical and
rhetorical methods of definition. These are discussed in Chapter
VI. In the following example, the first main point develops a
logical definition of jazz; the next two points use forms of
rhetorical definition: point II is definition by contrast, and point
III is definition by example (see page 82).

*Statement of purpose:* TO INFORM THE AUDIENCE OF
   THE ESSENTIAL NATURE OF JAZZ.
   I. Jazz is a form of popular music indigenous to
      the United States.
      A. Jazz originated in New Orleans.
      B. Jazz began just after World War I.
  II. Jazz differs from other popular music.
      A. It differs from Spirituals.
      B. It differs from Western Music.
      C. It differs from Folk Music of the hill country.
 III. Jazz takes several forms.
      A. Dixieland.
      B. Blues.
      C. Progressive jazz.

**Pattern of comparison and contrast.**     Speakers frequently
make use of the similarities and differences between two items
or concepts when an audience is familiar with one of them and
not familiar with the other. Comparison and contrast are not
only rhetorical forms of definition and forms of supporting

material (see Chapter VI), but they can also serve as organizational principles for an informative speech.

> *Statement of purpose:* To INFORM THE AUDIENCE OF
> THE CHARACTERISTICS OF A GOOD TEACHER.
> I. A good salesman must have three kinds of knowledge.
>    A. He must be familiar with his product.
>    B. He must understand the demands and requirements of his customers.
>    C. He must know the principles of persuasion.
> II. A good teacher will have similar kinds of knowledge.
>    A. He will know his subject thoroughly.
>    B. He will understand the needs of his classes.
>    C. He will be skilled in the principles of effective communication.
> III. A good salesman and a good teacher have similar personality traits.
>    A. Enthusiasm.
>    B. Honesty.
>    [And so on]

**Pattern of cause and effect.**      When a speaker wants to explain a topic in terms of what caused an event or when he wants to explain the consequences of some event, he will use a cause-and-effect order. You would employ this pattern to explain either the *causes* for the stock-market crash of 1929 or the *effects* of radioactivity on the human body.

## USING MULTIPLE PATTERNS OF ARRANGEMENT

In organizing an informative speech, you are not only trying to find *some* method of arrangement that will pull the points of the speech together, but you are also trying to find *the* method that best expresses and emphasizes the most natural sequence of ideas.

You need not confine your partitioning of an informative speech to a single method. It is quite possible that your ideas will

become clearer if you combine two (or even more) of the
methods mentioned. In some instances, the nature of the subject
itself demands multiple levels of arrangement. When, for example, you explain the steps in building an automobile on an
assembly line, you will necessarily combine chronological, spatial,
and topical elements in the sequence of ideas. The following
outline includes two methods of arrangement: topical and
chronological.

> *Specific purpose:* To INFORM THE AUDIENCE OF THE
>     PURPOSE OF THE THREE MAJOR HONOR SOCIETIES
>     OPEN TO SPEECH AND DRAMA MAJORS.
>  I. Phi Beta Kappa
>     A. First on campus—1906
>     B. Purpose—to recognize scholarship
>  II. Delta Sigma Rho
>     A. On campus—1916
>     B. Purpose—to recognize forensic ability
>  III. Alpha Theta Phi
>     A. On campus—1934
>     B. Purpose—to recognize dramatic ability

The speaker's objective is to classify the purposes of the honor
societies, but the chronological element in the arrangement of
ideas is valuable in strengthening the unity of the material.

In contrast, notice the lack of order in the following outline:

> *Statement of purpose:* To INFORM THE AUDIENCE OF
>     THE ESSENTIAL NATURE OF ATHEISM.
>  I. Early Greeks
>     A. Two meanings for atheism
>        1. Believing in foreign or strange gods
>        2. Believing that there are no gods
>     B. The original Greek word was "atheos"
>  II. Atheism and Communism
>     A. Associated with international socialist move-
>        ment
>     B. Part of the state philosophy of the Soviet
>        Union
>  III. Atheists and agnostics differ in their beliefs
>     A. Neither is convinced of the existence of God

B. Negative evidence sufficient for atheists
C. Proof one way or other needed for agnostics
IV. Atheism today

Ignoring the lack of coherence in the organization of sub-heads, look at the basic partition of the main points. The first main point appears to promise a chronological development. The second point shifts ground, however, and introduces what must probably be identified as a topical heading of the central idea. The third point introduces yet another pattern in the form of comparison and contrast. The fourth point returns to the original chronological pattern. The result is a mishmash of tangled ideas. Even if the speaker is successful in making clear each main point individually, his listeners will have only a confused notion of what atheism is.

It is clear, then, that imposing multiple patterns of organization on a speech is an advantage only as long as they are compatible and consistent throughout.

## NUMBER OF POINTS IN THE BODY OF THE SPEECH

There is no set rule for determining how many points there should be in the body of a speech, for the main points of a speech are determined by the nature of the subject. A reasonable number of main points would be from two to five. More than this number gives the audience too much to remember. Keep in mind at all times that you are trying to give your audience ideas they can carry away with them. The number of main points in the speech should be controlled to a large extent also by the time you have available for speaking. You should allow at least a minute to develop each of the major headings in the body. Thus, if your speech is to be five minutes long, then, considering the fact that you also need an introduction and a conclusion, four points in the body would be a maximum. Even in a seven-minute speech, three points are not too few. If you have more time, concentrate on extending the development of a few points rather than increase the number.

## Adding Supporting Detail

After you have established the basic partition through which you will develop the central idea of a speech, you are ready to develop these points by adding supporting detail. The partitioning of a speech creates an orderly structure that helps the audience follow the ideas and see the relationships among them; the supporting details are the sparks that strike fire to the cold logic of the outline. (You might review Chapter VI.)

When you choose supporting material for a speech, keep always in mind the fact that the key element in any speaking situation is the audience. Select material with the audience in mind. Use those materials which will best clarify your ideas and best sustain the interest of your audience.

Listeners usually grasp an idea more readily when it is associated with some object, person, or event which they already know or can easily comprehend. The more vividly your examples, statistics, definitions and quotations revitalize experiences which a listener has had, the better are your chances of making your speech interesting and clear to him. For this reason it is a good beginning rule of thumb to use at least one supporting detail for every idea you bring into a speech.

Variety in supporting detail is a further help toward building interest. A speaker who uses statistics exclusively, or only hypothetical examples, or nothing but quotations, may lose the attention of an audience because his materials lack variety. To be sure, having some supporting material, even if it does lack variety, is preferable to having no material at all, but get variety if you can.

## Preparing the Conclusion

When the ideas and materials of the speech have been organized, the conclusion is then prepared. The conclusion of the speech should contain a restatement of the purpose and a recapitulation of the main ideas. In short, it should be a summary of the speech. This much is necessary to assure clarity, but clarity itself is a minimal requirement. You can give the conclusion a personal touch and bring your speech to a graceful close by adding a story, a joke, or a quotation which illustrates the total idea you want the speech to convey.

## Preparing the Introduction

The last step in organizing a speech is developing the introduction. After the central idea has been logically partitioned; after the main points have been developed with clearly organized, interesting, and pertinent supporting materials; and after the conclusion has been planned—then the speaker knows to all intents and purposes what he is going to say. The major part of his preparation has been completed. The introduction of the speech is, in one sense, an added part. It is the part that prepares an audience to listen to the body of the speech. Every introduction, then, must accomplish two ends: it must gain the attention of the audience and it must disclose the subject of the speech. This much, then, must be included in any introduction: material to *gain attention,* and a *subject sentence.*

Over and above these two essential elements, however, some introductions include a third kind of material. These are the additional items of information which may be needed to clarify the subject sentence or to orient the audience before the speaker begins the development of the central idea. Such information is called *background material.*

### GAINING ATTENTION

It is often difficult for a speaker to realize that an audience is not ready to listen to him as soon as he is ready to speak. The speaker must *win* the attention of an audience before he can present his ideas. Talking serves no communicative end if the audience is not listening. Material must be provided in the introduction to catch the attention of the audience and direct its attention to the subject of the speech. Any of several means of gaining attention may be used. Here are a few: startling statistics, a story, an anecdote, a quotation, or a reminder to the audience of what it already knows about the subject of the speech. (See Chapter IX again, if you need to.)

Suppose you were planning to give a description of student government at your college. To show the importance of knowing what the student-body officers do, you might begin by pointing out the amount of money collected by the student body each year, and by showing the way this money is spent. Or you might recall the last campus election, or quote an authoritative statement about the importance of student-body government in college life. All of these ideas, and many others, may come to mind as means of gaining attention.

Despite the value of such devices for winning the ear of a listener, the speaker must avoid misusing them. Nothing must be done to interfere with the primary object of a speech—to communicate an idea. The materials used to catch attention must lead the audience *directly* to the central idea of the speech. Avoid the practice of using any introductory device that gains attention but fails to focus this attention on the subject.

A speech student in a class of businessmen persistently used some startling means of getting attention but consistently he failed to relate it to his subject. He would rise, for instance, go to the rostrum and say, "Bob, I disagree completely with you on that matter. If I've told you once I've told you a thousand times that you just don't know what you're talking about." A pause, and then, "Ladies and gentlemen, how much insurance does an unmarried man need? Here is a question I would like to speak to you about this evening." And so the speech would proceed. Needless to say his audience was bewildered. Bob would sit there waiting (with the rest of the audience) to find out what the speaker's opening remark had meant. They never did find out because it bore no relationship to the subject. It was nothing more than a gimmick to get attention.

A student once came into speech class and sought to catch attention by shooting an arrow over the heads of the students. The missile sent the class diving for the aisles. Another student pointed a gun directly at a girl in the audience and pulled the trigger. The gun had a blank in it but the experience was a great shock to the girl. Another young man caught attention by taking off his pants and ironing them. Many such incidents are fun to recall, but the speeches they introduced are long since forgotten.

## THE SUBJECT SENTENCE

The opening a speaker uses to catch attention brings him directly to a specific statement of his subject. The statement of purpose which the speaker formulates serves admirably to guide him in preparing his speech, but stylistically it leaves much to be desired. It will not be used in the speech in the form it originally takes. Instead, it will be replaced by a *subject sentence.* This, in effect, is the statement of purpose recast into a sentence of the sort the speaker might use in conversation. A speaker might construct this statement of purpose:

> TO INFORM THE AUDIENCE OF THE LEGISLATIVE, EX-
> ECUTIVE, AND JUDICIAL BRANCHES OF STUDENT
> GOVERNMENT AT HOWARD COLLEGE.

In a speech this statement of purpose would become a subject sentence and appear somewhat as follows:

> *Subject sentence:* Every student at Howard College
> should understand the job of the Student Council,
> Student Body President, and the Student Court
> if he is to know how our student government
> works.

## BACKGROUND MATERIAL

When an audience is not familiar with the subject at hand, it may be necessary to do more than state the subject sentence. When you choose a subject which is new to the listeners, you will often need to orient them to it. For example, when the Inchon landing was in the news there was no necessity for background material on a speech about it, but as the Korean war fades in our memories, it becomes more and more necessary to remind listeners of that earlier time. You would need to tell them, for instance, of the stalemated condition which existed in the war at the time this bold move was planned. By doing this, you give your audience a clearer picture of the main idea.

Such background material, however, should be limited to a few sentences and must not become an extended discussion. If you are talking about the basic plays of the T formation to an audience with little knowledge of football, you may need to explain the T formation briefly. If the audience knows so little of the subject that it takes a long time to prepare them for your discussion, it would be better to change your purpose to that of explaining the T formation itself. To spend three minutes of a five-minute speech in giving background is a waste of valuable time. If this much background information is necessary for the audience's understanding, then the speaker should revise his statement of purpose and make the background material the subject of his speech.

## Practicing the Delivery

At all times it is well to remember that a speech until its delivery is a growing thing representing your increasing awareness of the subject and the specific audience to which you speak. For this reason, your speech will continually change during the time you are working on it. You will be shifting points around, replacing one example with a better one, or finding new principles of partition.

Perhaps because so much of our training in school deals with written rhetoric, we sometimes come to think that a speech is something that we write out and read. As a result of this fact, we are tempted to prepare a careful outline and then when it is completed to stop revising it and begin to practice the oral delivery. But a speech is different from an essay. It will be judged by the impact its oral delivery has on the audience. Consequently, it should be tried out *orally,* in parts and in the whole, from the early stages of preparation. When the first rough approximation of your speech has been drawn up, begin to "talk it through." As you hear things in the speech you don't like, change them, replace them, improve them. The outline should be developed in the atmosphere of *oral rhetoric*. With this kind of preparation, a speech will come to be part of you; more and more it will grow into a communication that reflects your ideas, your knowledge, and your individual personality.

## SUMMARY

Of all the talking that goes on in the world each day, a large part is occupied with the transmitting of information. Informative speaking is an important process and therefore skill in this kind of communication is both necessary and desirable. To insure that the information he gives will be interesting and clear, a speaker should take six steps in preparing an informative speech:

1. *Select and narrow the subject, and formulate a statement of purpose.* The subject may be narrowed either as a whole or in its aspects. The more conventional methods are to narrow the subject to a specific segment of time, or of space, or to a sub-problem in a larger controversy, or to a single portion of a process. One or more of these methods of narrowing the subject may be used. A speech topic may also be narrowed by including in the discussion a series of treatments of selected aspects of the whole subject. Narrowing the whole gives a limited view of the subject by developing in detail a very restricted aspect of the subject; narrowing the aspects gives a broader view of the subject without sacrificing specificity and detail.

2. *Choose the basic method of partitioning the subject and determine the main points of the body of the speech.* One or more of several patterns of organization may be used to impose a clear and reasonable sequence on the ideas of the speech, both in the main points and in their subheadings: (a) Chronological arrangement; (b) Geographical arrangement; (c) Topical arrangement; (d) arrangement by Definition; (e) arrangement by Comparison and Contrast, and (f) arrangement by Cause and Effect. The total number of main points will usually be from three to five.

3. *Add the supporting details.* Use a variety of supporting

materials to bring your ideas sharply into focus for your audience.

4. *Prepare the conclusion.* Summarize the main points of the speech, including a restatement of the subject sentence; bring the speech to a graceful close.

5. *Prepare the introduction.* Plan to open the speech in a way that will catch the attention of the audience and, at the same time, lead directly into the subject sentence. When necessary, include background material to orient the audience to the subject of the speech.

6. *Practice the delivery.* Familiarize yourself thoroughly with the ideas and materials of the speech by "talking it through" from the early stages of preparation. With the contents thus firmly in mind, you will be able to deliver the speech with fluency, vigor, and conversational spontaneity.

## QUESTIONS

1. List the six steps in preparing a speech.

2. How may a subject be limited?

3. How can a speaker with limited time handle a broad subject?

4. Explain three of the five patterns of arranging the body of a speech.

5. Explain how a speaker gains attention in the introduction of his speech.

6. Differentiate between a specific purpose and a subject sentence.

7. What care must be taken in using background material in the introduction?

8. Explain how to practice the delivery of a speech.

## EXERCISES

1. Organize and deliver a five- to seven-minute informative speech on a topic selected from the subject matter of a course you are now taking

(other than Speech). Prepare the outline carefully and give your instructor a carbon copy of your speaking outline before you deliver the speech.

2. Select one item from the following list (or one supplied by your instructor) and prepare two statements of purpose for informative speeches on that subject. In the first instance, narrow the scope and limit the subject by using one of the methods explained on pages 326–327. In the second statement of purpose, do the like using another of the methods. Formulate a subject sentence for each statement of purpose.

| | |
|---|---|
| The liberal arts | Southern hospitality |
| Biology | The National Forests |
| The Civil War | College athletics |
| Summer jobs for students | Student government |
| Farming | Boating |

3. Illustrate with a brief outline each of the six methods of partitioning the body of an informative speech (pages 329–335).

4. Select an informative speech by one of your classmates and suggest how you might have tried to gain attention had you delivered his speech. Is your method better than his? Why?

5. With four of your classmates, select a subject for a symposium (each speaker delivers a speech on one specific phase of the general subject). Divide the subject into five subtopics. Let each speaker deliver a five- to seven-minute informative talk on a different one of the subtopics. The symposium topics might be:

(a) The basic beliefs (nature of man, God, and the relationship between the two) of the five largest non-Christian religions of the world.

(b) The main responsibilities of the five major executive officers of our state.

(c) The extent of the five major crimes in our city.

(d) The main ideas about writing of five contemporary novelists.

# SPEAKING TO PERSUADE

I. The nature of persuasion
   A. Persuasion defined
   B. Persuasion uses a variety of proofs
   C. The limitation of objectives
II. Organizing the speech to persuade
   A. Persuasive organization in general
      1. The introduction
      2. The body
      3. The conclusion
   B. Types of persuasive organization
      1. The deductive pattern
      2. The problem-to-solution pattern
      3. The reflective pattern
   C. Determining the best persuasive order
   D. Determining the placement of arguments
III. Summary, questions, and exercises

# Chapter **XVIII**

## SPEAKING TO PERSUADE

### The Nature of Persuasion

The speaker who undertakes to persuade a group of listeners often does so against a public habit of resistance and distrust. If a listener has a conscientiously formed view of what he should do or believe, what the school board or the city council or the state government or the president or the United Nations should do, he may naturally wonder why a speaker should propose a different view or plead for another course of action. What is the speaker's purpose? Is his argument for the alternative a truthful argument? Is he using tricks of rhetoric to deceive his listeners? And so on.

The clear recognition of the difference between honest and dishonest speech is ancient and long familiar. More than two thousand years ago, Plato severely drubbed those self-styled "wise men" who taught their students to use the trickeries and deceits of bad rhetoric. Plato's student, Aristotle, turned his enormous talents to the task of redeeming the art of speech from the scathing criticisms leveled at it by his great master. In his classic study of public address, the *Rhetoric,* Aristotle makes it quite clear that evil men may use speech to attain their selfish ends. One of the benefits of knowing the art of speech, he tells us, is to protect ourselves from the chicanery of others. There is no question, then, that persuasion can be turned to bad ends. But it must be recognized that the evil is in the user, not the tool.

Almost 200 years before Cicero began to produce in the law
courts of Rome the speeches that are today a part of the classical
tradition of Latin literature, Marcus Porcius Cato defined an
orator as "a good man skilled in speaking." Cicero himself accepted Cato's maxim and applied it to his own consideration of
oratory. So, more than a century later, did Quintilian, perhaps
the greatest speech teacher of all time.

As you begin your study of this chapter, keep in mind the pre-
cepts of the classical students of speech. Persuasion is an honorable act if it is practised by an honorable man. The writers of
this book are concerned with developing speakers of that kind.

## PERSUASION DEFINED

To persuade someone means to cause him to believe or act in
a certain way. In persuasion, a speaker presents to his listeners
impelling motivations and convincing arguments which cause
them to do or believe something. The effectiveness of persuasion
depends upon a speaker's ability to demonstrate to his audience
that the mode of conduct, the value judgment, or the factual
condition he proposes is expedient or good or true. In order to
do this, he must offer proofs. The proofs are not rigorous, however, in the mathematical or scientific sense, because proofs in
rhetoric are always to a greater or lesser degree tentative. There
is, in other words, no fund of absolute knowledge on which a
speaker can draw; neither can he develop absolute proof. The
tentative nature of rhetorical proof is discussed in Chapter X
(Argument: Logical Elements) as the concept of probability.

The materials a speaker uses, the examples he chooses, the
definitions he formulates, the comparisons and contrasts he
draws must be within the scope of his listeners' intellectual and
emotional ability to understand. The thesis he defends must
likewise be advocated within the framework of the existing ideas,
emotions, and experiences of his audience.

Here the term "identification" becomes useful. A speaker
identifies his proposal with backgrounds of fact and belief that a
listener already accepts as true, with the result that the listener
accepts the truth of the speaker's proposal as demonstrated.

When a listener accepts a proposal because a speaker has identified it with what the audience already believes, then the listener by the same act rejects the opposing point of view or disassociates himself from it. The point to be made here is that conflict is at the heart of any situation that requires persuasive discourse. The idea of conflict is inherent in the very process of analyzing a proposition to find the issues in it. To resolve these issues and prove the proposition, a speaker uses logical and psychological appeals in such a way as to cause his listeners at one and the same time to identify with the speaker's position on the issues and to reject the opposite point of view.

In summary, then, the speech to persuade can be defined as one in which a speaker selects the logical and psychological appeals through which a listener can identify his own ideas and experiences with the speaker's proposition. Through these appeals, the speaker motivates his listeners to reject all proposals save his and prepares them to act on it.

## PERSUASION USES A VARIETY OF PROOFS

A speaker will use a variety or combination of proofs to bring about persuasion. Logical argument, emotional appeal, and the personal influence of the speaker are combined to influence audience response. Indeed, they are all so closely intermingled in any persuasive speech that only the critic who is consciously looking for them can isolate one from another. In a single statement, the critic will often find evidence of each. Let's look at an example: When Winston Churchill became Prime Minister of England in the dark days of 1940, he assumed the fearful responsibilities of his office with a statement of policy that we know as the "Blood, Sweat and Tears" speech. The conclusion of this famous speech illustrates the intermingling of the different kinds of proof. Churchill says:

You ask, what is our policy? I say it is to wage war by land, sea and air. War with all our might and with all the strength God has given us, and to wage war against a monstrous tyranny never surpassed in the dark and lamentable catalogue of human crime.

That is our policy.

You ask, what is our aim? I can answer in one word. It is victory. Victory at all costs—victory in spite of all terrors—victory, however long and hard the road may be, for without victory there is no survival.

Let that be realized. No survival for the British Empire, no survival for all that the British Empire has stood for, no survival for the urge, the impulse of the ages, that mankind shall move forward toward his goal.

I take up my task in buoyancy and hope. I feel sure that our cause will not be suffered to fail among men.

I feel entitled at this juncture, at this time, to claim the aid of all and to say, "Come then, let us go forward together with our united strength."

Look at the individual paragraphs and sentences. Which parts are logical, which are emotional, and which rely upon the audience's acceptance of the speaker? All parts are a mixture of each of the kinds of proof.

## THE LIMITATION OF OBJECTIVES

The extent to which a speaker can hope for success in applying logical, emotional, and ethical proofs to a proposition must be kept in proper perspective. It is a misconception to think that a speech to persuade may be counted successful only if it causes an audience to change its ways. The dramatic picture of a speaker who meets a hostile audience and during the course of a half-hour address converts it into an audience of excited partisans is hardly accurate. The concept of the spellbinder who can mold audiences to his will on any subject is a myth. The persuasive speakers most celebrated in history have frequently had to be satisfied with the knowledge that they moved the members of the audience only a little way. As a persuasive speaker, your objective is to move listeners in your direction, however short the journey may be, or to stop, if only for a short time, their movement in another direction. There are many instances in which to expect more than this is to open the door to harsh disappointment.

## Organizing the Speech to Persuade

On September 11, 1941, President Franklin D. Roosevelt delivered from the White House a speech which has since been called "The Freedom of the Seas." In this speech, the President announced it to be the policy of the United States government to attack any German or Italian warship which entered what the United States had defined as her defensive waters. Previously, the policy of the United States had been to defend only her own ships from attack, but now she would protect all shipping in her defensive waters by sinking on sight any Axis submarine or surface raider. But notice the order in which the President presented his ideas.

He opened his speech with a detailed discussion of a number of unprovoked attacks on American vessels. He characterized these attacks as "international lawlessness" and as the manifestation of a design on the part of the Axis "to abolish the freedom of the seas and to acquire absolute control and domination of these seas for themselves." Next, he discussed the implications for America of the Axis plan. He pointed out that in time Germany would, through controlling the seas, be able to subjugate the United States. He said that something must be done: "When you see a rattlesnake poised to strike, you do not wait until he has struck before you crush him."

Only after he had elaborated this kind of background, building a strong case against the depredations of the Axis navies, did Roosevelt propose and defend the policy he had formulated. Why did he approach the subject in the way he did? Why did he withhold his statement of the proposition of his speech until so near the end? Why did he not state, bluntly and tersely, the policy of the American government? Because in September of 1941 there was a considerable segment of the American population who felt that if the United States could stay neutral, and would attack Axis ships only when and if they attacked her own, she could avoid becoming entangled in the war and live in peace with whatever victor emerged.

Three months later, the United States was brought into the war by the Japanese attack on Pearl Harbor. After this time, a policy of attacking the ships of the Axis powers could be set forth bluntly. There would be no need to prepare the audience to give favorable hearing to such a policy. But in September, the President had to adopt a speech organization that took into account the desire of his audience to avoid conflict. The organization he chose helped his audience to disassociate from the then current policy of defense and to identify with his newly established policy.

This example not only shows the importance of organization in a speech to persuade, but it also points out that the organization of a given speech will depend upon the temper of a given audience. Let's examine this latter concept in some detail.

## PERSUASIVE ORGANIZATION IN GENERAL

The general structure of the speech to persuade is the same as that for the speech to inform. Each has an introduction, a body, and a conclusion.

***The Introduction.***     A speaker uses an introduction to focus attention on his subject and to arouse the interest of his audience in it. In many instances, a speaker will include in his introduction a subject sentence stating the proposition he wishes to prove. In other instances, the speaker may want to withhold for a time the specific thesis. (Franklin D. Roosevelt's speech on the freedom of the seas is an example). In such cases the speaker substitutes for a clear revelation of his proposition a more general statement to let the audience know what the speech will be about. Let's look at an example of each of these situations. Subject sentence where the specific intent is revealed:

> The members of this union should support Congressman Bellinger because his voting record in the last two sessions of Congress indicates that he has consistently favored the position of the AFL-CIO on the subjects of labor, civil rights, public housing, welfare assistance and public works.

Subject sentence where the specific intent of the speaker is not revealed:

Since the AFL-CIO has clearly indicated its position on labor legislation, civil rights, public housing, welfare assistance and public works, we can tell from Congressman Bellinger's voting record how consistently he has favored the AFL-CIO point of view.

In both of the above examples, the listeners are helped to know what the speech is to be about, but in the second instance they are not immediately told whether Congressman Bellinger's voting record is prolabor or is not.

*The Body.*      In the body of a persuasive speech, arguments are stated and supported. The arguments and their supporting material are selected with an eye to influencing the audience to believe or act in a specified manner. Observe the fundamental difference from the informative speech. The latter appeals only to understanding and retention, and makes no effort to influence attitude or action.

*The Conclusion.*      The conclusion of the speech to persuade is less likely than that of the informative speech to be a strict summary. Since the arguments advanced in the body are designed to build to a single response at the end, the conclusion may contain little in the way of summary detail. It may be an appeal to action. Notice the conclusion to Adlai Stevenson's address at the Mormon Tabernacle in Salt Lake City on October 14, 1952.

Finally, then, let us recall that our basic faith in liberty of conscience has an ancient ancestry. We can trace it back through Christian Europe and through pagan Rome, back to the Old Testament prophets. It is by no means exclusive with us. It is in fact our bond of unity with all free men. But we are its ordained guardians today.

Let us lift up our hearts, therefore—glad of our strength, proud of the task it imposes. So far from being half-defeated, half-divided, half-bankrupt—while we are true to ourselves we can never be divided. And in the name of that burden we shall find the means and the determination to spend in money and in labor and in hard thought whatever is needed to save ourselves and our world.

Stevenson does not summarize his arguments as one would summarize the main points of an informative speech. In this stimu-
lating call for belief (and implied call for action—for their votes)
he does summarize the emotional feeling of the speech and in a
general way reminds his listeners of the main arguments:

1. That the United States has a great burden of leadership to
   bear.
2. That the (Republican) picture of a weak United States is
   inaccurate.
3. That the United States has the ability to carry its burden.

## TYPES OF PERSUASIVE ORGANIZATION

The general similarity of informative and persuasive speaking
in their basic organizational structure does not extend into the
partitioning of the body of the speech. Here, some essential differences may be found. The various structural patterns of the
informative speech (discussed in Chapter XVII) are not well
suited to the requirements of the persuasive situation. In persuasion, a speaker must prove; he must offer arguments and support
these with evidence. The clarity and interest so essential to effective informative discourse must, of course, be retained in the
speech to persuade, but in addition to these qualities, persuasion
is ordered to the further end of influencing belief and action.

The extent to which an audience influences a speaker in the
organization of his speech has been suggested in the preceding
section of this chapter. To accommodate the demands of a specific audience situation, a speaker may choose from a variety of
persuasive patterns. Three of these are of sufficiently general
character and widely enough applicable to warrant specific mention: the deductive pattern, the problem-to-solution pattern, and
the reflective pattern.

Any persuasive speech in support of any proposition may be
organized in any one of these three patterns. A speaker chooses
the one which he thinks will make his arguments most effective
for a specific proposition and with a specific audience. The question of which format to use requires some discussion and the discussion requires that you understand what the three patterns are.

***The deductive pattern.*** A deductive* pattern of organization is one in which the speaker states his proposition in the introduction of his speech and then develops a series of supporting arguments in the body. The main idea is revealed from the very beginning and the logical and emotional motivations are developed and heightened by building up subpoints. The speech concludes with an appeal for acceptance of the proposition stated in the introduction.

Suppose you were to speak in favor of a compulsory student-body fee to support extracurricular activities at your college. You look over your arguments and you find several good reasons for adopting the fee.

1. It will provide more opportunity for participation by all of the students.
2. It will provide a program of higher quality.
3. It will provide finances for some smaller activities which would not exist at all without funds from such a source.
4. It will mean better public relations for the college.

You also note that the one strong argument against this proposal is its unfairness to those who would not participate in student activities.

1. Students who aren't interested in student activities will have to pay for something they don't intend to use.

You recognize your reply to this objection:

1. Even those who do not use the student-body card benefit indirectly through the improved public relations of the school. (Note the relationship of this to Point 4 above.)
2. It is the democratic principle that everyone must share in the expense of maintaining the group when the membership of the group are agreed by majority vote.

* The term "deductive" is not to be identified or confused with that kind of reasoning which is called by the same name.

Here you have it, then: four arguments in favor and one against, with the answer to the opposition argument contained within one of the original arguments in favor, and the opposition argument further countered by an appeal to democratic principle. How might these be presented in the deductive pattern of organization? The following example is given to show the main points. (Obviously, if you were to give the speech, you would need evidence and supporting detail that are not shown here.)

### INTRODUCTION

I. The current student-body election has aroused the interest of us all.

II. I would like to enlist your support in favor of the compulsory student-body fee to support extra-curricular activities.

### BODY

I. It will provide more opportunity than now exists for everyone to participate.

II. It will provide financing for the smaller activities.

III. It will provide a program of higher quality than the present one.

IV. It will mean better public relations for the college, and thus eventually benefit even the students who do not participate in extracurricular activity.

V. The only democratic way to gain these advantages is with a compulsory student-body fee.

### CONCLUSION

I. Because of the opportunity it will provide for everyone, the aid it will bring to the smaller activities, and the better public relations it will bring to the college, all of us should agree to the imposition of this compulsory fee.

II. The way to achieve these advantages is for all of us to vote for the fee at the election so that we can all benefit from it.

*The problem-to-solution pattern.* In using the problem-to-solution order, a speaker, after getting the attention of his audience, presents a problem which needs to be solved. He then recommends a course of action and shows how it will solve the problem. He concludes with an appeal to act on the suggestion. The solution which the speaker wishes to propose is withheld from the audience at the beginning of the speech, at least until the problem has been presented. How long it will be withheld is determined by the situation. Here's how the argument in support of a compulsory student-body fee would look in a problem-to-solution pattern:

INTRODUCTION

I. The current student-body election has aroused the interest of us all.

BODY

I. One of the problems of this college is the lack of financial support for student activities.
   A. Currently the activities program is so limited that few students can participate.
   B. Activity is limited to events like proms and intercollegiate athletics.
   C. Little publicity is given to our school in the local newspapers because we lack a program which will draw the attention of people outside the college.

II. The solution to this problem is in a "yes" vote for compulsory student-body fee.
   A. It will solve the problems I have already discussed.
   B. It will help to put our activities program on a democratic basis with everyone sharing the load equally.

CONCLUSION

I. So support the solution to these problems—vote "yes" next Tuesday.

*The reflective pattern.* A third type of persuasive organization, the reflective pattern, also withholds the presentation of the solution until later in the speech. In using the reflective pattern, a speaker describes a problem situation and suggests several possibilities for solution. Next, he evaluates each of these. Finally, he proposes the one which he presents to his audience as the best. This form is compatible with a thoroughly objective approach to the subject. By the time the speech is prepared, however, the speaker's purpose is quite argumentative. Far from being purely analytical, he knows before he begins to speak exactly what course of action he will advocate. Everything he says is intended to move the audience toward accepting it.

Organized in the reflective pattern, the outline of a speech supporting a compulsory student-body fee would look like this:

INTRODUCTION
I. The current student-body election has aroused the interest of all of us.

BODY
I. One of the problems of this college is the lack of financial support for extracurricular activities.
  A. Currently, the activities program is so limited that few students can participate.
  B. Activity is limited to events like proms and intercollegiate athletics.
  C. Little publicity is given to our school in the local papers because we lack a program which will draw the attention of the people outside the college.
II. The causes for this unsatisfactory condition are two:
  A. Receipts from year to year under the voluntary student-activity fee have been uneven.
  B. The percentage of students who pay the voluntary fee is small.
III. We need some system which will satisfy two requirements.
  A. It should furnish enough money.
  B. It should furnish a consistent amount of money.
IV. The choice is between our present system and the proposed compulsory-fee system which will be on the ballot at the next election.
V. The new compulsory-fee system will best meet our needs and in the most democratic fashion.

CONCLUSION

I. When you go to the polls Tuesday, vote for the compulsory fee.

With this brief explanation as background, let's see how a speaker makes his decision about which type of persuasive organization he should use.

## Determining the Best Persuasive Order

This useful generalization applies to the organization of most persuasive speeches: To the extent that an audience knows in advance what a speaker's proposition is, or is informed on the general subject, or is unlikely to have strongly opposed attitudes regarding the proposition, the speaker may disclose his position toward the beginning of the speech. Suppose, for example, you are speaking to the members of the Westridge Women's Club, and they know that you are a member of the Committee for Proposition Seven on the November ballot. Because the audience already knows you favor Proposition Seven, it would be useless for you to postpone saying so. It would be better for you to acknowledge your stand from the beginning. Otherwise, there is danger that the listeners will be asking themselves throughout the early part of your speech, "Why doesn't he get to the point?" Clearly, your effectiveness would be injured.

Suppose you propose to speak in favor of putting more emphasis on scholarship and less on the so-called "frills" at your college, and that your audience analysis convinces you that the listeners are largely in agreement with your point of view. It is then quite likely that stating your proposition outright from the beginning would be most effective. Since your listeners already agree with you, the purpose of your speech is to strengthen their belief and to encourage them to support more actively its general adoption. Knowing your position will strengthen the audience's acceptance of what you say. The basis for their identification with your proposal has already been established. To demonstrate further the desirability of your proposal, you will take advantage of the identification they have already made with it. Open the speech by making it quite clear that you and they are agreed. Your arguments will develop the listeners' own beliefs in greater detail or give them new arguments to strengthen their conviction. To delay disclosure of your main point in such a situation decreases your effectiveness.

With an opposed or hostile audience, a deductive arrangement is somewhat risky. The listener who hears his firm beliefs controverted early in a speech will give the speaker's proposal a less than friendly ear. Should you speak to such an audience, you will fare better if you build favorable response to minor and less controversial issues early in the speech and thus set up a background of agreement that will help to support your position on the crucial issues.

Remember that frequently a speaker cannot hope to convert a hostile audience. Often he can only expect to temper its opposition. In an extreme case, a strongly hostile audience will not even listen to the speaker's arguments if he presents his proposition early. When the speaker withholds his thesis for a time, his listeners are more likely to listen at least until they find out where he stands. In the meantime, he may bring them to believe that his position does have some sense to it. In this way, the speaker may dampen the hostility of his listeners by moving them to reexamine or question their own convictions.

When listeners have little knowledge of the subject under discussion, the problem-to-solution or the reflective order will frequently be a wise choice, even if the audience is not unfriendly. Defining the problem first helps the speaker to establish the basis of his case and gives his listeners an opportunity to familiarize themselves with the materials under discussion before an attempt is made to crystallize their beliefs.

In general, then, the more the audience knows of the subject and the speaker's position on it the more he should reveal his position early in the speech. The less the audience knows about the subject or the more they would tend to disagree with the speaker's position on it, the more advantageous it becomes to delay stating his proposition and to develop his speech in either the problem-to-solution or the reflective pattern.

# Determining the Placement of Arguments

Once the problem of general arrangement has been resolved, a more specific question arises: "In what order should individual arguments be put?" Some will say that a speaker should save his strongest argument to give his speech a greater impact at the end. Another will claim the contrary, that putting the best argument first gives the speech a strong start. Both of these popular rules seem to ignore the fact that each speaking situation is unique. Each new audience, subject, speaker, or occasion demands that the question of placing arguments be answered anew.

When one argument depends logically on another, the problem is easily solved. The dependent argument must of course follow the argument upon which it depends. Before you can convince an audience, for example, that some federal system of medical care would alleviate the shortage of doctors in rural areas, you would need to show that in fact there is such a shortage.

When there is no direct logical interdependence to determine the sequence of arguments, that is, when each argument of a series can stand alone, an effective order may be determined as follows.

If an audience has little opposition to your point of view, you will probably find it best to put the argument with the greatest appeal to the audience first. Such a practice will produce a positive response at the beginning of the speech and that response will tend to carry over to the less conclusive proofs. If you have more than two arguments and two are especially strong, you can get an initial favorable response and a climactic impact as well by putting strong arguments first and last and sandwiching the weaker ones between.

With a hostile audience, you will want to use the less controversial arguments in the early part of the speech. Speaking to an audience strongly opposed to public housing, you might first show that the government already is engaged in many activities to which your listeners do not object, such as the post office. Then you can argue that it is within the philosophy of our society for the government to become involved in public housing.

Arguments which arouse the greatest disagreement are put last, not to build a crashing response, but to assure your case as fair a hearing as possible.

## SUMMARY

In persuasion a speaker selects arguments and motivations which will cause a listener to identify the speaker's proposal with what the listener already knows and believes. Proof in a persuasive speech is built on logical, emotional, and ethical appeals. These three elements are so thoroughly blended that one can hardly be distinguished from another. Success in persuasion is not always likely to be dramatic. With some audiences, even the most persuasive speaker can win no more than a slight shift toward his position.

Three different types of organization are useful in persuasion: These are the deductive, the problem-to-solution, and the reflective patterns. A speaker determines which of these to use for the over-all structure of his speech on the basis of audience attitude. To the extent that the audience tends to agree with the speaker or to know his position, he will find deductive organization most effective. To the extent that his listeners oppose him or have limited knowledge of the subject, he uses the problem-to-solution or the reflective order.

Three basic ideas about the placement of arguments in a speech have been brought out. When one argument follows logically from another, the more basic argument is presented first. When an audience tends to agree with the speaker, he puts the strongest arguments first. For a hostile audience, he holds the more controversial arguments until last.

## QUESTIONS

1. Is the use of persuasion suspected in our age?
2. Is persuasion an honorable purpose?

**3.** What is persuasion?

**4.** What is meant by "identification"?

**5.** Was Winston Churchill an emotional or a logical speaker?

**6.** Must a specific statement of what the speaker will prove be made in the introduction to every persuasive speech?

**7.** How is the deductive pattern basically different from the problem-to-solution and the reflective patterns?

**8.** What rule of thumb is useful in determining when a speaker should disclose his position?

## EXERCISES

**1.** Organize and deliver a five- to seven-minute persuasive speech. Turn in to your instructor a copy of your outline, a brief analysis of your audience, a brief statement of what motivation you will use and why you will use it, and a brief statement of what organization you will use and why you will use it.

**2.** Listen to some persuasive speeches in class. What persuasive order did the speakers use? Could you improve the speeches by changing the order?

**3.** Write a brief statement indicating what you believe to be the relationship between persuasion and honesty. Is a speaker dishonest if he "selects the logical and psychological appeals with which the listener can identify his previous ideas and experience"? What if the speaker doesn't agree with the listener's ideas?

**4.** Write a brief analysis of one of your classmates' speeches, evaluating the method of organization and the use of motive appeal in relation to the classroom audience to which the speech is delivered.

**5.** Formulate a proposition of policy from one of the general topics listed at the end of Chapter III. Sketch the outline of a persuasive speech on this proposition showing each of the three methods of persuasive organization.

# SPEAKING TO EXPLORE

*Chapter* **XIX**

## SPEAKING TO EXPLORE

One of the basic characteristics of democracy is that it conducts its business through a free and open discussion of ideas, in speech and in print. Thomas Babington Macaulay called this kind of government "government through speaking." And whether it operates through the instrumentality of a Parliament as does Macaulay's England, or through a Congress, a state legislature, a county board of supervisors, a city council, or a town meeting—whatever the instrumentality, a democratic government, indeed any democratic society, is carried on by discussion.

The need for some systematic verbal exploration of ideas is clear. There are many items of business to get done and many decisions to be made at every level of social interaction. The family has to decide how to spend its vacation, and how to finance the education of the children. The community must determine the best method of getting street lights and of eliminating juvenile crime. The nation must choose the best man for its president. The United Nations must articulate a policy for preventing or punishing aggression in specific parts of the world.

Experience shows, however, that no two persons will necessarily agree completely on the specific action that will best deal with a given problem. Conflicts of opinion are inevitable. Such conflicts are not in themselves undesirable. It is the concentration-camp, thought-police method of resolving the conflicts which is wholly bad. What intelligent man is willing to exist in an atmosphere wherein decisions are made by fiat and by force, unless perhaps he is the one who makes the decisions? There is

little doubt that establishing policy with talk is better than establishing it with guns.

This chapter is addressed to one of the methods for establishing policy with talk, namely, group discussion. The speaker in
group discussion has occasion to employ all that he may have
learned about speaking to inform, to persuade, even to entertain.
In a group discussion he will rarely make a specifically prepared
speech; he will make himself generally prepared to speak and
will make several speeches when specific occasion calls for them.
He will need to form them without rehearsal but with proper
attention to purpose, audience, subject, issues, attention, interest,
argument both logical and psychological, language, style, and
delivery: the entire range of the chapter headings in this book.
He will make these speeches within a pattern of reflective thinking and a systematic procedure applied to a group rather than
an individual. The activity of the speaker in an exploratory
group discussion is guided and formed by this procedure and
this pattern of thinking. They are the context of speaking to explore, and they impose on the speaker the qualities his speaking
must have. This chapter therefore concentrates on what this context is rather than on the details of what the speaker does in the
context.

## Exploring Problems through Group Discussion

Inherent in the idea of free, open consideration of conflicting
opinions is the concept of group participation. Co-operative exploration of subjects is often more fruitful of good than an examination of the same subject by a lone individual. In seeking
the answers to problems of fact, value, and policy, two (or more)
heads are better than one. Such explorations are called "group
discussion."

Group discussion can and should and does occur when problems of policy must be solved and when problems of fact and
value are examined. When two roommates in college consider
mutual vacation possibilities, they are engaged in group discus-

sion. The familiar college "bull session" on matters of religion, politics, and sex is a group discussion. Such discussions often jump from one subject to another without a predetermined pattern and without particular connection, but they are group discussions nonetheless. Group discussion may be found, then, whenever two or more people meet and explore a problem. Not all group discussions, of course, are as vagrant and as formless as the preceding instances are likely to be. Legislative committee hearings and business conferences, for example, are conducted in a much more formal manner.

A group enters into the exploration of a subject to achieve one or the other of two primary ends: (1) to formulate a course of action or establish a policy; or (2) to increase in the group (or in an audience) its knowledge of the subject under discussion.

You have heard of such *learning groups* as the University of Chicago Round Table, whose purpose is to provide information on a variety of subjects. Perhaps in some of your classes in social science or literature you will participate in group discussions that have the purpose of increasing your knowledge without attempting to solve any problem of policy.

Not only may discussion be turned to ends other than the formulation of policy, but policy discussions themselves may be a useful and fruitful experience even when they explore problems that do not directly affect the group. The decisions of a group, in other words, need not lead to immediate, observable action. Whether overt physical action is called for as a result of a discussion depends upon the power of the group to act. For example, the Executive Council of the Student Body at North Atlantic University decides that the student body will honor the graduating seniors by hosting them at a breakfast in the Student Union. The Council has the authority to act for the student body at large and is also empowered to disburse student-body funds. This decision can lead to specific, observable action.

These same students may be taking a course in Sociology. Their class asks itself how to improve race relations in the city of Parkland. It is doubtful that any conclusion they come to will have an immediate bearing on policy in that city. Nevertheless, the discussion is valuable. A problem has been posed and a reasonable solution has perhaps been proposed. The knowledge and understanding of the students have been increased. Thus, immediate, direct action is not required to make a group discussion successful.

The subjects of group discussions grow out of the personal, political, religious, and social problems that touch the lives of nearly everyone. They are problems of policy, fact, and value like those described in Chapter III (Selecting a Subject).

The principal concern of this chapter will be with exploratory speaking in its policy-forming role. It is more than likely that the great majority of discussions which engage you in the future will be aimed at the solution of some problem of policy. This emphasis does not mean that the informative aspects of group discussion are being ignored, or that in your class discussions you should not explore questions of fact and value. On the contrary, all three kinds of questions are valuable and interesting subjects for discussion. Keep in mind, however, that in order to resolve a problem of policy satisfactorily, it is necessary also to solve inherent subproblems of fact and value. Thus skill in solving all three kinds of problems is necessary for successful policy discussion.

## Reflective Thinking in Analyzing Problems

Various ways are used to analyze problems. Not all ways are desirable. Some involve a rough associational method of thinking, like that of students you may know: they choose to attend one college rather than another because it has a good football team, or because they know someone who goes there. They select their school without investigating such basic aspects of college quality as finances, curriculum, or the philosophy of the institution. National leaders, too, use associational reasoning when they approve an action (or reject it) without respect to its own merits as fulfilling the needs of their nation but rather because some other nation which they like or dislike is for or against it. Frequently, moreover, choices are justified by providing what sound like good reasons after the choice has been made. This latter kind of thinking, called rationalization, is another common flaw in policy making.

The better way to approach a problem of policy is a method called "reflective thinking." In reflective thinking, an individual or a group develops a clear understanding of a problem and analyzes it thoroughly to find the best solution. On occasion, however, a group may not be able to find a course of action agreeable to all its members. In such a case, they can at least develop a common understanding of the issues involved. The function of group discussion, then, is to find a solution to a problem through co-operative application of the principles of reflective thinking and, failing that, to discover, through the same procedure, the real issues of disagreement.

## The Pattern of Reflective Thinking

Reflective thinking as a pattern of systematic thought was described a half century ago by John Dewey. He enumerated a series of five steps in the process:

1. *A felt difficulty.* When we become aware of a set of conditions that disturbs us and sets us to wondering about how to improve the situation, reflective thinking can begin.
2. *Location and definition of the difficulty.* The next step in finding a solution to any problem of policy is to raise our awareness of the problem from the level of feeling to that of thinking. We become as fully informed about the problem as we can.
3. *Suggestion of possible solutions.* In the third step, we set up a series of possibilities for solution. These are proposals which, if put into operation, might solve the problems.
4. *Development by reasoning of the merits of the solutions.* Each of the possible solutions that suggests itself is tested and evaluated in order to determine which is probably the best. On the basis of the evaluation, a tentative choice is made.
5. *Further observation and experiment leading to acceptance or rejection of the selected solution.* No amount of reflective thought will bring a problem to an end. Only putting a policy

into action can really solve the felt difficulty. This is the final
test of whether the conclusion arrived at through reflective
thinking is a good one.

The pattern of reflective thinking outlined in the following
pages is only slightly modified from Dewey's original description
of how people think about problems. We will consider the group-
discussion process as developing through the following five steps:
(1) location and definition of the problem, (2) analysis of the
problem, (3) establishing goals, (4) determining the best solution,
and (5) putting the solution into operation.

## LOCATING AND DEFINING THE PROBLEM

Two difficulties are present in any problem situation that a
group can explore; these make it imperative to locate and define
the problem before useful discussion can begin. They reside in
the emotion-generating nature of the felt difficulty and in the
uncertainties and varied meanings of language.

"Thinking" is much of the time more emotional than rational.
Conduct is largely determined by emotional responses—people
do things because they *want* to; they make decisions and choices
on the basis of their *needs* and *desires*. This condition is wholly
normal. The purpose in group discussion is not to eliminate the
needs and desires on which decisions are based but to subject
them to a close rational investigation. Group discussion, carried
on by thoroughly informed people, with close rational scrutiny
of the "facts" and alleged "values" of proposed policies, is a protection against at least the grosser follies.

"Feeling" a difficulty, in most instances, means becoming irritated by something in the environment. The very irritation
obstructs rational thinking and thus may hinder the finding of a
sound solution unless the irritant is first located and defined.

Imagine a suburban bus station where wives in family cars
meet husbands as they return from the city. The streets are always congested; in time, the congestion develops into traffic jams.
Then, some rainy night, the buses can't even reach the station
through the jam of parked and waiting cars. The commuters in

the bus feel the difficulty; so do their wives, around the station or kept from getting near it by the traffic jam.

In what different ways may they react? In all likelihood, with some degree of annoyance. Despite this, they may meekly begin to seek ways to suffer along with the bad situation; change the dinner hour, take a later bus, take an earlier bus, meet the bus at another station. On the other hand, they may move from annoyance to fury, blame the traffic jam on the town police (perhaps the mayor is among the delayed passengers), and fire the police chief. Neither alternative is the result of a conscious effort to approach the problem reflectively. In each, the problem will have been met without thought: in the one by submission and in the other by blind rage, the people making no effort to understand the situation they faced. The course of action might be much better decided on the basis of an objective look at the parking situation in the light of the town's growing commuter population.

The inadequacy of language creates the second difficulty which makes location and definition necessary. Words mean different things to different people and to different groups of people. Joe, in the delayed bus, may remark to Fred, "Well, I guess this traffic is too much for our cops to handle." Joe intends to express compassion for a police force faced with an insoluble problem; Fred hears the remark as a too temperate complaint against inexcusable inefficiency. Even among homogeneous groups, a problem rarely presents itself with such clarity that there is immediate and common understanding of its nature. A group of people talking on any subject will think about the topic from differing points of view. When a man talks with others about a set of circumstances, communication often suffers for lack of common ground. Failure to clear away at the outset as many of the obstacles to communication as possible will do much to destroy a potentially good discussion. Consequently, locating the problem is necessary.

The various methods of definition are discussed in Chapter VI. The method to use is the one that will best clarify any vague, ambiguous, and unfamiliar words to the common satisfaction of the group. It is through the meeting of minds that the subject will be limited and defined. Since the members of the group have the "felt difficulty," only they can appraise or agree on the statement of the problem. And at the conclusion of this step of location and definition, the group should be in agreement about the specific subject under discussion and be prepared to analyze it with a minimum of confusion.

## ANALYZING THE PROBLEM

Analysis is the second step in the problem-solving process. Its function is to find the cause of the difficulty. The thoroughness with which this absolutely essential step is conducted determines as much as any other factor the effectiveness of the group in establishing desirable policy.

The first step in analysis is a review of existing conditions. When a doctor sees a patient for the first time, he needs to make a thorough examination. He takes the patient's history. Then he examines and questions the patient for symptoms: the patient's "felt difficulty." From history and symptoms, he endeavors to determine causes. This determination of causes is the important step in the process. The group discussing a policy question can be compared to a group of doctors in consultation. Both analyses require a thorough investigation of facts, a familiarity with conditions past and present, in order that the consultants may penetrate to the causes of the problem.

The causes determined must be sufficient; that is, they must account for all the symptoms and all the history. It is a common mistake to stop looking for causes while some significant symptoms remain unexplained. This mistake can arise from overlooking the symptom or from ignoring it when proposing the possible cause. It is a type of mistake easily made when considering research material from various sources. One member of a group might have studied material, for example, in a Brookings Institute report on urban blight. This would note and list various symptoms and perhaps submit several surmises or propose a single opinion as to their cause. Another might have studied an article on urban blight from *Harper's* magazine, likewise mentioning symptoms and submitting surmises or opinions about causes. The two could easily be in only partial agreement, and if your group were to choose the opinion of one about causes you should be sure it accounts for all the symptoms. Otherwise your group discussion might be made worthless because it neglects some aspect of the problem.

## ESTABLISHING GOALS

Before determining what solution will best meet a problem situation, a person or a group must have some standard for judging or testing the solution. For example, when you go to the store to buy a pair of socks, you may be thinking, "I want them to go with my blue suit, and I want the cheapest all-wool pair I can find." By these standards you evaluate the many different pairs of socks from which you can choose. That is, you determine the goals you want your specific choice to help you attain: three goals—socks to match the blue suit, socks to be inexpensive, socks to be made of wool. Your solution is to buy a specific pair of socks. At another time, you might want a pair of socks that would be long-wearing. This would be a new goal and might, therefore, cause you to select a different pair, that is, arrive at a different solution.

A more complicated set of goals would guide you in exploring serious social questions and the need for determining them would be more apparent. Your decision about the socks is based on an analysis, perhaps almost unconscious, of an existing need and its causes. Decisions about a social problem are similarly based on analysis.

In the same sense that the basis for determining the causes of a problem is an examination of symptoms, the goals of a discussion group are based on what analysis shows the nature of the problem to be. Once established, the goals serve as standards of judgment for evaluating potential solutions. Indeed, this is the reason the symptoms and the causes are explored in the first place—to know better what kind of solution to look for. Through analysis of the problem, the group distills the principles which will tell what a good solution must be.

Determining goals is frequently a difficult step in discussion because goals are not always made explicit outside of discussion.

When you are asked why you bought a certain pair of socks, aren't you likely to say, "Because I liked them"? Likewise you may support a certain political party, believe in stricter law enforcement, or want more government intervention to help our older citizens without clearly spelling out why. But there is a why—a goal or set of goals—and if someone insists, you can usually explain. However, if you are to be rational in your personal and group decisions, you must identify goals *before* you propose solutions.

To determine goals, then, is to develop a yardstick to measure the many possible courses of action which will be recommended. If the analysis of the problem has been thorough, the goals will be more easily determined. The more thorough and realistic the goals of a group are, the better are the chances of its choosing the most desirable solution to a problem.

## FINDING THE BEST SOLUTION

Determining the best policy requires an examination of the advantages and disadvantages of each possible course of action. Each is compared with the others to see which will best solve the problem, that is, achieve most satisfyingly the goals that have been established. If these are realistic, the best solution, thus found, is the one that most closely fits the specifications inherent in them; it is the one which most effectively cures the causes of the problem, and thus eliminates its bad effects.

All reasonable possibilities should be considered. That is to say, it is quite possible that the policy in force at the time the group meets (the *status quo*) might prove to be the most desirable. It is quite possible, in other words, that any proposed change would be for the worse. At any rate, the *status quo* should always be evaluated in comparison with the alleged advantages of any proposed change in policy.

## PUTTING THE NEW POLICY INTO OPERATION

The final step in the pattern of group discussion is implementation of any new policy. In this part of the discussion, the group examines the newly concluded policy to see what must be done to put it into action. The problem-solving group must find the most practical way, in the light of our criteria, to implement the solution.

In summary, then, the pattern of group discussion develops through the following steps:

I. Location and Definition of the Problem
(Clarify the limits of the problem and define all vague, ambiguous, or unfamiliar terms to the satisfaction of all the members of the group.)

II. Analysis of the Problem
A. Symptoms
(Examine the specific details and the *status quo* and the pertinent history leading to it, to find evidence of the nature of the problem and its severity.)
B. Causes
(Examine the symptoms and history to determine what cause or causes produced the undesirable elements of the situation.)

III. Goals
(Develop standards of judgment for the group. That is, phrase the specifications which enumerate the requirements for a good solution.)

IV. Appraisal of Possible Solutions
A. List the reasonable courses of action.
B. Evaluate each to see how well it attains the stated goals of the group.
C. Select the course of action which most closely achieves the goals.

V. Procedure for Putting the Solution into Operation

## Group Discussion in Progress

The final topic for consideration in this chapter is the discussion in progress. There is much speculation about the nature of group discussion activity. Some attempts have been made to examine this subject scientifically to learn more about the successful operation of group thinking. Knowledge in this area, however, is limited. Nonetheless, two areas of immediate importance can be identified: leadership and participation.

## Leadership—Procedural and Substantive

Discussions in democratic society invite two kinds of leadership: *Procedural* leadership determines the conduct of the deliberation (procedure); *substantive* leadership exercises control over the ideas (substance). The government of the United States offers an example. The Vice President, as President of the Senate, is the procedural leader of that body. He recognizes who will speak and decides actual questions of policy (substance) only when there is a tie vote. The President of the United States is more definitely a substantive leader. He and his administration initiate proposals, develop evidence, and try to lead others to accept their conclusions on matters of substance. The Speaker of the House of Representatives is a combination of the two: As leader of the majority party he exercises a great measure of control over the nature of the substance considered; at the same time he is the procedural leader in the operation of the House.

This distinction between procedural and substantive leadership may help to present clearly the role the leader plays in group activity.

## Leadership and Chairmanship

It is usual to think of a chairman, the person in charge of the procedure, as *the* leader of the group. In fact, however, he may not be the leader at all. That is, he may be assigned to control the group but actually be a mere figurehead, not leading the group but following the procedural and substantive suggestions of another member of the group. This other member is the real leader. In short, unless the appointed chairman guides the discussion procedure or the substance of discussion, or both, he is not the leader.

Leadership is a function of the group; that is, the members decide who will direct their thought. Leadership may change hands as the nature of the group or the area of discussion changes. The members of a deliberative body may accept the leadership of one person on one topic or on one phase of a problem and at another time turn for leadership to another member. The group decides not only whom they will follow, but also how much authority they will give him and how long they will accept him as their leader. It is useless, therefore, to talk about techniques of leadership. Essentially, the techniques of *leadership*, so called, are in reality techniques of chairmanship.

***Chairmanship—emergent and assigned.*** Your instructor may assign a chairman for your discussion group or let you elect one. He may also do what seems to invite chaos—have your group discuss without a chairman. Assigning a chairman, or electing one, tends to institutionalize the functions of the chair in a single person. Ordinarily a chairman is expected to concern himself primarily with matters of procedure, as does the President of the Senate. This restriction allows him to maintain an unbiased position in the group. He becomes an objective arbiter to whom the participants in discussion can turn in a time of disagreement about procedure.

Should your group, however, launch into discussion without a designated procedural leader, every member of the group must be prepared to assume the responsibilities of the chair. If you note, for example, that the group should move on to another phase of the discussion, you do not wait more than briefly for someone else to make the suggestion; you make it yourself. Perhaps someone else will emerge as leader, and thus you will not need to take upon yourself the procedural initiative. But every member must be prepared to act if the need for procedural leadership arises.

There are acknowledged and obvious disadvantages to a system of leaderless discussion. A struggle for power may develop among those who want to assume leadership. Power struggles can develop even when a leader has been assigned, but people in discussion are generally less likely to challenge a properly constituted authority than they are to challenge a leader who has no mandate from the group. However, there are also advantages to unassigned leadership. Chief among these is the fact that *emerging* chairmanship is more likely to produce the *real* leaders of the group—the leaders of procedure and substance that the members acknowledge. When it does so, profitable discussion is more likely to result.

Think of situations within your own experience. When you sit with a group of friends in the college cafeteria and discuss some campus problem, you do not elect a leader or call upon the student-body president to appoint one. Despite the lack of a formally appointed chairman, someone will emerge as leader of the discussion. Discussions do not fail because no leader is assigned. They may fail because the participants have insufficient knowledge, or because they don't think reflectively about the subject, or because they don't really want to engage in serious exploration of a problem. The success or failure of a group is not determined by whether the leader is appointed or allowed to emerge.

**The techniques of chairmanship.**    In a group discussion, the chairman is more a moderator than a parliamentarian. As such, he must do three basic things: (1) he must get the discussion started, (2) he must keep the discussion moving along efficiently, and (3) he must bring the discussion to a successful conclusion.

*Getting the discussion started.* The first of the chairman's three responsibilities, getting the discussion off to a good start, is probably the most difficult. Once it has been started and the group is functioning, the discussion tends to move along. In class discussions there will be a panel of participants, together with listeners who, for the most part, will be less informed on the topic than the participants. Whenever there is an audience, the chairman should introduce both the panel and the topic. His introduction of the question should be clear, brief, and interesting. He may give a short resumé of the history and background of the problem, or he may show briefly the nature and importance of the question. He will want to say enough in his introduction to make the problem meaningful to the audience, but he must remember that it is not his responsibility to analyze the problem. He should introduce the members of the discussion group to the audience by name and even if there is no audience, the group members should know each other by name. If they do not, it is the responsibility of the chair to introduce each one. This much is easy. It is a set of functions that must be performed, but it is not the vital problem in getting started.

Any serious fumbling by a chairman tends to occur in beginning the analysis of the problem. Visualize a situation in which the inexperienced chairman, having finished his introductions, assumes that the discussion will proceed spontaneously. He will be sharply forced to the realization that it will not; the members of the group are still waiting for some kind of starting gun. Hence the chairman may try to push the discussion off with the question, "Well, who wants to begin?" This will inevitably fail to get the discussion started.

It is true that some groups are eager to rush on; these may need to be held back. Most groups, however, have to be led into useful and worthwhile discussion. There are several ways of helping these less vocal groups to get under way.

A question, carefully designed to elicit an intelligent response, can be a useful device for getting started. This opening question should ordinarily be directed to the group rather than to an individual. It would probably be unwise to put any particular person "on the spot" this early in the discussion. Moreover, the question should be general rather than specific. It may well be that a specific piece of information is an item no one has at his fingertips. If they are asked for one, the whole group may freeze up beyond the point of easy thawing.

A useful maneuver for the chairman is to quote some statement referring to the problem at hand and ask the group for comment. He can cite some specific instance or illustration of the problem and ask for comment on this. If the topic is a broad one, he may want to ask for some specification or delimitation. In each of these cases, any member of the panel should be able to give a reasonable comment.

*Keeping the discussion going.* Once started, a well-informed group will usually move along quite briskly with a minimum of prodding from the chairman. His major functions, once he gets the discussion started, are to encourage general participation, to keep the discussion on the track, and to guide the group away from hasty, unrealistic action.

One of the main problems the moderator faces is that of keeping at least a reasonable balance in the amount of participation from each member of the group. There is, more often than not among student groups, at least one person who is too talkative and at least one who is too reticent. It is the job of the moderator to see that everyone participates, and that no one monopolizes the time of the group. If several speakers try to get the floor at the same time, the one who has, up to that point, spoken less frequently, should be given the opportunity to speak first. Sometimes real diplomacy is necessary to keep the discussion from becoming one-sided. Because the chairman is not a dictator, and should not be, his qualities of tact, geniality, and good humor come into play.

There are two dangers to be avoided. In curbing the overly talkative speaker, the chairman must be very careful not to offend. If he does, he stands a good chance of losing all effective contribution from a potentially valuable member of the group. On the other hand, in the effort to get some contribution from a timid person, the chairman is often tempted to ask a direct question requiring specific information. As we said earlier, this tactic is dangerous; should the person asked lack the necessary data, he will, in all probability, be even less inclined to speak thereafter. It is usually safe to ask for a comment or an opinion regarding an idea, a contribution, or data already advanced by another member of the group.

It is a great temptation in group discussion, because of the informality of the situation, and because of the group's easy familiarity with the detailed information it involves, to wander around the topic, digressing at length. Such digressions are often valuable in bringing out ideas and interpretations of data. Here again, the chair must determine when the digression is worthwhile and when it is a waste of time. The safest way to avoid wasting time in interesting but unnecessary and fruitless digressions, and perhaps most efficient, is to guide the group tactfully and courteously, but firmly, through the five steps of the discussion pattern.

One of the chairman's most useful devices is frequent brief summary of what the group has accomplished up to the point of summary. Then, to help keep the group on the track between summaries, it is advisable to make very short paraphrases of significant contributions as they are made. Such paraphrases are especially helpful if a speaker has held the floor for a comparatively lengthy statement. Brief summaries and even briefer paraphrases of individual remarks serve a triple purpose. They help to avoid needless repetition. They help to keep the discussion on the track. They point out areas of agreement and disagreement, and thus indicate the precise status of the discussion at any given moment.

Probably the most important function of the chairman in group discussion is to see to it, as best he can, that the group makes a thorough, impartial, and rational investigation of the problem at hand. More than this, it is important that there be a clear understanding of the areas of agreement and disagreement. To accomplish these functions, the chairman must see to it that all important points are heard.

Not only must these points be heard; they must also be examined critically and clearly. Both evidence and reasoning must be submitted to rigorous test. It is the responsibility of the chairman to see that the testing is done. Since he does not want to involve himself directly in argument, he can best accomplish this through the use of guiding questions. By means of such questions, he can accomplish several ends. First, he can make sure that all important facets of the problem are viewed. Second, he can require the members of the group to consider and comment on the evidence and reasoning of others. Thus he will avoid using questions that can be answered *yes* or *no*. Instead, he will raise the all-important questions of fact and value that must be clearly thrashed out before any group conclusion can be of real worth.

Ideally, the goal of any policy discussion is consensus, general agreement among the members of the group on what the best course of action will probably be. As we have pointed out, consensus is not always possible. Remember, a policy discussion comes about in the first place because there is conflict, an honest difference of opinion as to what policy should be adopted. There is nothing in the nature of discussion that inherently assures success in the effort to eliminate these areas of disagreement. No matter how conscientious a group is, no matter how impartially and reasonably its members investigate available data, they may still retain honest differences of opinion at the end of the discussion. No outcome of group exploration is more useless than a contrived or forced consensus. Differences of opinion are not to be strangled. The moderator will want to point out and stress the areas of agreement that do exist, but it is also important that the differences be brought out; otherwise, they can never be eliminated. Consensus is valuable only when it results from a realistic and rational adjustment of honest differences.

*Bringing the discussion to a close.* The time will come for deliberation to end, especially in class discussions where the bell rings at the end of fifty minutes. The type of conclusion the chairman will use is determined largely by the results achieved in the discussion. If the group has reached an agreement on policy, he can summarize the action recommended. When no conclusion is reached because still existing issues need further discussion, the chairman can put his conclusion into the form of a progress report.

## The Participant in Discussion

A group discussion can be conducted without a chairman but not without participants. The panel of participants is thus of far greater importance than the chairman in the success or failure of any group discussion.

In large measure, the success or failure of a group discussion is determined before the group meets. The degree of thoroughness with which each member of the panel prepares for the discussion is the determining factor. Let us assume, however, that all the participants in the discussion are well informed, and have followed the procedures for preparation outlined in earlier sections of this chapter. We may then ask, "What principles should guide the participant in speaking to explore?" If you conduct yourself in accordance with the following suggestions, you will be an effective member of a panel.

*Be open-minded.* You have heard of the man who says, "My mind is made up. Don't try to confuse me with facts." This sort of person comes to a discussion prepared to force his own opinions on the rest of the group. He knows what is "right" and is prepared to advocate it to his last gasp.

Impartiality and freedom from prejudgment should mark the thinking and speaking of the participant in group discussion. He does much to destroy the whole function of the group if he comes to the meeting prepared to defend his own point of view against all comers.

*Be responsible.* Each member of the group shares the responsibility of the entire group for concluding a policy. Being responsible, the individual participant will want to make the part he plays worthy of himself. The discussion speaker who accepts his share of the responsibility of the group will be eager to contribute to its effectiveness because he knows that he shares in any failure as well as in any success. There is no place in good discussion for the grandstander, nor for the speaker who hangs back and who is reticent or unwilling to contribute. Each member of the group must give what he has to offer, but, because he is responsible, he will think before he speaks and he will have adequate basis for what he says. He will both give and expect serious consideration of the problem.

*Be objective.* Objectivity shows itself both in the attitudes and in the language of a discussion speaker. In attitude he is impersonal and impartial. Many of the problems he will attack in discussion will touch his life directly. His own emotional involvement may then become a threat to his objective consideration of the problem. Issues are almost certain to arise. When they do, each member of the group must avoid the attitude that disagreement with his ideas constitutes a personal attack on him. Conversely, each must put his questions and criticisms on a basis that is impersonal, fact centered, and idea centered.

The language the speakers use can contribute significantly to the objectivity of a discussion. Avoid ambiguity, vagueness, and generalities. Define terms carefully. Even when a panel member feels strongly about a point, he can use language of moderation and avoid adding emotional conflicts to what may already be a complex set of rational disagreements. Try to make language as unemotional as possible.

Objectivity in discussion is by no means to be confused with apathy and lack of interest. Speaking to explore requires as much vigor, animation and enthusiasm as any other speaking occasion. But objectivity in language and attitude helps to avoid much of the ill will that can easily spring up when there are issues to resolve.

*Be co-operative.* Group discussion is by necessity co-operative. It requires the co-operation of all members of the group for maximum success.

Co-operativeness demands that the individual member of a panel be ready and willing to compromise when necessary and to retract when it is reasonable to believe he might be wrong. Ideally, he is firm in defending a position rationally held, but not blind to the possibility of his own error; he is willing to compromise in the sense of adjusting his own position to that of others but he will not abandon a well-supported position just to become "one of the gang."

*Be a good listener.* The participant should be an attentive, courteous, but critical listener. A good discussion speaker does not monopolize the group's time, nor does he seek to dominate the conversation. Being a good listener not only imposes responsibility but also brings benefit. It enables him to keep his contributions responsible, meaningful, reasonable, and relevant. One obvious mark of an inattentive, uncritical member of a group is an irrelevant comment. Contributions to the discussion are meaningful only when they are put into the context of what has gone before. Every statement should relate to the ideas then under discussion and not simply be dumped into the conversation.

## SUMMARY

The freedom that characterizes democratic society comprises the freedom to disagree. Conflicts arise over solutions to questions of policy, fact, and value. These conflicts are explored through group discussion—a process that assembles in a cooperative effort several informed persons who together search for solutions to problems.

Reflective thinking is the basis of problem-solving and takes place in five steps:

1. A "felt difficulty" is identified and defined as a problem.
2. The problem is analyzed to discover the symptoms that manifest it and the conditions that cause it.
3. The goals of the group exploring the problem are established as criteria for evaluating possible courses of action.
4. Alternative proposals for solution are weighed in the light of their comparative advantages and disadvantages.
5. Steps are outlined for implementing the proposal which appears to offer the greatest relative advantage and the fewest relative disadvantages.

Substantive leadership in discussion, control over the ideas, is usually emergent and shifting; it grows out of the group and tends to move from person to person. Procedural leadership, guidance in the conduct and progress of the group, is the responsibility of the chairman when a chairman is elected or assigned. When no chairman is specifically appointed, procedural leadership must emerge from the group. The responsibilities of the chair are primarily three in number:

1. To get the discussion started.
2. To keep the discussion moving along.
3. To bring the discussion to a close.

In group discussion, as in any other form of public speaking, it is a primary responsibility of the speaker to be well prepared. Once he comes to the meeting, he will contribute to the effectiveness of the discussion to the extent that he is open minded, responsible, objective, co-operative, and a good listener.

# QUESTIONS

1. What is a group discussion?

2. What is a learning group? How does it differ from a problem-solving group?

3. What is rough associational thinking?

4. What are the steps in reflective thinking?

5. Why must symptoms be considered in determining causes?

6. Why is the establishment of goals so difficult?

7. Why must the *status quo* be examined as a possible solution?

8. Differentiate between procedural and substantive leadership.

9. Distinguish leadership from chairmanship.

10. How should a chairman go about getting a discussion started?

11. How does the chairman put a stop to a discussion when no definite conclusion has been reached?

12. How does the chairman use the summary?

13. What attitude should a participant bring to a group discussion?


# EXERCISES

1. Make an analysis of some personal problem, using reflective thinking. How worthwhile do you find this method? What alternate possibilities can you think of as effective means of analyzing a problem?

2. With four or five other members of your class form a discussion group. Select a problem to discuss. Word it. Come to some basic understanding about what the terms of the question mean. Let each member of the group gather material and make an outline for himself. Present the group discussion in class a week after you have chosen the topic.

3. Observe the chairman of some group to which you belong. Is he the leader of the group? If so, in what way does he lead? If not, who is the leader and how does he take control? Write a short paper explaining what happened on the occasion of your observation.

# INDEX